War Stories of the Tankers

American Armored Combat, 1918 to Today

EDITED BY
MICHAEL GREEN

TO ALL THE U.S. ARMY AND MARINE CORPS TANKERS WHO HAVE SERVED AND FOUGHT FOR THEIR COUNTRY AND UPHELD THE PROUD TRADITIONS OF ARMOR AND THEIR SERVICE SINCE WORLD WAR I.

First published in 2008 by Zenith Press, an imprint of MBI Publishing Company LLC, 400 1st Ave N, Suite 300 Minneapolis, MN 55401

Zenith Press titles are also available at discounts in bulk quantity for industrial or sales-promotional use. For details write to Special Sales Manager at MBI Publishing Company, 400 1st Ave N, Suite 300 Minneapolis, MN 55401 USA

To find out more about our books, join us online at www.zenithpress.com.

Designer: Melissa Khaira

Printed in the United States of America

Library of Congress Cataloging-in-Publication Data

Green, Michael.
War stories of the tankers : American armored combat, 1918 to today / By Michael Green.
p. cm.
ISBN-13: 978-0-7603-3297-9 (hardbound w/ jacket) 1. United States. Army. Armored Force—History. I. Title.
UA30.G74 2008
358'.180973—dc22

2007027558

On the cover: M1 Abrams tanks on patrol in Baghdad. *U.S. Army*

On the back cover: M4 Sherman during a training exercise at Fort Knox, Kentucky. *Patton Museum*

CONTENTS

ACKNOWLEDGMENTS

Besides those individuals' stories that appear in this book, the editor would like to thank the following persons for their help in providing the contact points for the interviews. These include Jacques Littlefield, Dean and Nancy Kleffman, Charles Lemons, Candace Fuller, Richard Chegar, Randy Talbot, Steven Fixler, Sarah Ryan, Ron Hare, John Shay, David Smith, Edward Corcoran, Michael Flanagan, Gini Sinclair, Shane Lee, and Don Moriarty.

Organizations that provided help in collecting the stories for this book include The Patton Museum of Armor and Cavalry, the Patton Museum Foundation, the Fort Knox Public Affairs Office, *Armor* magazine, the Marine Corps Tanker's Association, the 69th Armor Association, and the Operation Tribute to Freedom Community Relations Division Office of Chief of Public Affairs.

INTRODUCTION

The Great War (later renamed World War I) began in the summer of 1914 with a series of infantry-dominated offensive operations by both sides. The allied powers, primarily consisting of the United Kingdom and France, and the central powers, led by Germany, which provided the bulk of its military might, both thought the conflict would be a short one, with the issues decided and the war ended with the proverbial "troops home by Christmas." Like two chess masters, both sides executed rapid advances with preplanned opening gambits. The opening moves resulted in decisive engagement along extended fronts, but both soon found themselves with insufficient resources to open new campaigns in what became a static battlefield. A bloody stalemate settled on the battlefields of western Europe, with each side losing appalling numbers of troops for little or no strategic gains, which would lead to resolution of the war.

The military stalemate in western Europe, which favored defensive operations over offensive operations, resulted from the newly developed machine gun and improved indirect artillery fire tactics. In conjunction with the widespread use of barbed wire and elaborate trench systems by both sides, the defensive battle lines of the opposing forces moved no more than ten miles in either direction despite the death of millions of soldiers, during the first two years of the war.

Such stalemates had occurred in earlier wars, albeit on a smaller scale. The solution to a static front has traditionally been use of mobility. Cavalry, mounted infantry, and horse-drawn artillery formations specifically designed for rapid movement had all been used effectively in both the American Civil War and the Franco-Prussian War. Such romantically named troops, referred too as lancers, dragoons, and flying batteries, respectively, had been the accepted practice for more than a half century. The battlefields of the Western Front were resistant to this accepted practice as the recently introduced machine guns of both sides raked them. In addition, there were elaborate barbed wire systems installed to protect the machine guns.

Artillery had been used extensively as a substitute for more traditional massed rifle fire to eliminate the machine guns, trenches had been dug to protect troops from artillery, and the whole landscape had been so thoroughly plowed by artillery, mortars, and entrenchment that the armies lived in a sea of mud. Re-establishment of mobility by traditional horse-drawn formations was impractical.

The British and French turned to the development of that new mechanical contraption, referred to by the British army as the "tank." Of the two countries' efforts, the British were the first to field the tank into battle in September 1916 during the last phase of the Battle of the Somme. The French first employed tanks in battle the following year.

Tanks seemed to present a combination of sufficient mobility to cross muddy fields, barbed wire entanglements, and trenches. They possessed sufficient armor to protect their crews against rifle and machine-gun fire, and all but direct hits from artillery. And finally, they could carry sufficient firepower to knock out bunkers and to sweep trenches of enemy infantry. This formulation of the tank as an embodiment of mobility, armor protection, and firepower endures to this day. The path from the first feeble implementation of mechanized warfare to the present has been neither straight nor easy, but the goal has remained constant from the first: to win battles, shorten wars, and ultimately save lives by eliminating costly battles of attrition inherent in static battlefields.

The United States declared war on Germany on April 6, 1917, and the first small detachment of American troops arrived in France in June 1917. When the number of American troops in France reached sufficient numbers, they took part in their first offensive operations in May 1918.

Seeing tanks as the wave of the future for armed conflicts, the U.S. Army sought to field American-designed and -built tanks. However, the lack of a suitable industrial base in the United States prevented this from taking place before World War I ended. As a backup plan, the U.S. Army took into service British-designed and -built heavy tanks and French-designed and -built light tanks.

U.S. Army tankers first saw action against the German army in western Europe on September 12, 1918. They would continue to battle the German army until November 11, 1918, when an armistice took place.

Although World War II began on September 1, 1939, with the German invasion of Poland, the United States did not officially enter the conflict until shortly after the Japanese attack on the U.S. Navy base at Pearl Harbor, Hawaii, on December 7, 1941, when war was declared on both Japan and its ally, Germany. U.S. Army tankers would battle the Japanese army while defending the Philippines between December 1941 and April 1942, before surrendering due to overwhelming numbers.

U.S. Marines Corps tankers would take the fight to the Japanese, between August 1942 and February 1943, during the successful battle for the island of Guadalcanal, located in the Southwest Pacific. In June 1943, U.S. Marine Corps tankers took part in the invasion and conquest of the Japanese-occupied island of New Georgia. In November 1943, marine tankers participated in the capture of the Makin and Tarawa Atolls in the Gilbert Islands, located in the Central Pacific. U.S. Marine Corps and Army tankers would continue to play a part in the dismantling of the Japanese Empire piece by piece until its surrender in September 1945.

On November 8, 1943, U.S. Army tankers landed on the shores of French North Africa and initially battled French forces fighting on behalf of the Germans. American tankers first met the more experienced German tankers on November 26, 1942. From that day on, until the surrender of Germany in May 1945, U.S. Army tankers would battle German tankers and give as good as they got. The mainstay of the U.S. Army tank inventory throughout the war proved to be various versions of the well-known M4 Sherman tank series.

Following World War II, relationships soured between the United States and its former wartime ally, the Soviet Union. The threat of a Soviet invasion of western Europe led by countless thousands of tanks and the resulting outbreak of World War III led U.S. Army tankers to concentrate on stopping such an assault until the Cold War ended in 1991, with the break-up of the Soviet Union. Rather than fighting on the plains of western Europe, U.S. Army and Marine Corps tankers would find themselves doing battle on the other side of the world. This would include the frozen mountains of Korea in the early 1950s to the humid jungles of Vietnam in the late 1960s and early 1970s.

American tankers would not see combat again in large numbers until Operation Desert Storm in 1991, when they forced the Iraqi army, under the leadership of Saddam Hussein, to end its illegal occupation of the neighboring country of Kuwait.

In 2003, due to a perceived threat, American tankers once again returned to the Middle East to both invade and occupy the country of Iraq. While the initial invasion of Iraq, referred to as Operation Iraqi Freedom, once again demonstrated the conventional warfare superiority of American tankers, the asymmetrical insurgent threat that evolved in the aftermath of the American military invasion of that country has forced those same tankers to constantly adapt to a foe that is constantly changing their tactics.

This book will attempt to capture in a series of representative stories from different conflicts, the experiences of American tankers, both U.S. Army and Marine Corps, from World War I through today. The stories themselves come from a wide variety of different sources, including interviews, after action reports, unit histories, *Armor* magazine, and written memoirs.

There are also stories of U.S. Army cavalryman, who became a part of the Armor Branch in 1950. Before that time, the cavalryman had their own branch.

Each story reflects the perspective of the individual, his position in the military, and his rank at the time the story took place. Obviously, higher-ranking officers have a much different view of combat than those of the enlisted personnel operating the tanks, as is apparent in the stories found within this book. Some of the stories are sad and reflect the nature of war, while others are humorous. Most provide examples of tankers overcoming various obstacles, be it the enemy, the terrain, the weather, or doing their duty as American fighting men.

The stories have been edited for the purpose of clarity, grammar, and to fit within the publisher's size and format restrictions.

CHAPTER ONE

WORLD WAR I (1914–1918)

///2D LT. PAUL HAIMBAUGH (U.S. ARMY)

The doughboys spring to their feet and start forward. You urge your tank on until you are nosing the barrage; ahead the German distress signals flare in the sky. In a moment the enemy barrage will fall. Here it is, and it's disconcertingly close. You think maybe you better zig-zag a bit, maybe you can dodge 'em. The doughboys trudge sturdily on, and here and there one sags into a heap (shell splinters). One shell nearly gets you as it bursts nearby with the rending crash peculiar to high explosive. Seems like it nearly lifts your tank into the air, as a dozen pneumatic hammers start playing a tattoo on the side and front of your tank, and splashes of hot metal enter the cracks and sting your face and hands. The infantry, a hundred yards back, is prone on the ground; too hot for them.

Well, it's up to you to locate the enemy machine guns and put them out. Observation from the peepholes reveals nothing. You pop your head through the trap door and take a quick look around. There they are.

A hasty command to the 6-pounder (57mm gun), and the tank is filled with the fumes of cordite. A hit and a couple of more in the same place, and the belt of machine-gun cartridges suffice to quiet that machine-gun nest.

"Come on infantry!" As the tank passes, you see the gray forms sprawled grotesquely around their guns. You are glad the "bus" (tank) is a male, for these 6-pounders certainly do the work.

Up ahead are a railway embankment and a sunken road, a likely place for machine-gun nests. Tat-tat-tat! They've already begun to strafe you. Slipping from your seat, you shout commands to your gunners. Picking their targets, they pepper away with the machine guns and 6-pounders. The noise is terrific; the tank is filled with cordite and gasoline fumes. There is a sickening smell of hot oil about. You are close now, so you order case shot; the 6-pounders rake the embankment and road with iron case shot, with deadly effect. The place is a shambles; gray forms sprawled in the road, huddled in gun holes, lying in position about their guns. It's war and you had to get them first. A half dozen Germans scramble to their feet with hands upraised, and you let them pass to the rear. "Come on infantry!"

Your tank surmounts the embankment and your hair raises, for on a ridge five hundred yards ahead are two 77s, sacrifice guns left to get you. Crash, a shell lands fifty yards to your left and short. Your starboard 6-pounder lets go. Crash, another one, which lands close, sends a shower of dirt and stones against the side of the tank. Working like mad, your gunner sends four shells after the two guns. Good work, for they are silenced. One member of the two gun crews is able to run away.

Beads of perspiration stand on your forehead. Hot work this. The combination of powder and gasoline fumes, the smell of hot oil and the exhaust begins to daze you, but you pull yourself together and rumble on. The infantry swings along behind, bombing dugouts and "mopping up," assisted by your running mate, a female tank armed with machine guns only.

It is a mile to your objective now, but it is a mile of thrills. You get shot up, put out a half dozen machine-gun nests; clean up another sunken road with machine guns placed every ten feet along it. A 1-pounder in a hedge scares you with several well-placed shots before it goes west (surrenders). Some German artillery observer, back, spots you and chases you over the landscape, dropping now a shell in front of and then behind you. Here is your objective! You wait for the infantry to come up, and your crew enjoys a breath of fresh air. After the infantry has dug in and consolidated its position, you turn toward the rallying point.

///SGT. CARL E. ROSENHAGEN (U.S. ARMY)

Friday evening, it was still daylight. Three of our boys from the 13th Crew, Company C, took a walk through the woods where our tanks were hidden and camouflaged. In a little while, they came back, one of them carrying a black cat in his arms that they had come upon in the woods. Jokingly the remarks were, "Well, a black cat on a Friday night for the 13th Crew sure portended good luck for the 13th Crew."

The next day we started out to take our place in the battle line-up. We stopped at a tank park or repair center, and the English mechanics mounted large fascines, large octagon squirrel cages about eight feet in height, made of heavy timbers and metal facings on the twenty-nine-foot-long tanks we used in this engagement. These tanks could not cross the twelve-by-twelve-foot antitank trench the Germans had at the point where we were to go over the top. The thirty-five-foot tanks could not be stopped by any trench, but the twenty-nine-foot tanks would nose down into the trench or against the other side of the trench, and there was no way for it to crawl out. By dropping this large fascine into the trench, the front end of the tank would not get below the ground level and could get across any trench. Guide rails, which sloped downward at the front end of the tank, were placed on the tank to hold and guide the heavy ditching beam if you were stuck where trenches ran close together and caved in from the thirty-five-ton load of a heavy tank or in bad mud. Chains held the fascine in place on top, and eyebolts on the chains came through holes in the top and front end of the tank. Nuts were then screwed onto the eyebolts extending through the roof of the tank, so that when the tank got to the edge of the antitank trench, we removed the nuts from the eyebolts on the chains and teetered the tank at the edge of the trench. This allowed the fascine to roll down and be thrown to the far side of the trench, preventing the front of the tank from going too deep in the trench, thus allowing it to crawl out.

While we were at this repair center awaiting the tanks to be rigged with all the necessary equipment, a firing squad shot a German spy dressed as an English officer; they also shot an English sergeant who had been caught robbing the dead.

I drove the tank after we left the repair center, and after dark we got into a couple of bad mustard gas attacks. It was sure a hardship driving with a gas mask on, for the manual labor required to drive a tank over rough territory with the heat of the motor and confined space inside made you perspire profusely. With both hands and feet working, it was next to impossible to keep the nose clips from slipping off. The gas burned terribly around our face and eyes, and to breathe through the mouthpiece and see where we were going was brutal punishment. It was impossible for the driver not to breathe in some gas.

We finally came to a halt to load up with gasoline, or petrol, as it was called. Aviation gas was used, and it was passed in two-gallon tins, man to man in a line to the back end of the tank. The gas was put in the outside armored fuel tanks, which were divided into three compartments. The refueling area was a short distance from the front lines, and artillery and machine-gun fire was heavy and well illuminated by German flares, causing several deaths and others in our battalion to be wounded. After refueling, we were briefed and then it was time to go.

"Zero hour" was 5:55 a.m. The artillery of both sides sounded as though the end of the world was here and the chattering of machine guns sounded like thousands of crickets to my ears. We had a hermaphrodite tank, that is, machine guns on one side and a 6-pounder Hotchkiss gun on the left side.

I had turned the driving over to Sergeant Barnard of Kokomo, Indiana, and I was in the observation tower standing on a platform over the transmission taking care of anything that happened and picking out targets for the gunners. Before we came to the antitank trench, we ran into about twenty machine guns corralled together, and they were firing against the right side of the tank. The whole inside of the tank seemed on fire from the sparks of the armor-piercing bullets around the gun slots, and through the other slots our gunners had to see their targets.

It was intense; one gunner lay back away from his gun, so I jumped down and took his place. Private "Wooden Shoe" Adams, he was called, from Indianapolis, Indiana, I believe, looked up from the gun he was on, and his face was a mass of blood. Seeing we could not cope with these machine guns, I pounded on the motor cowling, which is how we attracted the driver's attention, and put up my fist for a left turn.

He must have had his window or flap wide open and turned to the right, right into those machine guns, and he was badly hit. They hollered for first aid, and I jumped to him and said, "For God's sake, Barney, keep on driving until we get through this mess," and brave Barney did, turning the tank around where we were able to knock out the machine guns. We got Barney out of the driver's seat then, and I resumed driving.

This happened, I believe, in the first thirty or forty minutes, shortly after 6 a.m. We were in a bad fog and smoke screen; I remember seeing a fascine get knocked off or flying to pieces by a direct hit on one of our tanks. I thought, *Those boys are in a bad way for that antitank trench, not knowing what we were going to run into*.

Our 6-pounder gun was manned by Corporal Gagnon and Private Evans. They had made short work of the machine-gun nest, firing case shot out of the muzzle of the gun, as the Germans were not more than thirty or forty feet away from us. The artillery fire on both sides was terrific, and from what some English officers told us, it was the worst since the first Battle of the Somme, which had been the world's greatest artillery engagement on record until then.

By this time, the smoke screen and the fog had really worsened. There were some dummy tanks made of papier-mache and wood, which had a donkey inside them. These were used to draw antitank fire so that our observers could spot enemy antitank guns. We had arrived at the antitank trench, and I removed the nuts on the chains holding the fascine and teetered the tank plenty, but the chains snagged somewhere, and the fascine would not drop. I headed into the trench at an angle, and we bogged into the side of the trench. I worked and worked stabbing into the side of the trench, and dirt, stones, and everything just kept rolling on top, making it seem that getting the tank out would be an impossible job. The German infantry made it even tougher on our side without a six-pounder there. Being down in the trench, I guess, saved us from their artillery.

Having torn so much of the top of the trench away, we finally came out on a bias, as I swear we were tilted sideways at a forty-five-degree angle. I was looking for the tank to turn over on its left side, but we lurched out. How, I do not know.

Before we had gotten to the antitank trench, we had trouble with the infantry, our American 27th Division. Men were running in front of our tank, cutting us off from helping them against the German machine guns. Smoke and fog were so heavy now that we could not even see any of our infantry anymore, but because we had a timetable to get to Le Catelet, we continued.

We got to the outskirts of Le Catelet and it was lighter there, but we saw no supporting infantry. We stopped at the edge of the crossroads, and the boys opened the doors to let in some fresh air. Lieutenant Dunning and I were looking at the map we had spread between us when I looked up. In the gloom, I could make out some men running toward us. I thought they might be our men, and when Lieutenant Dunning grabbed the machine gun between us, I grabbed his hand saying, "Don't fire, they're Englishmen," but I was mistaken.

When Dunning went to fire the gun, it jammed, not even a shot came out. A German pushed his rifle into the front window on Dunning's side and shot a piece out of his nostril. I dropped into gear and gave the tank a leap as Dunning used his Colt automatic (pistol). I had, in the meantime, hollered to the men in the back to close the doors, even though I thought they were not Germans. We had a little commotion for a few minutes, swinging the tank around to get the Germans off the side machine guns so that our six-pounder could get to them. Our six-pounder crew was good and made short work of them.

After this, we drove the reverse direction, opposite the way we came by compass, which had been about northeast, taking a southwesterly course, hoping and watching for our infantry. We came to an abrupt ending of the terrain and thought it must be a stream or a gully. Visibility was nil, and after talking with Lieutenant Dunning, I teetered the tank, and that good old fascine we had cussed dropped off. I remember seeing it drop straight down. How far I do not know.

We backed up from there and followed along the bank until the terrain changed. Then a shell hit us on the right rear and tore a hole in our back end, busting our main water line running up to the motor. In no time, steam filled the tank so bad that I don't know how any of the rear crew lived through it, as we had our front windows open gasping for air. We came to the bottom of a ridge ten or fifteen feet high and tried to climb it, but the motor conked and knocked so bad and would not pull anything, even in the lowest gear. I shoved the gear in reverse and backed onto the level.

There were two terrific explosions outside of the tank, and then a shell hit us on top. I believe the motor casing saved us. We heard a big plop inside and we caught on fire; the whole tank seemed to be on fire. I climbed through Lieutenant Dunning's seat, the only way I could get out, and came along the motor by the six-pounder over the transmission when I saw the lower door open on the right side, and I slid out. In the smoke and fog, I could see two of our boys running away, I hollered to them, and they came back. Lieutenant Dunning got his face burned getting through and out of the tank. I was lucky as I kept my head buried in my arms and lost only some excess hair off my head.

The four of us ran for some small trenches we could see ahead, and while in there, the largest German I had ever seen made a running jump over us in the trench. I don't know whether he was a runner carrying a message, or if he had started to go to Berlin. German machine guns were firing a barrage, and we laid there concealed by the fog and smoke, seeing only the fire coming out the barrels of the machine guns.

We crawled on, and suddenly about 11 that morning, the fog and smoke screen started to lift. We jumped into some shell holes. We could then make out our tank about eight or nine hundred feet away. Lieutenant Dunning and I were in the same shell hole, not big. We didn't see the other two boys until later that night. Our tank was burning and blowing up all afternoon with smoke belching out. German planes were flying right over our heads, but they must not have seen us lying below. I think the Germans figured we never got out of the tank, as the door through which we fled was near the side of the ridge mentioned earlier, so they could not tell what had happened.

There was a battery of German 5- or 6-inch guns lined on top of that ridge, and that afternoon our artillery was trying to blast them out. There was a dressing station about 1,500 feet northwest looking toward the tank, but on top of the ridge and to our right a stream of wounded were walking toward it all day. Northeast of us was an old French cemetery, about a quarter mile away.

About 2 p.m. that afternoon, our artillery started a box barrage laying it where we were, no doubt intending to get the battery of guns on the ridge, but they laid their fire from the bottom of the ridge ahead of us to three or four hundred feet behind us, to the east of our guns. We were right in the middle of it! The box barrage was constant for one hour or more, and they were dropping all big shells every forty or fifty feet apart.

When they would get right in line with us, all we could do was push our heads against the sides of the shell hole. After three or four passes over our territory, one of the shells hit only a few feet away from us, digging a hole joining into our hole. Lieutenant Dunning was hit in the hand by a piece of shell. I pulled a big piece of shell away from my arm and body, but it hadn't gotten me. Lieutenant Dunning was in great pain, what with his burns, his nose, and now the hit in his hand. We had nothing to help us medically.

When the barrage finally stopped, a German from one of the gun crews walked toward us. He was an elderly man, walking real slow easterly with his head down. I had my Colt automatic in my hand, and I could have reached out and touched him as he passed by us. His mind and thoughts were apparently far away, or he could not have missed us, so we were fearful even after he disappeared from sight. We thought the other two boys had been blown apart from the box barrage.

After 6 p.m. it began to get dark, and we planned to go to the cemetery and come around behind the dressing station, when our own artillery started throwing a line of shrapnel about six or eight hundred feet south of us on the other side of the canal. We did not want to run into the shrapnel, but just as we were ready to start out on the alternate way, six or eight Germans from the gun crews were walking about fifty or sixty feet to the side of us, going toward the cemetery.

We then had to go toward the shrapnel barrage. We got up and started walking to where we thought our two buddies were killed, and they popped up as we neared them. We walked on to the Canal Du Nord and crept along its bank, which was well lined with bushes. We continued to creep along in the bushes until the shrapnel fire died down. We decided then to find out if we could get across the canal.

Two of the boys held my hands, and I lowered myself down feet first, trying to touch the canal bottom. I went to my chin but could not find bottom, so I had them pull me up, as the water was cold. We continued to crawl through the underbrush and could hear men talking and mess kits rattling. We crawled slowly, and I crawled a few feet at a time turning my luminous watch face back toward them.

Lieutenant Dunning and I stopped at a path through the bushes, and someone walked in front of me. I reached up and grabbed him by the neck, shoving my gun in his face, wondering what to do with him. I heard him mumbling as he was on his knees then, and I looked into his face and saw it was Daley, our big Irish crewman. I gave him Cain, whispering to him as we started out again.

I told them to snake along and not get on their hands and knees anymore. They would hold back fifteen or twenty feet, and then scramble to us. We came to a bunch of Quonset huts about fifty feet ahead of us, when two Germans came from the right of us, stopped at a clump of bushes, and started smoking cigarettes and talking for a few minutes. Dunning and I were close to the path ahead of us, when one German turned to the other. When he came along this path, I put my face down so he could not see me. The other German went straight ahead into a hut. The first German was still on the path, and I could have reached out and touched his shoe as he passed us. He made no signs of having seen us but continued into a hut about sixty feet farther to our left and ahead of us. I remember sliding across the path when flares lit up everything, because we knew they were hunting for us.

It had been drizzling rain for a while, black clouds moving fast, when it started to pour down. I heard someone say, "How many of there are you?" Then I heard crewman Daley say, "Two of us." This German spoke good English. They were about twenty or twenty-five feet away from us when suddenly the heavens opened up. Lucky for us the Germans did not look around, and they took our two men away. I'll never know how those two men of ours got ahead of us! About six Germans captured Daley and Capsticks.

I had dived into a small hole about fifteen feet ahead of the path where the Germans must have noticed us. Thinking I was on my own now, I got up and walked toward a road ahead. The rain had tapered off and I turned to the left on that road and started to walk along. I went down the road not far, maybe a hundred feet, and I was at the edge of the left side of the road when someone said, "What are you going to do?" I looked down on the side of the road, and it was Lieutenant Dunning. I said, "I'm walking," and he got up and we continued down that road together.

We saw woods on the right and we went into it, but there was nothing but real big shell holes filled with stagnant water, slippery clay footing, and one hole joining another. We could not walk without slipping and falling, so we gave up, leaving the woods and going back to the road again to continue on. We had no real sense of direction. The road started downward and was sunken and had dugouts along the left bank of the road, the way we were walking.

I saw someone standing in the front of one of the dugouts, and I walked up to him. It was so dark that I had to look up into his face before I saw the German helmet on him. We thought that we may have strayed into our lines, but saw differently then. Lieutenant Dunning was right behind me, and I said nothing, pushing my hand back to warn him.

We turned around and started up the bank of the road to the sound of roofing tin, which was covered by dirt. We ran along the edge of a woods in which they had ankle-high barbed wire. We tripped and fell over the barbed wire, then got up and continued running until we saw a small clearing with some shell holes and we jumped into one of them. It was drizzling rain, not too dark, though, and the fast-moving clouds were uncovering the stars and the moonlight.

Two Germans had come to the edge of the woods and were looking for us. I swear one of them saw us, and as he raised up his rifle, I could hear him as he moved the bolt of his rifle and brought it up to his shoulder. He held it there, peering through the gloom, and after a couple minutes, he lowered his rifle. They walked around a little, and we watched them go into the woods. We stayed lying awhile, as we thought they were hiding and watching for us. It was still squally, and the clouds seemed to be moving swiftly, big and black with the stars between the rifts.

While with an English tank company for experience, an English officer, commander of that tank company, taught me how to read directions by the stars using the Big Dipper. We had started crawling again from the shell holes, went a little ways, then I began looking for the Big Dipper. There was a ridge to our left, and as we lay there, I prayed for God to show me or just let me see that "seventh star" of the Big Dipper. I could only get a vision of no more than six stars. I fervently asked him to just let me see that seventh star! Do you know it was not long until my prayer was answered and we knew which way to go!

We went up in a stooped position along the ridge, the singing of machine-gun bullets over us, too close to stand or walk. The strange thing was that we were going correctly, but we did not know before this time. It was assurance to us that we had not gone deeper into the German lines.

I will never forget waiting for a glimpse of the tail of the Big Dipper, and the realization of what importance it had to us, per the teachings of my British tank commander. Four or five weeks before this I had been in his tank crew; I don't remember his name exactly, although a Sergeant Crofts, I believe, was one of the crew. I was saddened to hear that one of the crew was killed by a sniper. Another was wounded after returning from a tank action. They had been placed in a staff car, along with another wounded man who was being taken to a dressing station, when a shell made a direct hit on the staff car, killing both of them.

We got to the top of the ridge; below us we could see by the light of the flares and star shells that the territory ahead of us was trenches and barbed wire. We were back at the front lines again. There was an open space of probably a thousand feet between the bottom of the ridge and the front lines, and as we, back to crawling again, moved ahead, we encountered the bodies of many German dead. We snaked up to the rear of a big antitank trench and laid there for a while. *What to do* we wondered.

A little hill or small knob on the right side of us and a German machine-gunner, less than one hundred feet from our right, reeled off a belt of ammunition, I guess to keep any of our patrols away or to let us know they were still in the fight. About fifty or sixty feet to our left were some boards across the trench, running from side to side about four or five feet above the bottom of the trench; they were probably four or five feet below the ground surface. German infantry were under the boards, keeping dry, as it was raining and drizzling all the time.

We decided what to do; we jumped down into the trench, I boosted Lieutenant Dunning up, he crawled over the edge and reached down so I had to stretch my arms up, and he got hold of my hands. How he had the strength left to do that, I do not know, but somehow I also got out of the trench, and we both ran ahead and flopped down as a couple of machine guns started shooting up the ground all around us. We had slid into small shell holes and could not fit our whole bodies into them. Flares went up and they really lit things up, but due to the rain, I do not think they knew just what the matter was. After four or five minutes, things died down. We started to crawl again; we were trying to get through the barbed wire heaped up in front of us and were picking our way through it when they picked us up again and really tore the ground up around us. How we lived through that, I do not know. God had to be helping us!

We picked our way through several more wire barriers, and daylight was starting to break. We had gone through one trench where we had seen a cubbyhole in the side, but decided to keep going and continue down into a big dugout in another trench when we found loads of potato mashers, German grenades, so we turned away from there. We got into a trench, a short one it was, with dead machine-gunners in it.

A terrific shell or shrapnel fire had started, and we were caught in both German and our own shellfire. As we started up a dirt emplacement at the top of this trench, a shrapnel shell hit directly in front of me and exploded on the dirt. It really knocked me off my feet, about six or eight feet backward. I thought my legs had been blown off; Lieutenant Dunning ran to me, and we both felt around in the dark. I was okay after a couple minutes, just badly shaken up, with my leggings and pants legs torn up.

We got out of this trench and found the cubbyhole in the small trench we had been in before, then crawled into it wet, cold, and weary. It had water on the rubber sheet or poncho on the floor and we had to leave our feet sticking out, but we lay while the shelling went on and were so worn out that we fell asleep, dozing, each with his .45 in his hand on top of his gas mask.

How long we dozed, I do not know. The next thing I know or saw was an English soldier, rather five or six of them. One of them was pulling on Dunning's foot hollering, "Yanks! Yanks!" We were glad to see them! I saw two German machine-gunners strapped or bound to their machine guns, both of them killed by shellfire. There were a few more of them, all dead but not tied to their guns.

The English soldiers took us down into a big dugout where they had set up a headquarters of some sort and, man oh man, they gave us each a big glass of Scotch and a mutton sandwich before they started to question us. After giving them all the information we could, they showed us how to go, and we went to the rear to an English dressing station.

Later at another station, an American gave us a cup of hot chocolate, which made me sick, and I vomited, and then he asked if we had been gassed. We said, yes, and then he told us that drinking that chocolate was the worst thing we could have done. We had never encountered anything like that before.

We finally found what was left of Company C. I'll never forget, Lieutenant Cole grabbed me and hugged me and gave me a bacon sandwich he had in his hand. Before this, a Lieutenant General Reid, I believe of the 27th Yank Division, shook our hands and complimented us on what a great job our tanks had done. We then went to Major Harrison's headquarters and told them what we knew.

Lieutenant Dunning had big patches of white hair as it had turned overnight. They took him to the hospital, where they wanted me to go, but I said I was okay. Two days later, they took me to the hospital anyhow as I could not sleep. They gave me morphine tablets, but I still could not sleep. I could only see Germans chasing me and shooting at me, no matter what I did. They gave me more morphine, and then I asked for something to eat. They gave me a big bowl of hot stew. I fell asleep eating it and slept for thirty hours without wakening. More stew, and I went to sleep for another twenty-four hours. When I awoke then, I tried to get out of bed and found out I could not stand on my feet, so it took me another three days before I could walk again.

Got back to St. Emily about October 8, the day of the next show, and was back up to the front again for the next one on October 18.

Lieutenant Dunning came back to us shortly after that, and on about November 3, he came to me and asked if I would volunteer for a night attack taking the King's Own Infantry over the top. I agreed, and he told me to pick out the tank I wanted, but to save room for our first sergeant Carter and leave a place for two 6-pounder gunners from Company A or B, I do not remember which one.

The tank I picked out was the J23. It was a male (British-designed and -built) Mk V thirty-five-foot-long tank and had never been able to get over the top; it always developed mechanical troubles for the English and for us. I could never understand it, as to me it was the sweetest running tank then of Company C.

I got our crew lined up, we went over the motor, tuning it up, and on November 6 at 1:20 a.m. we went over the top again in a night attack leading the King's Own Infantry Regiment. We ran into a deep fog not long before we passed the end of the tape that had been laid to guide us to our correct positions.

We ran into terrific shrapnel fire and the Germans' timing was good, shells exploding fifty to seventy-five feet over the top of the tanks. One of the crew was wounded by the shrapnel. We went through heavy gas concentrations, which made some of the crew sick, vomiting and retching. The Germans were also throwing chlorine gas shells, which were deadly. At about 8 or 9 that morning, we came back a little way to let out the sick crewmembers and picked up replacements for them.

We went back, mopping machine-gun nests. We also found a battery of German field pieces behind an elevated railroad track. They were trying to knock us out, but they were not able to. One of two Germans under a tree threw a potato masher and hit the edge of the window opening on our right side. I saw him throw it, and I ducked down, keeping myself from falling by holding onto one of the handles placed inside the tower. I got hit in the left hand, nothing severe, just skin lacerations and a piece of grenade in my middle finger.

We also encountered a lot of antitank rifle fire and our magneto was shot off, but because of the double ignition system, we were still running on all six cylinders when we finished that night about 6 p.m. Those antitank rifles were bad actors sometimes, as they would come through our heaviest armor plate. The J23 performed beautifully and was able to lose the name of "the jinx."

When we looked the tank over the next day, we could see where we had many hits that night by shrapnel shells, knocking out our semaphore and tearing up our top ditching beam guide rails. We were told that our volunteer night show was highly successful. All twelve tanks came back okay. Our motor had actually been running for about twenty-six hours without shutting it off, never missed—a perfect performance.

Major R. I. Sasse was our battalion commander from the La Selle River attack until we arrived back at Fort Meade.

Colonel Patton came up to our front several times, as he and Major Sasse were working on a wireless communications system then. I became acquainted with Colonel Patton and later met him again at Longres, where we had stopped for delousing and clothing before we went to Marseilles for our embarkation to the United States.

Lieutenant Dunning was awarded the British Military Cross for officers only, and I received the British Military Medal. These were immediate awards and given in the field under the hand of General Rawlinson, Commander of the British 4th Army.

I also received a certificate from the British Tank Corps and a brown, red, and green whistle cord (lanyard), which represented the green fields of Flanders, the mud in Flanders, and the red for the blood shed in Flanders Field. The awards were for our September 29 action.

We headed back to Camp Meade in March 1919, and I was sent to Camp Zachary Taylor at Louisville, Kentucky, for discharge April 16, 1919.

///LT. HAROLD H. NEFF (U.S. ARMY)

The memories of my experiences in the tank corps are filled chiefly with the horrors of long, unending hours of fatigue, with the self-abnegation of a body of young Americans, who, eager to do their part in the liberation of the world, were forced, by the exigencies of circumstances. To spend many, many days here in sunny France, in comparative ease and comfort, while their brothers in arms were gaining laurels at Chateau-Thierry and at Soissons (France).

At last, the day for which so fervently had been yearned—as there is yearning for that of which one knows nothing—arrived; in the darkness and rain, we entrained our tanks for a destination unknown to us! High was the speculation whither we were bound, but great was the ignorance thereof—as always.

Finally, after hours of railroading, charmed by the sweet delights of "corn willy," (corned beef hash) and cold, cold tomatoes, by an occasional excursion from under the eye of the officers, in quest of tabooed cognac, Company B, 345th Battalion, arrived where it was to detrain. The night was black. On the horizon could be seen the sudden brilliance of uprising rockets; we knew we were there.

In the darkness and the rain, the (French-supplied light Renault) tanks crawled their way along the wobbly little cars, which made, by their cricks and cranks, our strong American lads long for something that was American and not "frog" (a derogatory term for the French). Of course, we execrated the French train crew for the small mishaps, and they as fervently execrated us for our too great desire for dispatch.

Into the unknown somberness of the night, we disappeared and meandered our way through the desolateness about us, between gaunt solemn of innocence and baby laughter, now stretched their gaunt arms into the sky, to say that war was grim. At last, as the day was breaking murkily, we hastily reached woods and hid ourselves within its deep seclusion—for we as owls and ghosts and bats are creatures of the night and dare not let the cock's crow find us wandering in the world of light.

It was for the Saint-Mihiel salient attack that we had come up.

After several days of incessant labor and discomfort, the time came for us to go over. Things went well, and due to the precipitations of the Boche (slang term for German soldiers) my company had no dire experiences.

From the Saint-Mihiel affair, after all the work to put our steeds of steel in mettle, we entrained again for parts unknown. The train conductor said that we were not going far from Verdun; our hearts were thrilled to think we were bound for a place so full of glory.

Again we disembarked. Again we worked. Again we lumbered up to the starting point in the blackness of the night. Stray shells bursting here and there in the blackness of the night told us that Fritz (slang term for German soldiers) was not asleep.

The first day of the attack, my company was supposed to be in reserve. After the attack had been well started, we crept along, over trenches, far away. The column stopped, as the leading elements were having great difficulty with a wide and deep trench. Suddenly, in the quietness that there was, crash went a shell right over there. We decided that it was best to scatter helter-skelter until a crossing could be negotiated. Machine-gun bullets started singing quite a bit.

Under the calm supervision of Colonel Patton, after several tanks had unsuccessfully attempted to cross and were ditched in the mire, the 1st Platoon of my company succeeded in passing and was sent up the hill to get "those machine-gun nests."

Before long, my tank, on account of various difficulties, met by others, was all alone. We kept on, not being certain where the Germans were, or whether any were really up there, and popped a few shots into all favorable cover. Suddenly, the front of the tank seemed ablaze with heat and smoke. I could not exactly understand what was going on. I inquired of the gunner if he was firing. "No," he said. Then I guessed. We advanced, but on account of the lay of the ground, could not exactly see what was before us. Suddenly, right in front of us, bobbed up, just like little Jack used to leap from the jumping box, a whole bunch of Germans running all hunched over, like little lambs, up the way. It was comical to see them run.

We kept on going, toward a village that lay high on a hill, fair and beautiful with its distorted and crumbling walls. Nothing could be seen on either side. We arrived on a high precipice and could find no course to descent into the small valley, from which the village clambered up the hill. At last, after patrolling hither and thither, we attempted what seemed to offer a fair method of descent and, much to our disgust, owing to crumbling of the banks of a ditch that was overgrown with grass and partially concealed, we suddenly turned topsy-turvy, and lay there in the hollow. Then, while we were still pondering what we should do with our overturned steed, up on the precipice behind us came the rest of the tanks and let loose on the village with all their guns, right over our heads. In addition, Fritz started back with a battery he had over there in the woods. The gunner decided to climb up after help, but when he stuck his head over, he saw all the guns of the tanks pointed right toward him and decided it would be, perhaps, the better part of wisdom to stay right where he was.

The next day, we finally succeeded in getting ourselves extracted. Several days thereafter, after various other experiences, both pleasant and unpleasant, the tread of my Angel—such was the name of the diabolic engine of war—got broken, away from the tank-a-drome, and I was left to guard it. Fritz was shooting them over pretty steadfastly. When night fell, I decided it best to crawl into her entrails and sleep there. During the night, while slumber-bound, Fritz was so unkind as to send over some gas, which sent me, in turn far to the rear, away from the boom of the cannon, to the mud of the hospital camps.

///SGT. ARTHUR SNYDER (U.S. ARMY)

Lieutenant Wood was on my right proceeding along a hedgerow from which the Germans were producing a severe machine-gun flank fire. My orders were to keep strict liaison with Lieutenant Wood's tank, and when I saw it change direction, I did likewise. If we had had radios, this would not have happened, because Wood was wounded and his driver, Corporal Rogers, was taking him behind the infantry assault line.

Then Rogers, who was only a kid in his teens, under great danger to himself, got out of his tank and crawled beyond the assault wave, endeavoring to signal me to proceed in the attack. Just at this time, a German shell exploded under the right tractor (track) of my tank, severing it in two like a knife cutting a piece of string. Of course, the tank could then go only in circles. Kelly (Snyder's driver) got it facing our lines. We got out through the driver's door and had a crawling race to the rear of our assault line. Here we found Wood and Rogers and their tank, the "Five of Hearts." I took command of it and, using Rogers as my driver, returned to the attack. The enemy machine guns in the hedgerow had been practically silenced, but the infantry could make little progress because of heavy frontal machine-gun fire.

As we proceeded in a frontal direction, we suddenly encountered, at close quarters, an extremely large machine-gun nest that was well constructed in a big shell crater. The position had undoubtedly been improved by field fortifications, and it contained at least three machine guns, maybe more.

We were fortunate that the position was not supported by any accompanying artillery piece, because in the fog and smoke we were practically on it (the machine-gun nest) before observing it. I saw a German raise a potato masher to throw at us. If he let go, it did no harm and we were causing confusion and damage in that nest with our 37mm fire.

The armor plate on those old French Renaults was good, but when we came to close quarters, the splinters from bullets hitting around the vision slits did considerable damage to our personnel. Wood was wounded this way. As Rogers and I were trying to get around the right flank of that big machine-gun nest, he was hit about his eyes with splinters. He fell forward in his driver's seat but, fortunately, did not stall the motor, which was an easy thing to do with those old tanks.

I knelt behind Rogers, cautioned him as to use of the foot throttle, and, reaching forward to the steering levers, steered the tank back to our lines. The blood from Rogers' wounds was blinding him, and when I left him at the dressing station, it was obvious that he was no longer fit for duty. I took the .45 pistol so the "Five of Hearts" would be sure to have a full complement of weapons, and then I looked for another tank mate. I was in the process of trying to get an infantryman, when I saw a runner wearing the tank corps armband (a triangular patch divided into yellow, blue, and red segments, similar to today's armor patch). I found that he was from the 345th Battalion and had become lost from his organization. He told me that he had graduated from our driver's school at the tank center at Langres, so I immediately pressed him into service as my third driver for the day.

We at once returned to the attack and found that the big machine-gun position had been taken. Some of its personnel were being taken to the rear as prisoners. We proceeded down the Exermont Ravine. At the bottom of this ravine is a stream, and to the west of Exermont was a stone bridge that spanned it. Orders had been issued not to use this bridge because of its being mined.

My driver and I were just getting ready to reconnoiter for a stream crossing when I was approached by a captain from the 16th Infantry. He informed me that his company was being held up by machine-gun fire from the other side of the ravine. I told him I would support his company as soon as I could find a place to ford the stream. He asked me why I didn't I use the stone bridge, and I explained the orders. He mentioned having received similar ones but had discovered that if the bridge had been mined, it was longer so. He asked me where my officers were, and I told him about my platoon leader having been wounded early in the morning. I did not know where any of the tank corps were as the "Five of Hearts" was covering a whole company front. I told the infantry officer that I would be glad to cross the bridge under existing circumstances, if so ordered. He ordered me so, with a smile, and the "Five of Hearts" crossed the bridge safely.

Upon gaining the heights of the north side of the Exermont ravine, we immediately contacted the enemy. The outposts gave way rapidly and several machine guns were abandoned. I have little doubt in my own mind that the enthusiasm to follow in pursuit made me go too far ahead of the infantry. The terrain flattened out, and there was little cover available, and though the going was rough, it afforded a rare opportunity to fire at moving targets. I fear that the backs of those Germans with their packs and heavy overcoats impressed me more than keeping liaison with our infantry. However, the party was not to last long, for when the cover was reached, we met with enemy resistance. Upon being fired on at close range, my driver was shot through the throat, and at the same time, our engine stalled. I made many attempts to crank it from the gunner's compartment, but to no avail.

We were in much the same condition as a disabled man-of-war. Our mobility was gone, and with it all chance of maneuver and the ability to seek cover. Our firepower was not far from zero because the 37mm gun was jammed in the depressed position from bullets fired at close quarters. Several times, I had to put my entire weight on the breech so as to elevate the piece, but now this had become ineffective. Our projectiles would hit the ground only a few yards from the tank. The turret could not be rotated because it, too, was jammed with bullets. To our left was a German 77mm field piece. There was plenty of ammunition beside its trail. The breechblock had been removed when the gun was abandoned, but now the Germans began to reappear. It was a local counterattack.

My wounded driver kept filling pistol clips, and I produced as much fire as possible with our pistols and the crippled 37mm. I paid more attention to the volume of fire than its accuracy for I feared the enemy would close in if the volume diminished. Three machine guns were set up at close range, just out of range of our piece with its limited elevation. The fragmentation of our shells did afford some protection, but I could not train this fire on the German field piece.

The constant hammering of these machine guns at close range was terrific. The hinges on the doors could not stand up under it for long, but it was the mushroom ventilator on top of the turret that gave way. I was hit in the back of the head with fragments of it and bullet splinters. The Germans did not attempt to close in; on the contrary, they began to give way and then fled. I have seen many marvelous sights of troops in action, and on parade, but I have never seen, or expect to see, a more glorious sight than our infantry advancing toward us at the high port (rifles held chest high, bayonets up).

The "Five of Hearts" and her crew had done their job, and our colors were not struck until relief came to us.

///LT. D. M. TAYLOR (U.S. ARMY)

About the rankest thing there is in this man's army is a big buck private or a noncommissioned officer detailed on duty as a runner at the front. Moreover, when such a man is on such duty with the tank corps, he outranks the German *Gott* (God) himself. One really cannot appreciate the amount of authority with which a runner considers himself invested until he has held such office with a brand new outfit on its first trip into battle. The writer was one such of the latter variety at the front in the Mihiel sector in the big drive, which started September 12 with a million-dollar barrage and wound up with a wild rush for souvenirs.

The writer never could understand what should cause any sane man to commence a story, such as he read some time ago, with the following words "dark and stormy night and rain it fell in torrents." That is, he never could understand it until the night of September 11, 1918, the year in which Gott deserted his company commander. Now he knows that the writer of those tragic lines must have been the advance agent who booked the night of September 11, 1918, on the Mihiel Salient.

On the afternoon of the 11th, when it became known in headquarters company of the 326th Battalion that the outfit was to go over the next morning the "goldbricks" (goof-offs) of that organization, numbering sixteen in all, including the writer, loudly clamored with apparently honest zeal to be allowed to take part in the picnic. Major Sereno E. Brett, commanding the battalion, had a peculiar habit of taking men at their words, so to be taken, given a few necessary instructions and detailed as a unit of runners to follow the major's tank. They were all equipped with the official insignia of the runner (red armband) so that if at any time during the engagement they should become wearied with the amusement of being shot at, they could depart hastily and boldly for the SOS (supply of services) without being picked up by the military police and herded back to the lines.

What with the protection of the red armband and the knowledge that the major had strict instructions to keep his tank at least a kilometer (621 yards) behind the lines, it seemed like a nice soft graft with a chance for some excitement and little danger. In this connection, I will say this much for the major: he complied strictly with these instructions right at the start of the fight. Leaving his tank at least a kilometer behind the lines as he had decided that means of locomotion was too slow, he hopped out calling, "Follow me," and beat it for a point about a kilometer ahead of the tanks.

But to return to our beginning, about 8:30 p.m., the tanks left their camouflaged position in the woods and started moving out for the jumping off place, about five miles up the line. When the procession started, it was as silent and secret an affair as any inner chamber session of the Masons or MPs Everybody who spoke at all spoke in whispers. No lights were shown, and all were careful to put their feet down gently in the mud holes to avoid creating a loud splash. However, by the time the outfit had reached the jumping off place, instructions were being howled back and forth. Cigarettes and flashlights were being used to guide the tanks into position, and pistols were being fired to attract attention. Barnum & Bailey's Circus never came into any town as well advertised. However, there was that million-dollar barrage to deaden these minor sounds, and as it happened, half of Jerry's (slang term for German soldiers) flock were already well on their way to Berlin by the time down H hour arrived.

About nine o'clock that night, it had commenced raining, and it rained such as it never had rained before the flood or since. Otherwise, Noah would have had the SRO (standing room only) sign hanging out long before he had sublet the contract for two by fours. The writer, being an American of the highly intelligent variety, started out without a raincoat, carried a full pack all night closely following the major's tank and arriving at the jumping off place thought to tie it to the tail of the major's tank.

At 1 a.m. sharp, the frequently aforementioned million-dollar barrage started. It was rather a disappointment in the way of noise to "our here" after having read a few of Irwin S. Cobb's and George Patullo's descriptions of a big American barrage. However, he was compensated for this disappointment by a sight on the morning of the 12th such as few men and neither of the aforementioned gentlemen can truthfully assert that they have witnessed. He saw with his own eyes an American aviator in an American plane on the front.

H hour was 5:30 a.m. About 5:15 a.m., Captain Weed approached me and conversed with him in the following terms: "Rush like hell down the line and tell 'blankety-blank' drivers to get their 'blankety-blank' tanks cranked up and be ready to start." He performed this little deed. The battalion moved out on time.

From that time on until about 7 a.m. that day, pandemonium reigned. The American soldier has frequently been heralded in history and fiction as an individual fighter, and believe me no one could accuse any member of the 326th Battalion Tank Corps that day of not being a true American. Never before or never since has it been my privilege to witness so much individual fighting at one time. In fact, the fighting became so individual in the course of the next half hour or so that it looked as if there were at least six different wars going on at once.

This can be said about the tankers: they were all and every one of them working with one purpose view, and that purpose was to get as far forward as possible in the shortest time possible and connect with Heine (slang term for German soldiers) even if they had to get out and walk. That is what the majority of them did. For the tanks after starting out the night before with no extra gas on board had only enough left in the morning to run a few kilometers. The Huns (slang term for German soldiers) had decided to counter our attack on this front by a strategic retreat, and the Renaults were never built for prize winning on a speedway. Nevertheless, with the aid of some good footwork, a good many of the boys did establish a liaison with Fritz (slang term for German soldiers), as can be proven by the fact that we secured that day that which the Americans had been fighting for—"souvenirs"—and a *beaucoup* of them.

Immediately, the major's first tank landed in a ditch and stayed there. He hopped out with his pigeon basket and grabbed the next tank in the column. Five minutes more and it was in a ditch, and in another three minutes his third tank was tangled up in the ruins of the village. Apparently, thoroughly disgusted with the turn affairs had taken, but secretly quite pleased that he could now disregard his colonel's instructions to stay one thousand meters behind and direct the fighting, he moved up on foot to the head of the column and, of course, the runners had to follow. The writer brought up the rear.

About halfway across an open field, the major passed by a shell hole and his nostrils caught a peculiar odor. Deciding it was gas, he gave the alarm. I got my mask on in less than five minutes—but not much less. If there had been any gas there, the great American public would never have the pleasure of reading this story. I decided, then and there, to, at the first opportunity, take a train for some good, reliable gas-school in the SOS and take about three weeks of gas instructions, feeling that I could in this way best protect Uncle Sam's $10 million investment.

The major's party traveled rapidly ahead for another fifteen minutes or so, and then halted. While the major made some reconnaissance of the terrain and the state of affairs in Jerry's front line, which consisted of a few machine guns and some 77s that the enemy had been unable to haul away and was manned by a few men who didn't know any better than to stay there. I was sent back to see if any tanks were coming up; about two hundred meters back, I found eight tanks, which were commanded by Captain Weed, who was in the leading one.

Captain Weed had halted his tank and was apparently arguing with himself as to which of several was the best place to cross a trench. I, by right of the red bandana wound around my right arm, decided for him and led him up to Major Brett as per instructions. The major having dispatched these tanks and several which followed to various points of the line, again moved forward until we reached a shallow trench. One man in the vicinity had his arm half blown off about this time, so the major decided that there must be some shrapnel flying about and ordered the detachment down into the trench. A Red Cross stretcher-bearer standing thereabout, a fellow about six feet, six inches, decided that this taking cover was all foolishness. About thirty seconds later, he changed his mind quite rapidly and tried to hide behind a clod of dirt about four inches high.

In a short time, this trench stuff grew too monotonous for the major, so he moved again. Shortly, eight reserve tanks, loaned to us by the 327th Battalion, arrived and the CO, having decided to take an active part in the picnic, secured himself a second lieutenant for a driver, climbed into the leading tank, and started off to hunt up machine-gun nests. We started to follow. The major ordered us to stay where we were as he was going off on a little personal affair. If some brigadier general had happened along about this time, we would probably all have been awarded the DSM (Distinguished Service Medal) for the promptness with which we obeyed these instructions. We did more than obey them; we moved back one hundred meters and crawled into a shell hole, opened up a couple of cans of corn willy and some hard tack, and held lunch. The line had moved so far ahead by this time that we feared that before the day was over, we would lose our 20 percent increase for foreign service.

After dinner, we moved up to locate the major. After traveling a couple of kilometers, we reached the brow of a slight rise just out of Nonsard and sat down to watch the waves of doughboys going by down the hill and into Nonsard. They came past us in squad columns. The first man in the first wave that passed us had his gun slung and was busy with both hands rolling a cigarette. The next man was busily engaged in carrying a head of cabbage in one hand and feeding himself hard tack with the other.

The writer was rather shocked and felt almost called upon to admonish these men for such disgraceful behavior in the face of the enemy. The enemy, however, were too busy to notice this breech of battlefield etiquette—both of them. Sergeant McGintey took one, securing a silver watch and a good German steel razor, and Major Brett shot the other one out of the church steeple in Nonsard, where he was busy firing his machine gun. Sergeant McGintey's prisoner was a man of apparently sixty years or so, who probably had been too tired to run with the rest. Neither the age, sex, nationality, or number of Major Brett's victim could be identified, as the major had made a bull's-eye in the center of the target with his little 37 (37mm tank gun).

We waited on the brow of the hill until the conquering heroes returned to seek a good, camouflaged position for the night. We then held a feast of canned tomatoes, corn willy, and hard tack to celebrate the victory. I was then dispatched to Essey with a message for the colonel. Reaching Essey, I stood at the appointed place to await the arrival of the CO until 6:30 p.m. I then decided that the message could not be of any real importance, so I found myself a billet and retired for the night. Thus ended my first, last, and only day under fire on the battlefields of France.

CHAPTER TWO

WORLD WAR II (1939–1945)

///SERGEANT BECKER (U.S. ARMY)

It's a funny thing being a tank commander. You have to run the crew, be stern, and show leadership. I had a new driver for an M3 (medium) tank. I told him to drive up a slope to a certain place and then stop. He got excited and went all the way up the hill. I told him to back up to the right place. He got excited again and went all the way back down the hill. He wouldn't listen to the interphone communication so I hollered to the 37 gunner to stop him. Finally, we stopped him, we drove to a safe firing place, and I asked him why he didn't pay attention to me.

Overnight, I explained how I wanted him to drive and how I wanted him to pay attention, and I told him if he didn't I would close his slot up completely and make him drive blind. That fixed him. I think I have a good driver now. I am lucky, as I have never lost a tank, but how I don't know. We saved two tanks out of the company.

When our platoon leader told us to withdraw by backing up, he became confused, perhaps because his gun was pointed to the side. Instead of backing up, he turned at right angles and ran up a ridge. He didn't come back.

I like the M4 tank. I look at the German tank and thank God, I am in an M4. The M3 is nice looking but should be three feet lower. I think we will lick the Germans in time. I think we are good.

///TECHNICAL 4TH GRADE ARISTIDE (ED) LAPORTA (U.S. ARMY)

After months of combat duty as a tank driver in the U.S. Army with the 1st Armored Division in North Africa, I was captured at Kasserine Pass by Rommel and company, but remained silent during interrogation other than my name, rank, and serial number. I was beaten and sent to a slave labor camp for six months in Reggio, Italy, then on to Stalag 3B in Furstenberg, Germany for seventeen months, and finally on to Stalag 2B in Bugenwald, Germany for four months until we were finally liberated in May 1945.

During these twenty-seven months as a POW, a special few comrades and I became known as "rabble rousers," always into some mischief! To maintain such a group of brave and special men, taking chances every day of being executed for sabotage, it took precise planning, timing, and security. During work, play, or exercise, we paired off in twos to "guard" the camp, doing whatever it took not to look conspicuous to the German guards.

My partner in guard was Robert Gearinger, better known as Lefty. During our long and lonely hours together, we did a lot of talking. No matter what the subject was, it eventually always came down to Lefty's wife, Betty, and his little girl, Patty, back home in Bloomsburg, Pennsylvania. He had never seen his little girl, Patty. During all our talks, I learned all about his family, friends, and hometown, the street he lived on, the gas company he worked for, the town square, and so on.

During our time as POWs, twenty-seven months, Lefty took ill a few times, nothing serious. After about twenty-four months, though, he came down with diphtheria and was put in isolation in what the Germans called a hospital. It was nothing more than a broke-down shack, no doctors, no medics, no nurses, no windows, and no bathroom facilities.

At night, I would sneak out of the camp and take Lefty whatever food I could find or trade for cigarettes to keep up his strength. One day, the Germans found our underground room under our barracks floor, where they found a radio receiver, a small-caliber handgun, hand grenades, an American flag, and other contraband. Remember, we were the rabble rousers! Well, the Germans had no sense of humor about this and ordered twenty-five of us before the firing squad, including Lefty. Only by the grace of God and a little help from an air raid by American bombers did we escape that situation. At that point, Lefty had been in isolation for about six days when a German officer informed us that we were being "transferred" to Stalag 2B in Bugenwald, an eighty-five-mile march in the dead of winter. He also informed us that whoever could not make the march would be shot and killed wherever they fell. We also knew that Bugenwald was one of the camps that had the ovens and gas chambers; we had no idea of our fate.

At this point, I asked the German officer about my friend, Sgt. Robert Gearinger, who was in the "hospital." He informed me that if he could not make the march, he would be shot, or if he were left here, he would starve to death or be shot anyway. I then suggested to the officer that I take care of Lefty, knowing that he could care less whether he was shot there or on the road. Well, when they brought Lefty out, he looked terrible. He was too weak to even stand, let alone walk!

So, what do you do with a friend who is facing certain death and has not ever seen his little daughter? You do what any red-blooded American would do, you carry him! It was snowing heavily and bitter cold. Therefore, I got the bright idea to build a sled. I got some boards from the wooden bunks, made two runners, and put on a form of seat, backrest, and footrest. I then tied Lefty to the sled so he would not fall off and made up a rope to pull the sled with. At 9 p.m. that night, we started out on our eighty-five-mile march.

I pulled that sled until 6 a.m. the following morning, about nine hours. At that point, we had reached an area where the snow was melting, so I could no longer pull the sled. The Germans were yelling at us, "Keep up, keep up, or you will be shot! Therefore, I took Lefty off the sled, put his arm around my shoulders, my right hand holding him by his belt, and kept walking. Every so often Lefty would ask me to just let him go and take care of myself, and I would say, "No way, buddy; we will make it together. You want to see your little baby, don't you?" I am leaving out the gruesome details of the march, as that would be another whole story in itself.

We finally reached our destination. Those, of us who made it were exhausted. Lefty said to me, "I owe you my life. I could not have made it without you." He went on to say how his entire family will be grateful, and that someday he hoped I would come to Bloomsburg, Pennsylvania, and meet them, especially his wife and baby girl. "She will call you Uncle Ed." I told him I don't know when, but one day, if we make it out of here, we will cross paths again, I promise!

We remained in Stalag 2B about four months, until one glorious morning we woke up and there were no guards in front of the tent. We went outside, and there were no Germans around anywhere. The gates were open unguarded, so we picked up whatever we had and started to walk toward the American sector, when thank God, we saw a convoy of American trucks coming to pick us up. The war was over. We were taken to a staging area, and a few days later, we flew to Camp Lucky Strike in Le Harve, France. There, we were put in different groups according to what part of the United States each of us was going to. At this point, Lefty and I parted company, as he was going to Pennsylvania and I was off to California. We said our so longs and promised that one day we would meet again. We boarded different ships and were on our way to the good old United States.

In California I worked about nine months for the Union Oil Company, but the transition from war to civilization was difficult. I was getting restless. I had many bad dreams and nightmares, tore up many bedsheets, and put my fist through the wall a few times. I needed time to readjust! One morning I went to my boss to discuss my situation. He was understanding and offered to send me to the company doctor. I said no thanks; I must work this out for myself. He gave me twelve months leave of absence with the promise that if I returned within the twelve months I was assured any job I wanted in the organization. That Friday I was paid, went right to the bank to get some travelers checks, then headed home to pack two suitcases. That night I hitthe road.

I was on the road about two months, stopping in about twenty states to visit my POW buddies. At this point, I was in New Jersey and on my way to Bloomsburg, Pennsylvania, to visit Lefty and meet his family. I never wrote or called him to say I was coming, as I wanted it to be a surprise. When I got near Bloomsburg, I put away all maps and his address. I knew just how to get there. I had a perfect picture in my mind!

As I approached town, I began to see all the landmarks Lefty had told me about during the war. I felt like I had been there before; I knew just how to get to his house. I drove up the driveway, got out of my car, and knocked on the door. A young mother and a little girl opened the door. I did not say, "Hello Betty." I did not say a word, nor did she, we just looked into each other's eyes. After about twenty seconds of total silence, she said, "Oh my God, it's Ed LaPorta! She put her arms around me and her head on my shoulder. Between sobs, she could not stop thanking me. "Had it not been for you, I would not have a husband and my baby would not have a father." At the same time, the little girl, Patty, was tugging on my trousers. When Betty released me a little bit, I turned to little Patty, patted her on her little head, and said, "Hi, Sweetheart!" She looked up at me with her big blue eyes and said, "Uncle Ed, thank you for my daddy."

This is an experience that after fifty-four years I still remember vividly and will never forget. We are still friends and see each other as often as we can. It was all worthwhile.

///PVT. CARL HALLSTROM (U.S. ARMY)

It was a good day, just right for an attack. The sun was out and the planes were up doing their job. They were like big birds in the sky, diving and spurting death from their wings. H hour was 10 . . . ten minutes to go. We were all set. Conversation lagged. Somebody would ask for a light, or for the time, but most of us were silent. By the time it was on minute to 10, sweat was dripping profusely from my brow.

Over the radio, a voice said, "Move out."

"Gun in working order?" asked the gunner. I gave him a nod and we were on our way.

I was looking out of my periscope, when I saw number one tank, which was in the lead, burst into flames. Five men bailed out and jumped for the cover of a ditch, just above the ditch, one of those hedgerows for which we had so much respect. Our own infantry was about four hedgerows behind.

Jerry was shooting at the five men from over the top of the hedgerow, so we sprayed the hedge with our machine gun. The tank commander spoke to the driver, over the interphone, "Pull up behind number one so that those five men can use us for cover."

"If we go up there, we'll get knocked off," said the driver, "Let's go anyway," said the commander. We made it okay, and the five men crowded behind our tank. Then we started back.

Through my periscope I saw a bright flash spurt from the hedge. It seemed like a ball of fire was hurtling toward us. Then the flames were roaring all about my body. The flames were licking at my face when I pushed my hatch open and dove out. I reached the ground ten feet below in one leap and started running. I believe my legs were in motion even before I reached the ground. The burning tank was only twenty-five yards away, parallel to the enemy line at a distance of not more than thirty yards.

I don't know how they missed us. Bullets were kicking up the dust all around us. Machine guns, rifles, burp guns, and every kind of small-arms fire was shooting at us. Once I glanced back over my shoulder at the tank we had left. Flames were leaping from the hatches, and the ammunition inside had started to explode. I could see the tracers from the machine-gun ammunition shooting out of the hatches.

At the end of the 125-yard stretch was a swamp. I dove in and lay there panting. I had run right in front of German lines for 125 yards. They were throwing everything at us but the kitchen sink. As I lay there, dirt from machine-gun bullets sifted down from a mound above my head and went down my neck. I had reached a place of comparative safety; at least Jerry could not see me. The only escape was through an old drain-pipe to my rear. It was small but I made it through, only to find three more just like it beyond. I got through two of them without mishap and crowded into a ditch, which lay between the last pipe and me.

I started to enter the last pipe, but a dead GI evidently had had the same idea, so my passage was blocked. Then I noticed I was not alone with my troubles. A couple of feet away laid a man with a wound in his leg. I helped him up, and together we made it across the field. I remember while passing a burning tank I said to him, "Don't worry fella, God is with us."

"You're right," he nodded, and together we stumbled across the open space. We reached a ditch safely, and I left him there with some dough-boys. Soon, I was rejoined by the rest of my crew. Together we made it back to the assembly area.

///PFC. ANDREW F. WOODS (U.S. ARMY)

Major Edwards came over by Lieutenant Guitteau's tank to confer with him. Major Edwards' jeep driver was with him, and I accompanied Lieutenant Guitteau. Edwards wanted Guitteau to race his platoon of five tanks into Herrlisheim at top speed staying close to the Zorn Canal, as far as possible from those guns that had shot up Company A. Then Major Edwards proceeded to affirm our judgment of him. Before this small group of ten to twelve soldiers, he emptied all his pockets of any personal effects and handed them to his jeep driver, who was staying behind, instructing him to send them to his next of kin. He would take his tank into Herrlisheim. Long faces abounded. Being a pragmatic farm boy, I looked up Maurice Storey, a good friend and the company armorer. He would be remaining behind also, and I did precisely what the major did.

We cranked up the tanks, with Guitteau's in the lead. Frenchie Dubois may have been a world-class goldbrick, but he was also an excellent tank driver and he got the most out of that tank.

We entered Herrlisheim from the west on a short street that runs into Rue de Gambsheim, just north of 36 Rue de Gambsheim. The home at this address is now occupied by Mr. and Mrs. Joseph Gries. In January 1945, Mrs. Gries was residing there as a sixteen year old.

Back up to the short street that runs west from Rue de Gambsheim, we paused midway on and Guitteau jumped out to confer with someone. I was looking about and things sure didn't look good. Artillery and mortar rounds and considerable small-arms fire were bursting all about.

I called over to George Cox, the gunner, and said it appeared prudent to finish the package of sweets my parents had sent for Christmas. While doing so we got into a discussion of the twenty-two cartons of cigarettes stashed down by the driver. Neither Cox nor I smoked, so we saved them should one of the crew draw one of those rare three-day passes to Paris. That issue was not resolved by the time Guitteau returned and had us pull around the corner and stop in front of 36 Rue de Gambsheim. The few minutes we stopped there, Guitteau was busy talking to the remainder of our platoon, which was just to the south of the last houses in the village. These tanks were trading fire with German tanks south and east of them. In 1945 houses did not extend far south of 36 Rue de Gambsheim.

While Guitteau, Cox, and Dubois (we were short a crewmember and left the bow gunner position vacant) were looking for the German tanks, I was observing in all directions. Two American infantrymen were digging a foxhole in the low vacant lot across the street. They were doing so with difficulty as they were trying to stay low to avoid the small-arms fire. Suddenly, I spotted a tank to the northeast three to four hundred feet away. My first thought was that it was one of ours; my second thought was to wonder where they got that good camouflage paint. Next thought (all in rapid succession): *it'ss not ours and I am looking straight down their cannon barrel!*

I shouted their position to Cox, and he had to bring our gun nearly halfway around. He coolly reached down and turned on the power traverse to get on them fast. I was throwing the cannon breech open for there was a high explosive round in it. All we had seen so far was German infantry darting about, and I was ready for them.

I pulled that high explosive round into my arms with my left hand over the soft nose to protect it from premature explosion. In all our training, we were told that there was a safety built into each round and that it had to be fired down the rifled cannon barrel for the centrifugal force to remove the safety. Most of us never quite bought that story, so we always handled them in a tender manner.

I sat in the center of the tank on a small jump seat with my back against the side armor toward the German tank. Just as I had the high explosive round cradled in my arms, with my left hand over the nose as I was going to put it back into the rack and replace it with an armor-piercing round, the German tank fired a round into us. The force of the German round slamming through our two inches of armor had a great, shocking effect. I was knocked off my small jump seat and was pitching toward the floor, cradling that high explosive round as if it were a basket of eggs.

First thought: *that round has cut me in half; I'm dying.* Next quick thought: *Why does everyone avoid death? This is the most serene moment I have ever experienced. I'm floating slowly through space.*

I do not recall hitting the floor. I must have been out for a few moments. Then suddenly I heard all these explosions. We were on fire and our supply of small-arms ammo was exploding rapidly. It sounded like a giant popcorn popper.

I shook myself a bit and realized I was not in half and our gasoline (100 octane) had to be burning and much of the fire was coming from below.

Already it sounded like a giant blowtorch. I was with it now and know we were fully loaded with cannon ammunition. I'd seen enough tanks burn to know when that ammo blew it often turned the tank upside down. It was time to leave!

I headed for the hatch just above my jump seat. When pushed up, it opened just enough to see that either Cox or Guitteau had pushed the large .50-caliber machine gun on top of the tank off of its mount enough to block my hatch. I looked to below the cannon breech. The fire was hissing through the floor, and I really didn't want to immerse myself in it. I tried to slide under the breech on my back, but it was not easy and too slow. As my head came from under the breech, I saw Guitteau appear above his hatch looking for me. He saw me coming and jumped off to get out of the way.

Coming off the tank there was a small garden tool building belonging to 36 Rue de Gambsheim, right next to the street. I ducked in there to take stock of the situation. My first shock was total lack of defense. I had left without my personal weapon, hand grenades, anything. Having been heavily dressed for January, only my face was burned. I was also denuded of hair, and my eyes were damaged so that my vision was badly blurred.

Cox came in the shed and he, too, was with nary a weapon. While in the shed, Cox told me Guitteau had gone to look for the company commander, Lieutenant Garneau. At this point, we did not know Garneau had been badly wounded by a shell burst or that Lieutenant Reitano had been killed. We started across the barnyard to take back lots out of town. We came across Dubois. One more soldier without any weapons.

We started over the fences. At the base of the fence, there would be a low cement wall, perhaps twelve to fifteen inches high, then a wire fence an additional six feet high. Climbing those fences with all that winter clothing soon became fatiguing. After each fence off would come one more article of clothing. At the edge of the village, I was ready for a foot race. We came this way to avoid all the firing in the streets.

At the edge of the village nestled in a corner by the Zorn Canal were the other two platoons of Company C. The three of us proceeded westerly along the Zorn, noting the elaborate foxholes left there by the German soldiers—as well as numerous German bodies.

When we reached the spot where the Zorn bends to a westerly direction, Dubois said we should turn straight south, away from the canal. I protested and wished to continue along the Zorn until we had reached the bridge we had crossed in the early morning. That would take us to Weyersheim. Then they said they both outranked me, a lowly private, and we'd go south to the Steinwald. I argued that somewhere in that vicinity was where Company A didn't return from. Then they became democratic and said I was outvoted two to one. At this point, I bid them good-bye and said I didn't expect to see them again if they persisted in their plan.

So, off we went in our chosen directions. After awhile, I looked to see if they were still in view. They were trotting diagonally across the terrain to catch up with me. By dark, we had crossed the bridge and were in Weyersheim.

My blisters were worse than Cox's. Neither was serious enough to be a worry, however. The seriously blurred vision was a concern, so we searched out a medical aid station where a doctor looked us over and patched us up. He assured me my eyes would heal rapidly and be normal in a few days. Thus reassured, we hitched a ride with a supply truck back to the village of Gries, where Company C headquarters platoon was waiting out the battle. Due to my limited vision, this battle was over for me. Four days later, when the company, less casualties, reassembled, Vickless said I'd be joining his crew. That is another story of adventure.

///SGT. HAROLD G. BRADLEY (U.S. ARMY)

We had been fighting for seven days. We had never seen any fighting until that time, but it doesn't take long for a man to learn what the "scare" is. We were drawn back after the seven days were up, but not to rest, just to get ready to draw some more tanks. After we had drawn our tank, orders came down for us to attack. Well, we knew a little of what was going on. We were to jump off at 0600 hours, the next morning. I was tank commander, and it was my first time at it in combat. I didn't know what my reaction would be.

The time came and we were on our way. The ground was covered with snow and it had frozen. All our tank would do was slip and slide all over the road, but we had our objective to take before night. As we moved along, we picked up our infantry. We had our plans all fixed up for how to attack, but things didn't work out so well.

We had a little bad luck; one of our tanks hit a mine and was disabled, so it couldn't go any farther. So, we had to go on with our other four tanks. We hadn't gone but about a half mile up the road until the TDs (tank destroyers) started to move out, and the first one pulled out in front of our lead tank by mistake. When it did, Jerry had some 88s on our objective and they caught the TD, and it exploded about the same time it was hit. That was a good Jerry trick, to knock out the first tank, and then start at the back of the column and try to get it. Then he would have the rest of them where he wanted them. But the gunner must have been off a little, because I was the third tank back and he started throwing them at me. I could look over the side of the tank and see those 88s plowing up the dirt along side of my tank. I counted seven or eight of them, and every one seemed like it was getting closer. One did get so close that it almost covered me up in the turret of my tank. I finally got the tank under cover. All I can say is that the gunner must have been poor or the Good Lord must have been with us.

///TECHNICIAN 4TH GRADE EDWARD J. PAVEL (U.S. ARMY)

About five miles out, we came to a small town. We didn't go in because one of the line companies was having a little action fighting a few tanks and Jerry infantrymen. While waiting on the edge of town, I felt uncomfortable. We were parked out in the open, no cover to get under, and there was a good field of fire from the woods and town around us. The order came to move out again. I felt better. Slowly we moved into town, came to a cross road, and a Jerry laid there wounded.

We crossed and went about two hundred yards and stopped. The order came down again, watch out for bazooka men. This time I felt worse. We sat there for about twenty minutes, when all of a sudden we got hit in the track and support roller. Both of them broke, but it stopped the shell from going into the engine. I had a feeling we were going to get hit and damn near wore the periscope out of its sockets looking around. At the time we had infantrymen on our deck. They unloaded quickly for they saw the damn ball of fire coming at us. Soon as we were hit, the tank commander gave the order to move out, not knowing the track and support rollers were broken. He wanted cover quick so we could possibly get a shot at them. We started out and rolled off the track. I realized this quickly and yelled for them to bail out. The infantry boys were off the deck, and I expected another shell to tear into the tank any second. Four of us got out not knowing that the other was hurt. For no sooner I hit the ground than two rounds pierced the side of the tank. Finding out that one was missing we pulled him out, got the medics, and had them look after him.

The column moved out again, but we had to stay for the track was broke. The column was gone, and just a few jeeps and trucks came on. Things had quieted down, but Jerries kept coming down the road, their hands over their heads, yelling, "Comrade," to every Yank they saw. They had no guards, no nothing to keep them from taking off again, but they didn't. I know they were glad for the war was over for them. It was over for me for a while, but only until my tank was repaired and ready to go again. I got one of the shells that smashed into the tank. The other broke to pieces. I had one shell to take home and a patch on the side of my tank to remind me of my narrow escape.

///PVT. HARRY HEWITT (U.S. ARMY)

There was a thick soupy fog on this particular morning, which made visibility beyond a couple of yards impossible. We had no complaints, as we knew that any antitank guns would be blacked out. We pulled down the road in column and halted about two hundred yards from a hedgerow. On our immediate right were approximately forty-five or fifty wounded and dead Krauts. I noticed one woman in the lot who had been wounded in the hip. We were sitting there waiting for further orders when this gal picked up a carbine and opened fire on the infantry. She dropped two of them, when an M1 (rifle) barked and she rolled over. An order came for us to move up—two tanks on the right and the remaining two on the left. I recognized Lieutenant Ayers' voice, which never varied or seemed excited when things got rough. We didn't button up because we were afraid we might miss a bazooka-man who might be wandering around . . . opened up at two thousand yards with our 76s firing continuously for fifteen minutes. An order to cease fire came through.

I had been sick the night before, and I was still shaky. I had to get outside and heave. Sergeant Dubbert okayed the move but told me not to stray off too far. The infantry had flushed the area around us so, I climbed out without looking either way. I walked about fifteen or twenty feet, bent over, and let it go. As soon as I was finished, I spotted a Kraut lying there with a small .32 automatic (pistol) beside him. I reached over to pick it up and froze in my tracks. Directly behind were five more with carbines, lying on their stomachs ready to fire. I lived my whole life in those two seconds or less. I didn't have my grease gun (submachine gun) with me, not that it would do me any good against five carbines. An infantryman opened up with an M1 and dropped three of them. Sergeant Dubbert (my tank commander) opened up with his carbine from the turret, and the other two fell over. I gave the infantryman the .32 and made a hasty trip to the tank. I was through collecting souvenirs for that day.

///PVT. JAMES FRANCIS (U.S. ARMY)

It was the day after my twenty-second birthday, we seemed to be out for a country drive, and I was quite at ease. My parents had sent me a pair of warm navy gloves. They were both working at the Corpus Christi Naval Air Station in Texas. Leslie Miller was our tank commander and leader of the 2nd Platoon of Company A. He had recently been promoted from staff sergeant to second lieutenant. I can't recall the names of the other members of the crew, and that's a shame. We had a brand new M4A3 (Sherman medium) tank, which replaced the one we lost at Herrlisheim.

As gunner, I had a limited view of the outside world through my two sights, but I believe we passed a hill on our right side, and then made a right turn around the base of that hill. The narrow road then ran straight for a short distance into a small town. Only years later at a reunion did I learn the name of that town.

I was jarred out of my relaxed state by a flash of fire across our front, from left to right. I turned on the power traverse and spun the turret to the left. (I wonder now if the driver had his hatch open and his head out.) Across an open field, maybe seventy-five yards away, I could see two 88mm guns firing at us. None of our guns were loaded—when driving in column, only the lead tank was allowed to have the cannon and machine guns loaded and ready to fire. I yelled to the loader for an HE (high explosive) round and signaled with spread fingers.

Maybe there were only AP (armor-piercing) rounds in the "ready rack"—at any rate, the loader opened the door into the underfloor ammo compartment and pulled a round up from there. As he yanked it up, the turning turret caught the brass case, and the round came apart! He had only the HE projectile in his hands, and powder grains poured from the case over the floor and into the lower ammo rack!

One of the 88s hit us then, but the shot didn't penetrate the crew compartment or anything flammable. I wonder now if the 88mm gunners didn't have any AP ammo and fired at our tracks and wheels with just the HE they had. Our tank careened to the right into a ditch, and we stopped abruptly, tilted over at about 45 degrees. Lieutenant Miller yelled for us to get out, and the four of us obeyed his command, "Yes, sir!"

There was rifle and burp-gun fire coming at us now. (German machine guns fired so fast we called them burp guns.) Instead of jumping into the ditch, we scrambled up the hill to our right and made it to the top. The loader was limping heavily; he must have been hit. Panting and looking around at one another, we thought we had made it to safety.

We had not; a German called in accented English, "Come on boys, come on." We had run smack into an observation post on top of the hill with a machine gun. An older German noncom was in charge, and he held fire instead of shooting us down. Perhaps we five owed our lives to that man.

In my jacket pocket was a .32-caliber pistol taken earlier from a captured German officer. I quickly decided not to go for it—that little pop gun wasn't much of a weapon against a burp gun already aimed at us.

After dark we were marched down the hill and into town. The part of our column of tanks, which hadn't been caught in the ambush, had withdrawn. Everything was quiet. I wonder now about the loader—I think we bandaged his leg with the small first-aid packets we all carried, and he was able to walk. In the town, we lined up against the wall of a building, while a young German soldier strutted back and forth. No doubt, he was crowing about the huge number of American tanks he had destroyed that day. He was wearing a black uniform with a skull and crossbones insignia on the jacket lapels. I learned much later that the black uniform and *Totenkopf* (Death's Head) insignia indicated that he was part of a Panzer (armored) combat unit. When he finally ran out of steam, we were herded into a dark cellar with another crew and some Polish men who were apparently forced labor on the local farms. Once during the night, I was briefly permitted to go up the stairs to take a leak. I got to see just how big the muzzle of a rifle looks when it's only four feet away, pointed at your guts, and held by a nervous youngster. He was shaking so much that I was afraid he might accidentally pull the trigger. I didn't waste any time.

Just before daybreak, we recognized the sound of Sherman tanks approaching. We crept up out of the cellar and found the Germans were gone, leaving us behind. A column of our tanks entered the town with no resistance. I can't remember what unit they were from. I was handed a grease gun and detailed to escort a German medical officer while he went around the town giving little more than first aid to wounded German soldiers left behind for us Americans to take care of. I remember well one poor man who had been shot through the jaw. The German doctor was quite satisfied to become our prisoner and get out of the war. I even let him go back to the house where he been staying so he could say good-bye to the family and gather up his gear.

Later that morning, we walked back to our tank and found it to be completely looted, including our field rations and my new gloves. The engine access doors were open so we looked in. Looking carefully, we saw several concussion grenades rolled back into a corner, almost completely out of sight. We did not start the engine to drive the tank out of the ditch.

///CAPT. JOSEPH J. GRAHAM (U.S. ARMY)

It must have been about June 1941 that I decided to join the army. A few weeks after signing up and not too many days short of my twenty-fourth birthday, I received my induction orders and reported to Fort Dix, New Jersey. After ten days or so at Fort Dix, there was a posting of the names of those warehoused at the base. My name with many others was on a list for Fort Knox, Kentucky, but none of us was aware of what really went on there. When we concluded our march to the waiting troop train, a group of officers who looked like real army officers instead of whatever it was the reception center had as officers met us. A major was in charge of the group, and he addressed the roughly five hundred of us who were about to be put on the train. "Gentlemen, you are on your way to the Armored Force Replacement Training Center (AFRTC) at Fort Knox where you will be trained as tankers. You are going to be a part of the army's elite troops.

Welcome to the army's best." So the guy who did not know a screwdriver from a wrench and who had never driven a car in his life was about to become a tanker. My God, tanks; I had hoped I'd be sent to the signal corps.

What happened in an AFRTC? Basic training, obviously consisting of a tough physical training program, which ended up with a forced twenty-five-mile hike with a full field pack (forty-five to fifty pounds) designed to rid us of our civilian flab plus instructions on how to shoot the rifle, pistol, carbine, Tommy gun, and the .30- and .50-caliber machine guns. We had to shoot the machine guns from the ground because the obsolete tanks we had available to us did not have guns mounted in them. The army did not have enough guns to go around even at its training facilities. We were taught how to be soldiers; how to make our bed; how to keep our equipment orderly in our foot- and wall-lockers; how and when to wear our various uniforms; how, when, and whom to salute and other military courtesies; even how to keep clean. Those who did not keep themselves clean received a bath with the strong soap we used to clean and bleach our wooden barracks floors, and the scrubbing during the bath was done with the tough floor brushes.

Of course, there were training sessions in map reading, enemy aircraft and vehicle identification, identification of poison gas along with gas mask drills, and vehicle driving (jeeps, trucks, halftracks, and tanks). The first vehicle I ever drove in my life was a tank and, believe me, I was a disaster! "What do you mean, corporal, when you say, double clutch?" And we marched, marched, and marched. "What the hell are we marching for when we're supposed to be tankers," I said to myself repeatedly.

I guess that I showed enough promise as a trainee and soon became an instructor at the replacement center. Most of the noncoms and officers of the center knew they had a nice safe berth, and they had no desire to leave for other duty elsewhere. With my instructor's duties, I went through three different groups of recruits plus my own recruit session. It was sort of like flunking kindergarten a couple of times, so I was bored with the repetition. I sincerely wanted to get into a combat outfit and be an officer. Shortly afterward, I was enrolled in the armored force OCS (officers' candidate school) about halfway into November 1942.

After becoming an officer, I finally got into a combat outfit in early 1943, the 781st Tank Battalion. The first mission given to the battalion was to test tanks for the armored board. Actually, this was an important assignment in early 1943, because the army had not decided on a specific tank model to ask American industry to produce for our prospective European Campaign.

Under the supervision of the armored board, it became the job of the 781st to test the various models provided to the army by four different Detroit automobile manufacturers and to pass on our test results to the armored board for the final model choice decision. Chrysler had a Mickey Mouse tank powered with five engines, all on one crankcase. I remember another tank whose power came from a radial Lycoming engine. General Motors had a diesel-powered tank, and Ford had a tank with an all-aluminum 500-horsepower engine. We did not test motors only. We had records on just about everything in the tank: gun mounts, the effectiveness of the guns' stabilizing gyroscope, turret-traversing mechanisms, steel versus rubber tank treads, filters, and what have you. The army wanted the best possible model tank with the best possible equipment. We ran ten tanks of each model, and we ran them rain or shine, twenty-four hours a day, seven days a week. Sometimes we drove on dirt roads, sometimes we ran across country, and at other times we ran on highways. By far the best performer was the General Motors diesel model from both a performance and a maintenance standpoint. The Ford tank model received the nod because the petroleum industry would not be able to produce enough diesel fuel to supply both the navy's heavy requirements and the armored force's considerable needs. The testing went on from early March until about September 1943.

Another important job assigned to the 781st, this time my Company D only, involved sending us off on secret duty outside the United States.

What was this important task? The military commands wanted to conduct tests in Canada to determine if tanks and infantry could successfully work together to attack enemy positions while our forces were under a blanket of dense smoke. There had been a good deal of success (defensively) with this tactic during the Battle of Britain. Because Britain's ports and shipping were being dealt devastating blows by the German Luftwaffe, the Brits developed and used huge steam generators into whose steam emissions they injected sprays of diesel fuel to make the steam heavy enough to hug the ground. They sited the generators where the generators' diesel-impregnated steam would blow over a port denying the German aircraft the ability to see their intended targets. The prevailing winds in Europe are, we were told, mostly west to east, the ultimate direction of the intended Allied assault on Germany, so it was decided to test the generators with live tanks and infantry to see if we could develop offensive tactics that could be used successfully in the future ground war in Europe.

It wasn't until around mid 2000 that I came into possession of an unofficial history of the battalion, written after I was discharged from the army, that I learned for the first time the tactics we had developed had actually been used successfully, thank goodness in actual combat in Europe. That story of my battalion entitled "Up from Marseille" notes: "During this time, 'D' Company was at Camp Wainwright, Alberta, Canada. Using GI smoke generators, they worked with elements of the Royal Canadian Army on tank-infantry operations in smoke. Some of the techniques developed by 'D' Company were used successfully by the British Second and Canadian First Armies when they crossed the Rhine."

After the armored board project and the trip to Canada was finished, we seriously went on with the job of making ourselves combat tankers. We had loads and loads of firing practice, up-to-date enemy vehicle and aircraft identification, map reading, maneuvers to practice tank combat tactics, and so on. However, we could go only so far with our training at Fort Knox because the post was solely a tank facility with no infantry troops with whom we could train for our ultimate combat mission. Training with infantry was essential because the 781st was one of a number of so-called separate tank battalions.

Separate tank battalion to the army meant we were not a part of any of the much more sizeable armored divisions of about twelve thousand men and more than three hundred tanks. Our future role in combat was to be assigned by an army (four star) or corps (three stars) general to one of the infantry divisions under his command. These assignments were to be mostly (but not always) in attack situations. In the European campaign, we served with five different infantry divisions. So, in November 1943, we moved to Camp Shelby, Mississippi, to train with the 69th Infantry Division based there.

This may be a good time to describe what it is a separate tank battalion, such as the 781st would add to an infantry division. Three companies labeled A, B, and C, each had eighteen Sherman tanks. These tanks weighed thirty-two tons and mounted three .30-caliber machine guns and a 75mm main gun. Each separate tank battalion's Company D had eighteen M5A1 Stuart tanks each of which weighed sixteen tons. The Stuarts also had three machine guns, plus a 37mm main gun. The Shermans could get up to about twenty-five miles per hour while the Stuarts could get up to fifty miles per hour.

I cannot remember how many thousands of rounds of machine-gun ammunition we stowed in the Stuarts. I know we never ran out of ammo in any combat engagement. I do remember we stowed a bit less than 150 rounds of 37mm ammo and, of that, we had about sixty high explosive rounds, thirty or so rounds of armor-piercing shells, ten or so phosphorous shells for setting buildings on fire, and the balance in canister ammo, which consisted of one hundred steel balls within a light aluminum casing. The canister made a shotgun out of our big gun. We later found the canister ammunition dreadfully effective against enemy infantry who were charging our tanks.

Unlike the Sherman that had three men in the turret, consisting of the tank commander, loader, and gunner, the Stuart had only two men in the turret, the gunner and the tank commander who doubled as the loader. Due to this turret arrangement, the tank commander on the Stuart was like a circus ringmaster. He had to look up so he could command the tank and he had to go down inside the turret to load the 37mm main gun or the machine gun. This made the job difficult to the degree that, in the latter and more fluid stages of the war when Company D led the 7th Army's advance into southern Germany and Austria, I could not command the entire company and feed ammo into the guns at the same time. Instead, I rode in my jeep and kept in touch with the tanks through my jeep's radio. For a bit more protection in the jeep, I had a machine gun welded onto the top of the jeep's radiator. My jeep driver and I both had a carbine and a submachine gun within instant reach.

A little about the way the tank commanders operated: To see the enemy in combat, it was impossible to fight with your overhead hatch closed. When I rode in my tank, which wasn't often, I always had my turret hatch open. Most all of the 781st tank commanders went into a fight with their heads out of the open turrets. Yes, I did lose staff sergeant Williams, one of my best men, killed when a Panzerfaust (the German equivalent of the American bazooka) hit his turret. One can't tell but I feel it was likely we saved more men than we lost because of the better vision from the open turret in spite of the increased exposure to the tank commander.

The same Ford 500 horsepower aluminum engine we had tested in Fort Knox in the early days of our battalion powered all the Shermans of the other tank companies. They were extremely loud. You could hear them long before you ever see them. It was impossible to sneak up on the Germans in a Sherman. The German Tiger tanks were the same, so I guess we came out even on that score.

The Stuart in contrast came equipped with two relatively quiet Cadillac gasoline engines of 110 horsepower each. Because of this fact, it was often possible for us to maneuver some of our tanks to sites from which, with a squad or two of the 100th's infantry on our back decks, we could dash into a German position. The infantry would grab a couple of Krauts, throw them on the backs of our tanks, and rush back to our own lines with the prisoners who could have valuable information for the intelligence officers.

Most of our tank noise came from the slap, slap, slap of our treads, so it was possible to sneak up on the enemy under some conditions, as did one of my platoons. On one occasion, the Germans had a couple hundred troops on our side of a river when they began to dig in for the night. Unless something was done to drive them out immediately, they would have a sizable force on our side of the river soon. I'd like to say I had a part in what happened next, but I cannot. One of my platoons took their five tanks and, with minimal infantry support, performed an unforgivable tank tactic that met with terrific success.

They moved slowly from a protected wooded area out across a big open field to try to sneak up on the Germans while they were busy digging their foxholes. Why didn't they dash across the field with their tanks? There was deep snow on the ground, and the snow muffled the slap, slap, slap of the tank tracks. Our tanks were painted white to blend them into the snow. Before the tanks left the cover of the woods, our gunners had put canister ammunition in the breeches of their guns and they had their ready racks loaded with more canister. All three machine guns in each tank were in the full load position, meaning they fired with a touch of the trigger. Incredibly, the Germans had not posted any guards who could have alerted them. Our tanks were not seen until they opened fire on the Germans from about fifty yards away. It was no match, and now it was the Germans' turn to run. The canister ammo made big shotguns out of our 37mm main guns and the Germans suffered terrible losses. We didn't lose a tank or any infantrymen.

One episode produced a lot of talk among the officers of the 781st around this time. Two of my tanks had their tracks blown off on a road just a bit east of the Maginot Line and on a slanting hillside facing the city of Bitche where the Germans still held out in force. This was at the time of the well-known Battle of the Bulge up north of us, when the fighting in Alsace was as intense as it was up there in the Ardennes, and when we knew we would have to withdraw for several miles similar to the retreat the U.S. Army made in Belgium.

We had to get those tanks back. Except for the tracks, the tanks were in good condition, and we didn't want the Germans to lay their hands on them after we retreated. Captain Vinnie Donise, the battalion maintenance office, and I furtively moved up on foot to get close enough to the disabled tanks to see what we could do to retrieve them. While we were making plans for the retrievals, we drew rifle fire and had to jump into a ditch from which some of the infantry had made a stand for several days and from which they had just retreated. To get back to the safety of our lines, we had to crawl up the ditch on our stomachs for about a hundred yards until we reached a point where we could get up and run for it. The infantry had lived in that ditch for several days and it had not been possible for them to dig a latrine. Vinnie and I had to report to the battalion commander to tell him what our plans were for the retrieval of the two tanks. Our appearance and our odor caused a lot of comment.

Did we get the tanks out? Yes, we did. Once again, and on the following day, division artillery helped immensely. We had to use two of our huge tank retriever vehicles, which were even noisier than our Sherman tanks. To mask our move to the vicinity of the disabled tanks, division artillery hit the Germans. They also used smoke shells to mask the retrievers' crews from small arms fire while we were hooking the disabled tanks to the retrievers. Just as the last tank was being hauled over the hillside, the smoke cover lifted and one German 88s opened up on us with a couple of shots, but they missed by about forty yards.

The Germans were always a methodical bunch, and a couple of sharp guys in my company helped us take advantage of that fact. A group, who were in foxholes along the bank of the Neckar River, noticed something.

At just about 2 a.m. each morning, they could hear the clop, clop, clop and squeak, squeak, squeak of what was likely some horses and wagons, and the sound appeared to come from the road on the other side of the river directly opposite the town I was in. After a couple of nights of hearing these sounds, we felt we were seeing a definite pattern likely to be repeated at the same time, on subsequent nights. In daylight, we moved a couple of tanks to positions from which they could sight (aim) their guns on the road on the opposite side of the river from where it appeared the sounds had come. The tanks fired some tests shots just over the road, and, when we were satisfied we were on target, we let the tanks sit in their positions confident that if there was to be any more 2 a.m. clop, clop, clop, we could hit them with our first shots—whatever it was we had been hearing.

No one touched the tank's guns. We also had our mortar guys fire a couple of test rounds intending for them to fire parachute flares over the opposite road to permit our men to see the intended targets after we heard the possible targets coming. Most everybody stayed awake and we waited. Soon, 2 a.m. came and so did the methodical Germans. We could hear the squeaks and the clops. When it seemed to be the correct time, it was "Mortars fire." Up went the flares, and suddenly, it was daylight across the river and we could see three horse-drawn wagons plopping along the opposite road. I called out the command, "Fire," and boom, boom, boom went the tank guns. The wagons had been heading for Heilbron, and judging from the huge explosions that took place, they were hauling ammunition to their troops who were facing another American unit. Almost immediately, my radio crackled with someone calling from regimental headquarters, "What in the Hell is going on over there?" My response was, "Just doing our job, sir."

Shortly after that, we got orders to go east and a bit south and bypass the large German city of Ulm. We were under orders to head for a bridge over the headwaters of the Danube River just east of Ulm. I had a narrow escape there: Close to the bridge was a small village. As we approached the village, a man who told me he was the *Burgermeister* (mayor) of the village met us. I really don't know what he was wearing but he, apparently, felt he needed to look official. Whatever it was he was wearing, he looked more like the doorman at the Waldorf-Astoria. He told me there were no soldiers in his village (he was telling the truth) and he would direct us toward the bridge. He climbed up on the front of my tank, which was a violation of the rules of warfare on my part because you are not supposed to expose captured enemy to any danger. However, I felt comfortable with this man so I acceded to his request that I give him a ride to his village. He pointed to the approximate location of the bridge, and it was here I began to feel uneasy. For about a quarter mile, the road going out of the village ran parallel to some heavy woods bordering the river. There was about fifty yards of open area between the road and the woods until the road made an abrupt right turn directly into the woods about where the *Burgermeister* said the bridge was located (and so did our maps).

I had about ten tanks edge out of the town and give the woods a real bath in machine-gun fire. Then, I took the five or so other tanks, and we made a dash for the bridge with me in the turret of the lead tank. When we made the sharp turn into the woods, my driver yanked back on his steering brakes to stop the tank. Dead ahead of us and stretched across the road and only a few yards in front of my tank, was a heavy log tank barrier. In a foxhole next to the barrier was a German soldier aiming a Panzerfaust. Just below the soldier's steel helmet was a bullet hole between his eyes. He couldn't have missed with his Panzerfaust, and he would have blown my tank to pieces. Just as we pulled up at the tank barrier, the Germans blew the bridge sky high. We dismounted the crews from a few tanks and had no trouble cleaning out the few Germans remaining on our side of the river. I think the soldier with the Panzerfaust had been the only one with any fight left in him.

I also remember something that happened in a little German town we drove into. It had a military school. Most of the soldiers who had been there had likely climbed into civilian clothes and had hit the road to head for their homes but there were still some of them around. A few of them had hidden in homes, and because we had no infantry with us that day, I dismounted about five or six tank crews and led them in a house-to-house search for them. The few we found had no fight in them so we rousted them out. One home had its door locked, and I told one of my sergeants to kick the door in after I shot out the lock. I then planned to jump into the home with him following me in. We did that, and I jumped into the house with my gun firing. Fortunately, out of the line of fire of my bullets, there was a mother and three little girls kneeling on the floor of the hallway crying, "Please, please." They probably thought we would act as German soldiers had in the areas they had conquered. I felt awful. I asked if any soldiers were present. The mother answered no. I believed her as she was too scared to lie, I merely said in German, "God Bless," and we left, and then went to the dark side.

We were close to the end of the town when a German soldier stepped out from a house and shot at me with his rifle from about twenty yards. He missed badly. Almost as a reflex, I fired my submachine gun and hit him with a good burst. In desperation, the Germans were scraping the barrel for soldiers with old men and young kids. The soldier lying on the ground in front of me was only a teenager. In awful pain, he was crying, "Mother, mother." We yelled, "Medic!" and the corpsman came promptly. He examined the young boy, and looking up at our group of filthy tankers sadly shook his head. There had been only about a dozen times in the entire war in which I had occasion to fire a personal weapon such as a carbine or my submachine gun. In every other instance, others were firing at the same uniformed figures as I was and I had always tried to kid myself that the others hit them. I had fantasized that I could go through the war without personally killing anyone. The fantasy was over. It has stayed with me all my life.

May 9, 1945, sticks in my mind as the day we call V-E Day. We would have to wait until we licked the Japs before we had V-J Day and end the war. Naturally, we had to have a celebratory parade so we could thumb our noses at the Austrians and bring ourselves closure. The 103rd Infantry Division and all of its attached troops, about fifteen thousand men, tramped down a couple of miles of Innsbruck's main drag, the Marienstrasse, an attractive cobblestone street lined with beautiful, centuries-old medieval buildings. We had an impressive parade with all the infantry in clean combat uniforms. The men were all clean-shaven and, presumably, bathed. The "Big Brass" was on a hastily constructed reviewing stand draped with American, Canadian, British, French, and Soviet flags. As each unit went by the reviewing stand, the "Eyes Right" command was given with all heads snapping toward the reviewing stand and with unit flags being dipped and the reviewing officers returning the salutes. We looked like what we were, a conquering army giving the finger to the Austrians who had so enthusiastically supported Hitler.

///PVT. TOM SATOR (U.S. ARMY)

I joined the U.S. Army in May 1943 and took my basic training at Fort Knox, Kentucky. Eventually, I ended up in England as a replacement, and then transferred into the 4th Armored Division, assigned to the 37th Tank Battalion, Company B, in September 1944. I became a loader on an M4 tank, although I did spend some time at the other crew positions in the tank.

The 37th Tank Battalion was commanded by Col. Creighton Abrams, who was my hero because me he was such a courageous man. He always sat on top of his tank's turret with his legs dangling down. That's what I remember of him, with a helmet on his head, a microphone in his hand, and a cigar in his mouth, plus a red scarf he always wore. From the top of his tank, he commanded the battalion in combat. He'd look out over the field, and there was always something—artillery or machine gun or something flying about. But he always sat up there and never got wounded to the best of my knowledge. I've never met anybody so brave, I really haven't. On top of that, he was a wonderful human being.

Abrams used me as an interpreter because I could speak good German. Whenever we captured officers or higher-ranking enlisted men, he would call me and ask, "What did he say?" or "Ask him this or that," and I would translate for him and tell him what he wanted to know. I guess he took a liking to me, which I was happy about.

Some of the German officers we captured and did not want to talk to a skinny little Jewish kid, but a jab in the gut with the barrel of my Tommy gun usually convinced them that I was not going to take no for an answer.

The first time I came under fire happened during the Battle of Singling, in early December 1944. My tank was coming out of the woods, and I saw some bright balls slowly floating across a valley in my direction. I was sitting next to my tank commander, and I said, "What are those?" He looked at me somewhat sadly, because I'd never been shot at before and said, "What the hell do you think those are?" Those are German tracers and they're shooting at us.

That was my first real combat experience. Up to then I wasn't really too scared or concerned, but after you see some of those things coming at you, then the whole thing changes quickly and you have a sudden desire to leave. After we pulled back from the Battle of Singling, we had only three or four tanks out of a full company of fifteen tanks divided into three platoons of five each. I now know that we were up against the German 11th Panzer Division, equipped with Panther tanks and various self-propelled assault guns, as well as dug-in towed antitank guns.

I remember that the December 1944 Battle of the Bulge was cold. It was so cold that the turrets of the tanks froze in place on many an occasion. The worse part was that the army hadn't supplied us with winter uniforms yet. We didn't get any winter gear until February 1945.

During the Battle of the Bulge, the Germans had captured some M4 tanks from the 9th Armored Division, which they decided to use against us. We found this out when my company parked in a snow-covered field, near some woods. All of a sudden, a large tree started to sway along the wood line near my tank. We all knew that only a tank could do that to a tree that large. Everybody in my tank started screaming at the gunner, "Did you see that tree?" At that moment, the tree fell down, and a Sherman tank, with a German cross on its turret, came out of the wood line. My tank commander hollered out the approximate distance to the gunner, and he opened fire. In a span of ten seconds, I loaded five AP rounds into our 76mm gun. I had never moved so fast in my life before then or since. The gunner of our tank put those five rounds into the enemy Sherman tank turret. A couple of the German tankers got out of the destroyed tank, but we nailed them with some HE rounds.

Sometime after that my tank was hit by a mortar round that blew off the tank commander's cupola and the .50-caliber machine gun, located on the top of the tank's turret. Luckily, my tank commander survived that with only a ringing headache. After he came to his senses and wasn't seeing stars anymore, we decided to keep going. We went around this town in our now damaged tank and thought we saw our armored infantry taking some prisoners out of a warehouse. We were wrong, and as we sat there in our tank wondering what to do next, a German Panzerfaust hit the gunner's side of the tank.

The only thing I remember after that is a big red flash, and I ended up on the snow next to the tank, as did the tank commander. The driver and the bow machine-gunner bailed from the tank, right away, when we were hit. The tank didn't blow up, luckily, so we climbed back in and got out the gunner, who had part of his left calf torn off by the Panzerfaust when it penetrated into the turret of our tank.

After we got out the gunner, I ran over to the platoon leader's tank and climbed on top of the turret to tell him to send the medics, but he wouldn't open his hatch. I pounded on his hatch with my fists and said, "Call the medics; we need the medics." He still wouldn't do anything. Captain Leech then came over and gave us permission to evacuate; we went back across the town to an aid station and surrendered the tank to the maintenance guys.

After that, we got a new tank, and I went back on the line. By the way, this happened Christmas Eve, because it was December 24, 1944. On New Year's Eve, we were told that a kitchen truck would come up, and we were to get pancakes, bacon, and real eggs the next morning.

Everybody in the company was elated about the prospect of hot food. So, we all decided to dig a large trench for the kitchen truck, near a clump of bushes, the only cover. Everybody turned out, and we started digging, but the soil was impossible. Finally, they brought a backhoe in to dig a hole for the kitchen truck and that is where we put it. We then camouflaged the truck from enemy observation, and the cooks dug foxholes near their truck.

Around midnight, we had one of the few air raids that the Germans executed during the Battle of the Bulge. They came over and started dropping bombs. One of them hit, maybe five or ten yards from my tank, which shook us up a little, but it didn't last long. They fired machine guns, too, and then it was over.

There was one last big explosion, so we looked around to see what that hit. It was the clump of bushes, were the kitchen truck sat. No tank was hit, just the kitchen truck, which got a direct hit, and it was burning. The whole company stood around, and you'd never seen a sadder sack of GIs, all crying. That was it, because the pancakes, eggs, and bacon went up in smoke, and I can still smell it. When I think about it, I still like to cry.

On a less dangerous occasion, my company captured a liquor warehouse. We were already halfway to Germany, and there wasn't much resistance. It was a sunny afternoon, and we went into this village and stopped for a smoke outside of our tanks. There was this Russian with a big beard. He had stuck his face out from a building, and I spotted him. He motioned to me. Of course, everybody grabbed their guns, because they didn't know who he was. It turned out that he was a Russian soldier who was a prisoner of war of the Germans. He greeted us as liberators. He came over and kissed us on both cheeks; he spoke a little bit of German and said, "You want to have something to drink?" We all said, "Of course, we want something to drink." He said, "Come with me."

He took us right around the corner where there was this building, which turned out to be a German warehouse, full of liquor. Whiskey, Schnapps, wine, you name it. We all went in there and stuffed our jackets full of liquor bottles. Just about that time, somebody came over and said, "Sator, Colonel Abrams wants you at the battalion to talk to a German prisoner." I got into a jeep, and as I was driving back to the battalion, I kept drinking. By the time I got to the battalion, I was drunk. Somebody told me where the battalion headquarters were; it turned out to be a nice house. I went in, and it was beautiful; it was everything the warehouse should have been. There were bedrooms to the left and right. I remember there was one room with a bed in it with white sheets, and I couldn't believe it because I hadn't been in any bed for a long time. I went in there and saw this bed, and I was, of course, by that time, pretty well oiled and I guess I fell into the bed and went to sleep.

The next thing I remember is some guy slapping the hell out of me and cussing me out. "You drunken so and so, what are you doing in my bed?" It turned out to be Colonel Abrams' bed. I sobered up pretty quickly, I guess, because I remember he grabbed me and said, "Come on with me." There was a German who he wanted me to talk to, but I can't remember exactly what it was; all I know is that after awhile he said, "Get your rear end back to the company." He never mentioned it again. I thought I was going to get a court-martial, but he never mentioned the incident again. To me he was the bravest, and fair and concerned about everybody.

///SGT. NELLO J. FASOLI (U.S. ARMY)

During the Battle of the Bulge, our platoon was advancing to take a town. A Royal Tiger was spotted, and I was sent up to knock it out. Getting into a good position, I fired five rounds, hitting it three times but not knocking it out. The next thing to happen was that the enemy was firing at me, knocking down two large trees in front of me as I took cover. I then took two TDs (tank destroyers) up and showed them where the tank was. They were knocked out, and I had to run back to my tank under artillery fire. I had to hit the ground twice on the way back.

Later, the enemy tank being knocked out, I was told to advance into town. Passing the burning, knocked out Jerry tank, I started around the curve, and there stood another Royal Tiger, fifty yards away. I fired at it, while the 88 was being traversed to my tank. The large tank and long gun made me feel like my days were over. I had many narrow escapes that day and was lucky to get out alive, whole, and with only a scratch on my face.

///LT. MARVIN W. ORGILL (U.S. ARMY)

As long as you are in the seventh or eighth tank, you feel good. Everything's fine; you feel as safe as in a church. Then the colonel gets on the radio and says to you, "Move up to the point of the column." Then everything changes.

You move up and the leading tankers wave as you pass and you grin back, but you feel like a fake because you don't feel like grinning. You get up there, the radio comes on, and the battalion commander wants to know what is holding up the column. So do the combat commander and the company commander. You say to yourself, "Why don't those guys relax?" You say over the radio, "My platoon is moving out."

Behind you, four other tanks cruise fifty yards apart. You watch every bush, tree, house, and hole in front. You call over the interphone (intercom) and tell the driver to kick it up to fifteen miles per hour. The radio squawks and the battalion commander comes on. He wants to know what's holding up the column. You call him back and say, "Dammit, nothing is holding up the column; you're moving fifteen miles per hour." He calls back and wants to know why you can't make it twenty. You bang the microphone back on the hook and don't answer.

You begin to get that tingling feeling in the back of your neck. There's no good reason for it, but you get it, and whenever you feel it, you usually run into trouble. You tell your gunner to spatter the patch of woods ahead and he does it with his machine gun. Other tanks join in. Then from the woods comes a spurt of flame. If you're lucky the shell misses. You talk your gunner into the target, and in five seconds he fires the 75mm.

He fires again and his second shot is on the target. Three more rounds go out fast. Your platoon has deployed to the right and left and all are firing now. Suddenly, there is an explosion in the woods, and a German vehicle ahead begins to burn. Two more explosions and two more fires, your stomach begins to uncurl. All the tanks are firing. They shoot up everything in front, and nothing shoots back. For the first time you notice that you are sweating and trembling. You don't say anything, but you reach down and give a pat on the shoulder to your corporal gunner. He turns around and grins.

///CORP. CLARENCE SMOYER (U.S. ARMY)

I was a gunner in Company E, 32nd Regiment, 3rd Armored Division, and we were one of the first crews to get the M26 Pershing tank. After we got the new tank, they took us out to a valley to test fire the gun before we went into combat. They started us off by having us shoot at houses that were about 1,200 yards away.

Once we began hitting the houses with our 90mm gun, they made it even harder for us by telling us to shoot at the chimneys on the distant houses. The chimneys soon began disappearing in a series of explosions. They kept increasing the target distance on us to test our skill, and for the final one they chose a house 1,500 yards away with two chimneys. I remember announcing that I was going to attempt to get the first chimney on the right side of the house. I fired, and the chimney went up in pieces. The one on the other side of the house was a red brick chimney, and just the top of it stuck out over the roof. We set up and fired, and the red brick flew all over the place. I then heard people cheering, saying what a great gunner I was.

From there we went on to the German city of Cologne. As we approached the city, there was a great deal of artillery fire. Our battalion leader got on the radio and said, "Gentlemen, I give you Cologne; knock the hell out of them."

As we approached the city, we found that the Germans had jammed streetcars underneath the overpasses to slow us down. They weren't much of a problem to deal with, and we pulled them out with cables. As we continued into the city, they stopped us at an intersection. I don't know why. Being in the tank half the time, I didn't know which direction I was facing, but I could see the Cologne Cathedral to my left. We sat there quite awhile, and as the Germans soldiers came into the intersection, we fired on them.

Eventually, a German tank (Panther) came around the side of a building; by the time we got an armor-piercing shell into the cannon, he realized that there was a bunch of us over there and he backed up. We fired armor-piercing shells through the building that he backed up behind, thinking we might get a lucky hit and knock him out, which we didn't.

After awhile we went down one street, and Company F went down the street beside us, which was the street that the German tank had backed down to the cathedral on. It now sat in front of the cathedral and everybody thought it was knocked out. A Signal Corps cameraman had gone ahead of us and was up in a building shooting pictures of our tanks when the German tank suddenly opened fire on our column and knocked out a tank, the lead tank. One man climbed out of the top of that tank, with a leg missing, and then rolled onto the ground and died. That same man had just heard from the battalion commander three weeks before about receiving his battlefield commission. I heard that two other men in that tank also died.

When the lead tank was hit, they radioed us to go down another street, to take out the German tank. Somehow or another the German tank crew knew what we were doing; they came up to the intersection approaching and were waiting for us. Our plan had been to come up to the intersection corner and slowly pull around just far enough to see where the German tank was, and then let me turn the turret and get a shot off. After that, we would quickly back up.

As soon as our driver saw the gun on the German tank, less than one hundred yards away, instead of stopping the tank to give me a chance at a shot, he floored the throttle as fast as he could through the intersection, and I fired on the move and hit him right below the gun shield. Because we weren't sure if we killed everybody in the tank, we fired two more shots into it, and that was the end of the German tank and crew.

///BRIG. GEN. ROBERT L. DENIG JR. (U.S. MARINE CORPS)

My happy day arrived on September 15, 1941, when Company B, 2nd Tank Battalion, was organized, and I became commanding officer. First Lieutenant Cohen and fifty-nine men were assigned with me as the initial compliment. Ten (M3) light army tanks arrived by rail in San Diego on the 19th, and we received them the following day. Captain Swencesky was then assigned to the company. Later, Second Lieutenant Schmidt and twenty-three men, all from Paris Island, and five lieutenants joined; by the end of September, the tank company was slowly being built up to strength. Our biggest problem was the lack of tools, equipment, manuals, and so forth necessary to maintain the tanks. Finally, by the end of October, the company had received some manuals and blueprints but still no spare parts.

On October 19 I received word from Joe Burger that my nomination to be an observer at the 1st Army maneuvers in North Carolina during the period November 22–23 had been received. I would be assigned to a tank organization at these maneuvers. I decided that it would be well to ask the division to grant me leave so that I could go to headquarters at the conclusion of the maneuvers in Washington, D.C., to discuss the material requirements of the tanks. Burger said that he would try to have the orders modified so I could take this side trip to the headquarters and have it included in my orders.

During the last week of October, the transmissions in the tanks began to experience problems. The manufacturer representative from Timken (they makes bearings) said that it was to be expected, as all of these transmissions were of faulty army ordnance design, and that his company was unable to correct it because the army didn't want to stop production to make the necessary changes. The representative told us how to remedy the situation so we dead-lined all the tanks for modifications, which took about three weeks to complete.

On November 1, Warner Brothers movies, who made the movie *Halls of Montezuma,* took some pictures of our tanks to be used for effect in the movie. Then some photographers from the press arrived to take stills of our tanks for a Marine Corps supplement of the Sunday, November 9, edition of the San Diego paper.

On November 10, I received orders to proceed to Camden, South Carolina, and to report by November 22, 1941, to the 1st Army as an observer at their maneuvers.

I took advantage this time, to go via Washington, D.C. in order to spend a few days with my parents. The orders also included that after the maneuvers I would proceed to New River and spend a week with the East Coast tank unit station there. Included in the Marine Corps observer contingent from the 2nd Division was Colonel Burke, Major Burger, and Capt. Ben Powers. I departed San Diego on the *Santa Fe Scout* (a passenger train) on Saturday, November 15, and arrived in Washington the morning of the 19th. I was met there by my father, and after breakfast went to headquarters. In the afternoon I saw Colonel Barrett, the assistant to the commandant, and informed him of Colonel Lockee's request that my orders be changed so that after the maneuvers I would be able to return to headquarters to discuss the requirements of the tank units of the 2nd Division. Then I would return to San Diego. Colonel Barrett agreed that it was a good idea and had my orders so modified. I then left Washington by train for Camden on Friday night, the 21st, arriving there the following morning. I requested assignment to the 2nd Armored Division because the 66th and 67th Tank Regiments from Fort Benning were units in that division, and I knew some of the officers while I was stationed there going to school at Fort Benning.

At lunchtime, I saw Ben Powers from the 2nd Marine Division Scout Company. His unit, as I was to observe, was a reconnaissance outfit, which he had heard was about a hundred miles from Camden. I joined the 2nd Armored Saturday afternoon. Fortunately, his headquarters was near Camden. The maneuvers went off in grand style. The weather was cold, and having come from San Diego I was not properly prepared. So, the first thing I did was to find a store to buy some long john underwear. I also borrowed a tank jacket from the unit to which I was attached. In all I gained a lot of knowledge from my assignment, and it was a lot of fun to be with a number of the army friends who were with me at the same tank school class in Fort Benning. I can't recall how long the maneuvers lasted, but I think they ended about noon on Friday, November 28.

I returned to Washington by train and spent the week of November 30–December 6 at headquarters discussing the equipment required for a tank company, maintenance problems (including the lack of trained mechanics), and so forth. During this period, the quartermaster department made reservations and obtained tickets for my return to San Diego by rail for the evening of Sunday, December 7. This was quite fortunate when you consider what happened on that date.

On December 7 my parents had a luncheon party for the Marine Corps general officers on duty at headquarters and those at Quantico, plus some colonels and navy fliers. This party was held at the Army Navy Country Club, as I was then a member. The Commandant of the Marine Corps, General Holcomb, was not present. As I recall he was somewhere in the valley of Virginia for the weekend. Guests were to arrive around noon, with a luncheon to be served between 1 and 1:30 p.m. The seating of the guests was on time, but just as everyone was seated, my father was called to the phone. Later, he told me that's when he found out about Pearl Harbor. The last guest, a navy lieutenant, Allen Brown, arrived at about this time from the Navy Department, where he had been on duty until noon. He told me later that prior to leaving the department he and others were aware that something was in the air, but no one could guess what. When my father returned to the table, he asked the assistant commandant and a couple of the other generals present to join him away from the table. He then told them about Pearl Harbor. A few seconds later, the club radio announced the bombing of Pearl. Pandemonium! The luncheon was hurriedly served and hastily eaten, and within thirty minutes we had all departed for our respective posts. My mother and I stayed at the club to square things away before I drove her home at Arlington Heights, which is only about fifteen minutes from Marine Corps headquarters.

I packed my bag, called Union Station, and confirmed my train reservations. Around 6 p.m., I was driven to Union Station to catch the Pennsylvania railway train to Chicago, where I had to change to the *Santa Fe Scout*. The station was jammed with people hurrying about. Those arriving by train were either trying to find transportation uptown or to obtain reservations to continue their journey. Others, arriving like myself, were either going to the counter to obtain tickets or trying to find out the gate numbers to catch their trains. As I had already my ticket, I went directly to the correct gate and was told that the train would depart on schedule. I went back to the car, said good-bye to my parents, and returned to the gate. Prior to leaving, my father gave me a portable battery-operated radio, which was used during the train ride west to keep abreast of the news.

The following day, about an hour before the train arrived in Chicago, I heard the president speak to Congress about the attack at Pearl; he said that there was a state of war now in effect between the United States and Japan. As you may recall, in those days trains did not go from coast to coast, one had to change in Chicago. My train arrived about 1 p.m. and the connecting train, the *Scout*, left around 10:30 p.m. that evening. The train ride was interesting, especially on Tuesday and Wednesday when we crossed the prairie states. At each stop men would board the train for a ride to the nearest connecting railway. They seemed to be either regulars on duty, volunteers, inductees, or reserves called to active duty. They were heading for either the recruiting station, the recruit depot, or a permanent post station.

It reminded me of my experiences in Italy in 1935, when I was returning to the States from Shanghai. I was en route from Milan to Venice by rail. The Ethiopian–Italian War had started, and reserves were being called along with inductees. The train made numerous stops, and at most every crossroad, so it seemed, we took aboard these young men. Then, a few days later, on my trip from Venice to Budapest while the train was in the foothills of the Alps, alpine troops would get aboard heading for their concentration points. All of this made me feel strange, as my passport, although it was a diplomatic one, had in it my picture in green U.S. Marine Corps uniform. I was wondering all the time if they would consider me an embassy spy.

The Santa Fe train finally arrived in San Diego on the afternoon of Thursday, December 11. Mary met me and drove me to our home in Kensington. I phoned Major Burger, the division adjutant, and reported in. He said that things were relatively quiet and for me to remain home until the following day. So I called Capt. Al Swencesky, who was my company exec and maintenance officer. His office was at the recruit depot, the only place with maintenance facilities for our tanks. He said that I should report in for duty, that Captain Powers had his reconnaissance cars scattered all the way from the Mexican border to San Juan Capistrano on lookout for Japanese raiding parties. Furthermore, no one was certain if the Japanese would make a landing. I told them that I was reporting in the following day—and that was that. He was insistent so I said, "If the Japanese land give me a ring, and I will join you at the depot." They didn't take this very kindly, and I think that he never got over it.

The following day Friday, December 12, I reported in to special troops and joined the rest of the gang on the routine of two days in camp with a third afternoon and night at home. We spent our entire time at camp, so it seemed, in preparing tables of equipment, organization, and the like, along with drawing supplies to put us on a war footing. My company, along with most everyone else, was intense, and it was a cold December on the mesa. Kerosene heaters for the tents were finally issued.

The light tanks with which we were equipped were powered with Wright seven-cylinder radial air-cooled aircraft engines, and the radios were those used in naval aircraft. Our engine mechanics were from motor transport and were not trained or skilled in aircraft engines. Radio repairmen were not available. Either my visit to Marine Corps headquarters or my constant requests for skilled personnel paid off, because the Marine aviation squadron stationed at North Island transferred to us a few mechanics and radio personnel to tide us over until tank personnel could be trained. I think that General Vogle had something to do with this help that we received. In addition to paperwork, we continued to train our tank crews in driving and gunnery. On December 20, Col. Maurice Holmes relieved Colonel Lockee as commanding officer of special troops. On Monday, December 22, the 2nd Tank Battalion was created with Major Withers the commanding officer.

Our battalion consisted of Company A in Iceland, Company B with Captain Denig in San Diego, along with Company C, Captain Swencesky, and the headquarters company. The same day a meeting was held in camp by the division. All units were represented and most officers were present. At this time Colonel Larson, who I think may have been a brigadier general by this time, selected units and officers for the newly created 2nd Brigade, which was being activated for duty in American Samoa. Captain Swencesky was nominated to command the tanks assigned, but Larson said that he wanted Denig. I was elected along with Company B to join his brigade. After the meeting, the command went on a schedule of one day that is twenty-four hours in camp, and the following day, after working hours, home for the night. This continued until we sailed for Samoa in January. When I say "sailed for Samoa," I mean that is where we thought our destination was, up to this point. The destination was either Alaska or Samoa, but nobody said exactly where we were going to go.

Our table of organization and equipment called for the company to take 50 percent replacements in weapons; thirty days of ammunition for our 37mm guns, .30-caliber machine gun, and .45-caliber Thompson submachine guns and pistols; plus gasoline for thirty days of combat. In those days, the tank company consisted of about 132 enlisted and six officers. All maintenance and repair was to be done by the company maintenance section, which amounted to about twenty men total.

The following will give you an idea of the amount of equipment for which we had to contend: eighteen tanks, plus nine spares for a total of twenty-seven; twenty-seven Thompson submachine guns (.45 caliber), one per tank; twenty-seven 37mm guns, one per tank; about a hundred pistols (.45 caliber); 135 .30-caliber air-cooled machine guns, five per tank; five spare barrels per gun. A total of 675. Eight trucks (two-and-a-half ton, each with a .50-caliber machine gun, plus five spare barrels. A total of forty. One reconnaissance vehicle, one-half ton, spare tires and so forth, gasoline, and ammunition for all to last thirty days, and each man had his rifle and bayonet. To this must be added the repair equipment: a machine shop, tents, cots, sea bag, ammunition, galley gear, dishes, most everything else you can imagine necessary for living in the field in a remote place such as Samoa. In addition, we were ordered to take clothing for both cold and hot climates, as some thought we may go to Alaska. Most of this gear was procured and loaded on the ships, but was eventually lost, misplaced, or abandoned before we left Samoa for other places in November 1942.

Somehow, all was loaded on the ships: the *Lurline*, *Matsonia*, and I think *Monterey*. My company officers consisted of 1st Lt. A. J. (Jeb) Stuart (the exec), 2nd Lt. R. K. (Dick) Schmidt, 2nd Lt. Louis Metzger, and 2nd Lt. G. B. Thomas, platoon commanders, and Warrant Officer Charles Oliver, the maintenance officer. I, along with Metzger, boarded the *Lurline* (SS *Lurline* was a Matson Line ship), and as luck would have it we were assigned to a Lanai suite, which included a balcony. We went to war in grand style as you can see. The other company officers were assigned to the other two ships, two to each ship. Civilian crews were still aboard, and on our ship, this included room stewards. We soon found out that all one had to do was to press the suite's call button and a steward would appear. We ordered what we desired, including drinks, and signed the chits as U.S. Marine Corps. This lasted for about three days until the brigade quartermaster found out and put a stop to our fun.

These three Matson steam ships had been requisitioned by the navy for use as transports. About all that had been done for conversion prior to our arrival was to paint the hulls and superstructure gray and to convert the large shipboard reception rooms into troop quarters by installing tiers of bunks. The first-class galley, being the largest, was used to feed the troops. The officers used the second-class dining room and its galley. The food was excellent, as it was that used for the first-class passengers on the Hawaii–San Francisco run. We ate like kings, to say the least. During the first few days aboard ship, all hands rested as we were exhausted from the long hours spent in the preparation for embarking, loading, and so forth. The *St. Louis*, which survived Pearl Harbor without damage, was one of our escorts. We departed San Diego on the morning of Tuesday, January 6. The convoy headed about due south, in order to avoid suspected submarines and to approach our destination from the south.

On January 12, 1942, we crossed the equator, and each of us who were Polliwogs were initiated into the realm of Neptune by the Shellbacks. A lot of fun. While at sea, we held school drills for the troops. But on the whole, everyone took it easy, as we were well aware of the problems awaiting us at our destination, which had not been officially announced, but was believed to be Samoa.

I'm not certain of the date of our arrival, but a few days before we arrived there, we were told of a Japanese submarine lobbing some shells over the mountains to the north of Pago Pago Harbor and into the beach area. About twenty miles from the harbor entrance, the *St. Louis* catapulted a seaplane, which went airborne. It then made a circle and landed alongside the ship. Later, either it or another seaplane was launched, and I was told after our arrival in Samoa that the pilot wasn't told of his destination and his radio silence was in effect. He had to land for instructions. Eventually, the planes were launched, three or four of them, and they remained in Samoa as our reconnaissance air arm.

The transports anchored in the harbor and unloading began. The first night when we had the bulk of the tanks and trucks ashore, we moved them off the only road from the harbor to the west, where we were told to spend the night. This was done to permit trucks to move gear along the very narrow dirt road. I selected a coconut grove in a flat valley between two rather steep hills. The footing looked good, and none of us realized that the raining season was upon us. Nor did we have any idea of the amount of rainfall that occurred in Samoa each year. We were later told that it was about 350 inches per year on Rainmaker, the high mountain just north of the harbor. After we got sort of settled down around 8 p.m., it began to rain, the nice valley became flooded, and the ground turned into a sea of mud. This wouldn't do, so I ordered that all the tanks and vehicles be moved back onto the road. What a job that this turned out to be. In one case, it took two tanks to drag one out of the mud. We learned our lesson quickly that night. The next day I found a dry, elevated coconut grove farther away from the beach area, and we had that area assigned to us. We remained at our coconut grove for about two weeks.

During this period the village chief, who owned the coconut grove in which we were living, called on us with his high talking chief to pay his respects and to tell us that he was glad to have us as his guests. He also told us that we could eat as many of the coconuts as we desired. A few days later, the brigade issued four bottles of beer for each member of the command. These were the first refreshments we had had since leaving the transports. It was good even though we had no ice.

About February 8, permanent campsites were selected for each platoon and company headquarters. Lieutenant Schmidt's platoon was assigned to support the infantry on the eastern end of the island. Lieutenant Metzger, near the harbor and airfield under construction, and Thomas, near the company headquarters, which was located at a village called Ili Ili ("Little Pebbles"), about three miles from the harbor.

Because of the terrain, the tanks were assigned the task of defending likely landing beaches in support of the infantry and the defense battalion. Revetments were improvised so that the tanks could be used as mobile pillboxes and anti-boat guns. Prior to our arrival, a civilian contractor had the task of building an airport between Pago Pago and Ili Ili. The platoon on the western end and the middle platoon had the task of assembling or assisting in the defense of the airfield, if requested. Later a CB (U.S. Navy construction battalion) unit came into Samoa and took over the airfield construction.

The tank company attempted to improve their combat efficiency by training drivers and with gunnery practice, but as the brigade was distant from a base of supply, for either the United States or New Zealand, we were told to keep expenditures of gasoline and ammunition to a minimum. The gasoline for the tanks was high-octane aviation gas, and the containers were five-gallon square cans of a commercial type. After a few months the cans began to spring leaks, so we had quite a time obtaining used fifty-five-gallon drums to transfer this high-octane gas into. Another bad feature was the fact that this high-octane gas could not be used in trucks, as it would ruin their engines.

Around the middle of February, the brigade staff had settled down and decided that we were more or less on garrison duty. Therefore, in the future, all requests and issues had to be formal and in due form with signatures on most everything. At the same time, a shuffle of men and equipment began to take place. The first change in my company was to transfer my corpsman to the medical company. Then, brigade decided that Jeb Stuart, who had just made captain, should be shipped into the infantry. Somehow, I got them to reconsider this and they let me keep Stuart. Next, they decided that I should give up my trucks and drivers to the motor transport company. After much discussion, I put an end to this idea, but it was required to make my trucks available to the 8th Marines when they needed extra wheels. At first, this was a nuisance, but eventually I managed to set up a routine with the regiment.

Life went along a leisurely pace for about four months when the brigade staff decided that the tanks could be better employed in the defense of Uea, Wallis Islands, which was being garrisoned by the 7th Defense Battalion and one battalion of the 7th Marines from British Samoa. Consequently, in June we loaded our tanks and equipment on a cargo ship and set sail on a two-day voyage to the Wallis Islands.

The brigade reached Samoa on January 21, 1942. During the period February to September, promotions of both officers and men came rapidly. About the time we went to Uea, a school was established by the brigade on to Tutuila to train selected noncoms for promotion to reserve officers. I sent two sergeants, both by the name of McCann, and they passed with flying colors. About a month before we left for Uea, I was promoted to major, and Lieutenants Metzger, Schmidt, and Thomas were promoted to captains. Now we had one major and four captains in the company, a regular Mexican army. At this time, through the aid of Capt. Bill Baker, the commanding officer of the engineer company and a good friend of mine, we managed to electrify headquarters section of the tank company. We were the only camp, except for brigade headquarters, with such a luxury. It was a great help as it gave all of us a chance to read and to take it easy at night. Also we were able to show movies once a week with a borrowed projector to the delight of not only the marines but the natives as well. One fill of gasoline in the tank on the generator ran it from sunset until about 9:30 p.m. each night, when it ran out of gas and shut down. Prior to this great improvement, the town's chief built a hut for the officers of headquarters as a hangout. We put down a cement deck, fixed up a lawn, and Stuart planted some flower seeds that he had sent from San Diego. It was a regular country club. One of the bad features of Samoa was the dampness, which in addition to causing rust on most everything, seemed to rot our tents and clothing and cause mildew to form on most all of the equipment. This problem kept all of us busy attempting to preserve our gear and clothes. After we settled down and were quite comfortable, we were upset when we were ordered to move to Uea, Wallis Island.

While the tank company was in the San Diego area, we were unable to fire the 37mm guns or the machine guns mounted in the tanks, as there was no suitable area or gunnery range. We did manage, however, to drive the tanks, but it was mainly done with the hatchets open. Only when we got to Samoa were we able to do any amount of driving or gunnery. After the first night on Samoa, when we had so much difficulty in getting the tanks out of the muddy valley, we moved to a larger coconut grove in a valley called Mormon Ranch. The ground there had better drainage and was drier, but with all the rainfall in Samoa, it was still muddy and unsuitable for tanks. After a couple of weeks, the company was assigned the task of supporting the infantry in the defense of certain areas. As a result, Lieutenant Schmidt and his platoon were assigned to the eastern end of Tutuila and established camp at a village called Amuli.

Lieutenant Metzger was assigned a central area to support the infantry defending the area where the airfield was being constructed. He made his camp at a village called Pabaiai. Company headquarters and the 3rd Platoon were assigned to the western area, and they took up their camp in a town called Ili Ili, which had an abandoned church that we were able to use as a maintenance shop and storage facilities.

The merchant ship with our company aboard arrived at Uea after a two-day voyage, passed through the reef to a large lagoon, and anchored off Gahi Beach. Like Samoa, it was a nice place to view from the sea. In the center of the island was a large mountain, which looked as if it were a thousand feet high. Lieutenant Colonel Wilbur "Big Foot" Brown came aboard to welcome us. He was on the staff of the 8th Defense Battalion, whose commanding officer was also the island commander. The units assigned to garrison the island were the 8th Defense Battalion, one battalion of the 7th Marines, and now one company of tanks. Sending the tanks to Uea was a rather good idea, as the terrain there was more suitable for tanks and the rainfall was not as heavy. Colonel Brown being an artillery officer was well aware of the problems connected with the movement of heavy equipment. He informed us of an area suitable for our camp, which he had selected, and a tank park. He took me there later that day. He also informed us that our supplies, food, clothing, and so forth were to be turned over to the island command to be issued upon request. Having been through this pooling of supplies in Samoa before, we were prepared for this event, so we had extra food squirreled away in our tanks and other hiding places. Prior to departure, we obtained extra dunnage (wood) lying about the dock of Samoa, and en route to Uea had talked the ship's captain out of other dunnage that he had aboard. This lumber, even though it was of poor quality, would help us build a fine camp later on. When Colonel Brown saw the dunnage, he said that it, too, belonged to the island command. I objected. After a short discussion, we made a compromise, because I figured out that when he said "island command" he really meant his own artillery outfit. So, we divided the dunnage between the two of us and moved it from the beach as soon as any of it landed and said that mum was the word on the dunnage.

Late in September we were relieved by the 2nd Separate tank company, a unit attached to the 22nd Marines. This regiment relieved the 7th Marines on British Samoa and sent one of its battalions and the tank company to Uea. Our tanks and gear were loaded on a large barge, which was towed to Tutuila by the fleet tug *Turkey*. As I recall, it took two trips to move the tanks. The trip was rough, at least the one I made. All hands, including the tug's captain, got seasick. The *Turkey* bounced up and then smashed down on the other side of large swells because the heavy tow behind them held back the tug. Finally, the company got together once again, and at bivouac area north of the airfield in Tutuila we were attached once again on September 29 to the 8th Marines. This time we had no problems as the reinforced regiment had been directed to prepare to load out for parts unknown, but most of us were of the opinion that New Zealand was the destination. We were told to forget about the special garrison gear and load in such a manner that we could unload rapidly over a beach in an area that was not too friendly. In other words, not an assault landing, but perhaps a reinforcing operation. During this period, as I recall, a navy transport heading for the United States came into Pago Pago Harbor to pick up people and to drop some supplies. We were aware of a fierce naval engagement off Guadalcanal, but no one knew the extent of our losses, if any, as all the details were kept quiet in fear of the Japanese gaining information. Just after the transport dropped its hook, the word was passed that those who wanted to go ashore could do so. They must, however, fall into muster at designated places. I couldn't imagine that anyone who went ashore wanted to stay in Samoa, but anyhow, the bosun on the loudspeaker could be heard for miles. Then he said survivors of such and such a ship form in a certain location. He continued on until at least three or four ships' names had been announced. This, then, let everyone ashore know how severe our losses had been. I've always wondered if the skipper of the transport ever got into difficulty over this oversight.

About October 22, the 8th Marines, Reinforced, embarked; I can't recall what ship my company was loaded onto, but I remember that I was aboard the *American Legion*, a transport manned by the Coast Guard. And the crews for the landing crafts were surf men from the lifeguard stations. The convoy headed in the direction of New Zealand. Just prior to our embarkation Admiral Halsey succeeded Admiral Ghormley as commander of the South Pacific, and shortly thereafter the 1st (Marine) Amphibious Corps was formed. Somewhere along the line our destination was changed we headed for New Caledonia and then to Guadalcanal.

Our stop in New Caledonia was brief, about one day. I guess we went there to join a convoy because of the Japanese naval activity in the Guadalcanal area. We arrived at Guadalcanal on November 4 and disembarked. All of the 8th Marine reinforcing units were assigned to the 1st Marine Division. My company joined two tank companies of the 1st Division at Henderson airfield. Major (Harvey) Walseth commanded one company (A Company) and was the senior tank officer for the 1st Division, and he was in charge of both of the 1st Division tank companies. I was a senior to Walseth, so the division kept the two units separate. However, our mission, along with the other two tank companies, was to defend the airfield against any paratrooper attack and to reinforce or operate with the infantry units when directed. Also the landing beaches were rather close to our bivouac area, so we were told to prepare to help out the infantry if any landings were attempted in that area.

As it developed our first problem was being in the receiving end of a couple of naval bombardments during November. The first occurred on November 12 when I was in the division medical battalion hospital with malaria. Some Japanese battleships and cruisers decided to work over Henderson field, and the hospital was located in the line of flight of the shells. The hospital consisted of three shacks that the Japanese had constructed from packing crates during the construction of the airfield and some tents erected by the medical company. Our troops had constructed a number of shallow air-raid shelters that had some overhead protection. When the shelling started, those of us who could make it unassisted went to the shelters, and stretcher cases were moved by corpsmen and others who were able to assist. The Japanese fired illumination shells and high explosion, which as you can well imagine made quite a racket. This went on for about an hour, and I was glad to be released from the hospital a few days later so that I could use the deep and well-constructed shelters that the tank company had built soon after our arrival. In addition to the shelling, we were subjected to numerous air raids during November and December, which always seemed to occur at dawn, noon, and midnight. Our antiaircraft guns always fired at them, and I believe eventually got one.

During November my company assisted the ground personnel of the marine air squadron at Henderson field in building machine-gun ammunition (belts) and moving it to the airplanes for loading. It was a continuous demand for all planes to remain in air and be on the attack against enemy naval forces, especially transports ferrying Japanese reinforcements into the island. And the squadron personnel needed help because of this around the clock operation. The terrain where the battles were fought on the ground was not suitable for the employment of tanks. Along the coast it was swampy with creeks and rivers and either coconut groves or heavy underbrush. Most of the flat area was shallow, then it abruptly sloped up to steep hills and into ravines. The light tanks were not heavy enough to push their way through the underbrush, and the small 37mm turret gun did not have enough charge in the ammunition to do much damage to emplaced machine-gun positions. Consequently, the tank companies remained in the area of the airfield doing odd jobs, logistic jobs, on call.

One of the nuisances was the rats. They seemed to love the bindings of books. After reading a book, it was necessary that it be placed in a drawer or some rat-proof area. Otherwise, the rats would find it and start eating. Sometimes it turned out to be a rat race to see if you could read the book before the rats ate it.

On December 8, 1942, the command of the island passed from Vandergrift to Major General Patch, U.S. Army, and the 5th Marines sailed for Australia. Soon thereafter, the remainder of the division left and the 2nd Division then became a division of the XIV Corps.

On January 16, 1943, I was requested by the corps to support the advance of an infantry unit. A platoon of five tanks was assigned the task. Because of the heavy brush and lack of communications between the tanks and the infantry, the tanks got too far in advance and had no close fire support. One tank was damaged by the enemy causing the crew to abandon it. Two .30-caliber machine guns were removed and set up in order to engage the enemy. The platoon leader, Lieutenant Hanson, with his and another tank, joined the firefight, but they, too, were damaged by enemy action and abandoned. The three tank crews, twelve men, engaged the Japanese for about an hour with .30-caliber machine guns and Thompson submachine guns, when, under the cover of direct fire from some half-tracks, Lieutenant Hanson led nine of the twelve men back to their own line. Hanson then called in artillery fire to check the enemy from overrunning the abandoned tanks and the three men guarding them. Finally, the infantry advanced forward and beyond the tanks. Two of the tanks were successfully withdrawn.

During this attack, two tanks of the platoon managed to advance along the coast. One went about eight hundred yards into a Japanese bivouac area before withdrawing. The other destroyed seven machine-gun emplacements. Although it seems as if some damage was done to the Japanese defenses, really nothing much had been accomplished, except to prove that the light tanks needed clear terrain for movement. The area in which they were used was about the only suitable area along the coast, and, as you see, they were ineffective. The 2nd Marines was withdrawn from Guadalcanal the day before this engagement. Two weeks later the Japanese began their evacuation of Guadalcanal. The 8th Marines and its reinforcing elements were ordered to load out about January 28 , destination Wellington, New Zealand. There we rejoined the 2nd Tank Battalion after an absence of one year.

Our trip south was made in our old friend, the transport *American Legion*. During the Guadalcanal operation, it became apparent that light tanks, with their 37mm guns and .30-caliber machine guns, were of little value in the jungle, because they were not heavy enough to push their way through the heavy underbrush. In addition, the 37mm gun did not have enough explosive power to destroy machine-gun emplacements or concrete bunkers. Because of these defects, it was decided that medium tanks with 75mm guns would be the main battle tank for the U.S. Marine Corps. In addition, by this time suitable landing craft had been developed for landing operations. Medium tanks were employed during the attack on Tarawa with great success. Soon thereafter all marine tank units began to be re-equipped with mediums. This took a period of time to accomplish and the 4th Tank Battalion was equipped with two light companies and only one medium company during the attack on Roi-Namur.

As I recall we arrived in Wellington, New Zealand, on February 17, 1943. Thereafter, I was transferred to Headquarters 2nd Division Special Troops and given command of Camp Central Park in Wellington, New Zealand. It was here that the division band, military police company, supply personnel, and other supporting troops were billeted in.

I recall an incident that occurred during our loading out at Guadalcanal for New Zealand. Lieutenant Foos, the company maintenance officer, and myself went aboard the *American Legion* during the afternoon because of difficulties experienced during the loading of the tanks. We had been aboard ship for about half an hour when we noticed that the ship had gotten underway, along with all the other transports in the area. As we rapidly went south and Guadalcanal vanished into the distance, we found out that a Japanese task force of cruisers and destroyers had been located to the north. Later it developed that the Japanese were there to screen their own activities. Consequently, sometime during the night we returned to our anchorage and began loading operations early in the morning.

The voyage from Guadalcanal to New Zealand was uneventful. As it happened I was once again on the USS *American Legion*, APA 17. The ship's captain who brought us to Guadalcanal was still aboard, but this time he was a passenger. His relief had finally caught up with him at Guadalcanal, and he was happy to be taking it easy and heading back for the states. After a few days, he began to agree with our complaints and joined us in griping about the lousy chow and accommodations that the ship had for its passengers. I've always wondered if he remembered that experience when he assumed command of another APA.

The convoy arrived at Wellington, New Zealand, about February 16, 1943, after a cruise of about nine days. The tanks and equipment were off-loaded and the company moved to a tank park outside of Wellington. I reported to the commander of special troops and a few days later was told that the tank battalion would be commanded by Major Swencesky and that I would be executive officer of division headquarters battalion and camp commander of Camp Central Park in Wellington. I was disappointed with this assignment, as I had been looking forward to commanding the tank battalion. I must say, though, that I think a friend at division headquarters was instrumental in having me transferred so I would have a nice billet in the big city after spending thirteen months in the bush.

CHAPTER THREE

KOREAN WAR (1950–1953)

///LT. ROBERT W. BAKER (U.S. ARMY)

On September 20, 1950, at 1100, I reported to Lieutenant Colonel Lynch. He gave me an order to follow his I&R (intelligence and reconnaissance) platoon north out of Poun. We were not to fire unless fired upon. He said we were going to link up with the 7th Infantry Division, but we had no idea where they were. At that time, I reminded him about the need for gas for my tanks for such a long move. He said that someone would take care of it.

We left Poun at 1130, with the I&R platoon in the lead. We reached the outskirts of Chongju at 1430. Crying women reported that their families were held captive and that if we entered the city, they would all be shot.

Lieutenant Colonel Lynch personally ordered me to lead into Chongju with my three tanks, and he and the I&R platoon would follow. When I arrived inside the town, it was deserted except for a few civilians.

They said the North Korean Reds (slang for communists) had left. This I reported to Lieutenant Colonel Lynch, who with the I&R platoon then entered the city. We left Chongju with the I&R platoon in front. Although no enemy forces were visible, North Korean Red flags were in all of the towns.

At 1800, after a distance of sixty-four miles, I stopped the convoy and asked how far we were going. At this time, Lieutenant Colonel Lynch reported that we would be continuing on and that we had to link up with the 7th Infantry Division between Osan and Suwon. I asked for gas again, as I knew my tanks could not make it. No one seemed particularly interested, so I started walking to the rear, having all the trucks pull over as I did. I had passed about twenty-five vehicles when Lieutenant Colonel Harris called me and chewed me out for closing up his column. I reported to Lieutenant Colonel Harris that I was out of gas and was trying to find some. This was about 1815. At about 2000, gas arrived at the head of the column. After I gassed up my platoon, the 2nd Platoon was to split the rest, though there was a shortage.

About that time the I&R squad, which was seventy-five yards in front of my tank, reported North Korean Red soldiers with rifles were proceeding south on the road, and when they saw us they ran.

A short time later, the I&R squad came running past us and reported that an enemy T34 (Soviet-made) tank was coming down the road. We immediately manned our guns. Then two trucks came around the corner, one with equipment and the other with personnel. When they saw us, they abandoned their vehicles and one ran into an I&R squad jeep in the road. We thought it might have been the 7th Infantry Division, so we held our fire. As it was dark at this time, we put up a flare to determine the type of vehicle.

At one time when we were parked for gas, I was at the CP (command post) jeep, when radio messages concerning lights were held. Lieutenant Colonel Lynch personally ordered me to turn on my lights. He also informed me that I was to lead the column with my platoon and that the

I&R squad would be pulled back. I informed him that I thought we may be going a little slower as I had to recon my own route and bridges and our way through towns in the dark. I also asked him if I could shoot known North Korean Red soldiers, if I thought it necessary. He said yes. He asked me to push right along as we had to make contact. I asked him how and where we were to make contact, and if there was some way of sending a message that we thought we were going to meet the 7th Infantry. He reported the 7th Infantry Division had been in Osan and had pulled back, but for what reason he didn't know. Still no enemy situation, except we did know that the Red soldiers weren't retreating here, but heading south.

Just as we were ready to pull out, a captain from Lieutenant Colonel Lynch's jeep came up and said, "Go slow for about ten minutes and then highball as fast as you can!" I informed him that I would give him all my tanks had.

Right after we started, we passed a few abandoned trucks on the road. Just before we got to Chonan, we started passing soldiers. I reported this to the tanks in the rear. I called on the SCR 300 (radio), but received no "Roger" (confirmation). I waited for the convoy, and at one time, I could see about twenty sets of headlights.

The city of Chonan was full of soldiers all standing around in groups; I passed right on by them, as the town was quite complicated, my map was poor, and there weren't any civilians. I stopped and asked a North Korean Red who was sitting on guard which way it was to Osan. He pointed that I was going on the right road. He recognized me and started to run away, so I had to shoot him for fear he would warn people up the road in town. Just outside of the town, we caught up with what I estimated to be a company of infantrymen walking north in full uniform with camouflage. We sprayed them with .30-caliber machine guns and small arms. All along the way between Chonan and Osan, we saw soldiers at bridges, on motorcycles, jeep trucks, bicycles, and carrying supplies. We shot them up, however, not shooting the trucks and jeeps unless someone was in them. I figured if we captured them, then we could use the vehicles. We ran over one soldier when he collided with another in the road. We stopped several times to let the convoy catch up, when I could see many headlights behind me.

The last time I stopped for a long time was north of Osan and just past the railroad crossing. We stayed there for a few minutes until it was determined that the vehicles were behind us. Radio contact had been out, but my orders were to highball until we met the 7th Infantry Division, and because nothing was bothering us, I went on.

About three to five miles north of Osan, I received my first enemy fire. As I had seen many enemy tank tracks along the road, I knew it best not to stop and get the whole convey ambushed. I sincerely believed they were right behind me. After we went past the fire from the enemy, I came upon M26 (Pershing) tank tracks, but we were beginning to get more fire. (I found out later on that it was small-arms and 75mm recoilless rifle fire from the 7th Infantry Division.) The 7th Infantry tanks reported that the only reason they kept from firing on us was our headlights, excessive speeds, sounds of motors, and finally a WP (white phosphorous) grenade lit up the white star markings on our vehicles. One tank commander allowed my first tank to go through and was going to get the second; they had no idea we were anywhere near them and had received word that we were thirty to forty hours away. They had AT (antitank) mines supported by AP (antipersonnel) mines, and AT guns all on the road, just a few hours before we arrived. The only reason they took them down was that they were going to attack at 2400 with tank and infantry.

I left Ipchonni at 2030 and arrived at the battalion CP, 31st Infantry Regiment, 7th Infantry Division, at 2226, a distance of forty miles. The reason I was able to go so fast was because of a combination of clear moonlight, fresh enemy tank tracks, which made detours easy to determine, and expert tank men and tanks. Had not every man been alert, calm, and knowing his job perfectly, we would have been lost. My platoon had not had any real rest for more than a month except Sergeant Riffle and myself, who had slept for the three days while we were in the hospital.

I would like to get some awards for these tank commanders and drivers, because without them we would have never been able to do what we did. At the time these orders were given to me during the operation, I thought they were the damnedest I had ever received. Not only did we go 106 miles through enemy territory, but also we ended up being shot at by another division who had little knowledge that we were coming. Had not pure luck and something bigger than bravery and God been with us, I'm sure my whole unit, including others in the company, would have been wiped out in the worst massacre of the war. Because everything came out so well, I feel the least I can do for my men is to get them some awards that prove they have guts, which are hard to find at times.

One man was killed in the rear tank, which we figure was from an 85mm shell from the rear. He was in the TC's (tank commander's) seat driving to spell off his driver on this zero to thirty-five miles per hour, one-hundred-mile jaunt. We tried frantically at the 7th Infantry Division front to reach the convoy. My SCR 300 was working, and the M26 outfit tried it. I gave my crystal to their communication (section), and they had a radio on all night trying to call. I kept a man on all night trying to call on my 526 and 300 radios, too. They were trying all the channels in the 610 to get the air tactical officer on his radio. They tried to get a plane up, but they didn't have any lights. They tried sending out relay 300s down the road up to the edge of enemy territory.

At 0200, I couldn't take it any longer, and I passed out. I gave all the poop I could to them, and they called off the attack. I'm sure that if we had not gotten through when we did, they might have attacked right into our whole column, because they didn't have any idea we were near.

At 0630 the next morning, I was ordered to the rear and was told they had made contact with Task Force Lynch and that I was to revert to their control until the road was open. I told the 31st Infantry Regiment what I just wrote. They gave us some POWs to clean the blood and brains from my one tank, and others to clean the rest.

At about 1100, I met Major General Barr and about twenty correspondents. I told them what happened, and they were all amazed. They took many pictures, including TV and newsreel. I don't think I could count how many. General Barr personally shook hands with my entire platoon. They took several pictures with the general and me in front of the lead tank, which had the markings 1st CAV-70th TK and "Don't shoot" on it. The PIO (public information officer) said these pictures would be flown to Tokyo and then radioed home for all the stateside papers. They asked questions about even small details. One correspondent passed around a bottle in order to get stories from my men. The next day *Time* and *Life* reporters came and got all the stories again. Several correspondents drifted in and out all day.

That night Lieutenant General Almond called for me and asked, "What are you doing here?" I told him the regimental commander had introduced me as the liaison officer. General Almond then gave me a message to take back to my commander, which was in gist. "Tell him I have met the enemy and am annihilating him, and I will continue to do so. Also, I am going into the west and will do so and that I don't need help up here and to go some other place!" I started to tell him who I was, and he said he didn't care how or who I was, but to take back that message, and he left. I asked the executive officer of the 1st Infantry Regiment what the hell was going on. He said that General Almond was all pissed off at the 1st Cavalry Division. That was all he had heard all day—and that he had dressed down someone else earlier. Apparently, he reported heavy fighting around Suwon and here 1st Cavalry Division tanks and four jeeps were putt-putting right through it. In addition, I told Lieutenant Colonel Rogers about General Almond and the General Barr incidents and about getting orders to barrel down the road with lights on.

I am still finding out what happened along the column, and apparently, the 6x6s could not keep up, and the column must have been thirty-five miles long. They said they were fired on at 2400 to 2430 south of Osan, and I had passed it about 2200. General Barr personally directed a picture of the platoon and lead tank to be sent to Fort Knox to be preserved. He also said General Patton would have been proud of us.

Corporal Lorelli kept a list of my tank's fire. List of damage by 1st Tank Battalion; seventy-nine men shot, eight carts shot up, four motorcycles shot up (one full of riflemen), two jeeps run over in middle of road, five trucks shot up, eight trucks passed up, four bicycles! We shot at them over the side of the tank but didn't take credit for those hit in the dark. These were all in the tank lights. Loss: one casualty, one .50-caliber machine gun, and four cupola glasses, revived commo (communication) system, one hundred years of growth, many more hairs. End!

///COL. WALTER "MUMU" MOORE (U.S. MARINE CORPS)

September 11–22, 1952, my unit participated in the 1st Marine Division's contribution to the final offensive operation of the war on the northeastern front. The 1st Marine Division attacked the North Korean hill/ridge positions that we referred to as objectives 673, 749, and 812 in a column of infantry regiments. This ridgeline ran roughly in a northwest direction and was heavily defended by the NKPA (North Korean People's Army).

Early D-Day, September 11, 1951, the 1st Regiment led the way, capturing the hill known as 673, then it was the 2nd Regiment's turn on the fortified slopes of hill 749. The 3rd Regiment attacked the hill known as 812 and won a victory over the NKPA forces. The enemy fought much like their old Japanese mentors, giving no quarter and not expecting any.

My tanks were in the fight continually. We initially supported the 1st Regiment in the attack on hill 673. I had tank liaison teams with SCR 510 pack radios situated with the forward infantry elements. These liaison teams were our eyes and ears and the reason we could shoot over the heads of infantry marines without causing casualties. This, of course, was accomplished in close coordination with infantry unit leaders, right on the spot! Unlike hills 749 and 812, the enemy bunkers on hill 673 were pretty well exposed to the 90mm flat trajectory fire of the tank guns.

Distances from my tanks in the valley to the impact areas varied from four to five hundred yards. One must remember that a high-velocity 90mm tank gun was an accurate weapon at these shorter ranges. Our SCR 510 radios were often unreliable, but thanks to a stash of light combat wire and sound phones, I was able to keep in touch with my liaison teams up front. Because radio communications went out on a regular basis, using wire and sound power, though unorthodox, worked pretty well for us.

The light wire we used was vulnerable to tank treads and enemy mortar fire. This meant people under my command, such as the intrepid Sgt. C. B. Ash, made numerous trips laying wire under fire to keep communications open. I usually placed myself with a rifle company commander officer or on the battalion observation post where I could coordinate activities with the battalion commanding officer. In this terrain, being in a tank would hamper my ability to keep in close touch with my customers, the infantry.

In order to keep constant pressure on the enemy, we used the processing system developed on fighting the Japanese defensive system on Okinawa. *Processing* meant shooting in relays. This kept at least one tank platoon on station firing on call during the daylight hours. Due to the good relationship we maintained with the infantry regimental and battalion commanders, I was able to keep the three tank platoons from each of the infantry regiments. Small wonder we expended an average of seven hundred to one thousand rounds of 90mm gun rounds per day. That doesn't include the thousands of rounds of .30- and .50-caliber ammo expended. We had ammo, and we used it!

Mainly because of the intervening terrain, it became more difficult for my tanks to support the marine infantry regiment assault on hill 812. Thanks to the initiative of my men, we solved that problem. How? By using the two company headquarters tank dozers and an armored engineer tank bulldozer to cut a tank track that traversed up the side of the ridge, a hairy experience under even the best of circumstances. Later in the winter months, this technique became standard operating procedure.

Contending with snow and ice, we actually cut roads up to the top of these ridgelines. These pine-covered ridges were at least one thousand yards in elevation. We tried everything we could to get our tanks to support the infantry in their mission "to kill or destroy the enemy."

Accomplishing this feat was done despite a few influential senior officer nay sayers who kept telling me, "You're crazy MuMu, it can't be done." These are the guys who referred to tanks as the "sick beasts of Korea." How wrong they were.

The NKPA had burrowed deeply into the slopes of hill 749. When the marine infantry regiment assigned to capture that position launched a series of attacks, the enemy unhesitatingly called down their own artillery upon the exposed marines, inflicting severe casualties on them. Eventually, Company C tanks were brought into position and fired 720 rounds of 90mm ammunition into six large bunkers.

I was firing about one thousand rounds a day of 90mm ammo. I got my tanks up on places using dozer tanks to cut roads, if you want to call them that, along the sides of places where you could get direct fire over the top of the infantry into these bunkers, maybe seven hundred yards away. When the winter came, we actually cut roads up the top of these ridgelines, at a thousand yards in elevation, to use tanks to attack these heavy sets of bunkers.

On the northeast front in the dead of winter, we conducted aggressive raids to inflict casualties and destroy enemy positions. The costs were inevitable casualties and wrecked tanks. We had a fair number of casualties; I even got myself shot up there. As the battalion S3, you must know what is going on. Curiosity can . . . kill the cat sometimes.

As the story goes, I was still a company commander at heart, and Charlie Company just happened to be the tank company supporting the marine infantry regiment in an attack on a position that we dubbed this rock pinnacle "Luke's Castle." We had a platoon of flame tanks working in tandem with our gun tanks supporting the marine infantry in their raid on the castle. The attack started at first light, January 5, 1952.

This castle was a pinnacle sticking straight up in the air. We could see the heat emanating from the inside. The NKPA had a cozy place in there until we wrecked it for them. The flame tanks got close enough to the pinnacle to shoot their loads of flame. Out the back of the tank, you could see the North Koreans running in a panic silhouetted in the snow, some with their ammo bandoleers exploding because of the napalm. The ridge was so narrow here that only one flame tank at a time could operate without sliding in the ice and snow into the deep canyon below.

The success came with a price, though. One of our flame tanks hit a mine backing out of his firing positions a mere fifty-five yards or so from the pinnacle. After several vain attempts to pull the crippled vehicles out using steel cable hooked to the tank, the company commander and I went out there to see what could be done. This was done under small-arms and mortar fire coming from the NKPA positions to the rear of the pinnacle. Time was of the essence because it got dark extremely early.

Our tank crewmen and maintenance men made another valiant attempt to hook up the disabled tank. Thank God! It worked! They literally dragged this thirty-five-ton M4A3 medium flame tank with two M46 tanks pulling in tandem. We could not use a World War II–designed M32 retriever designed for such work. Why, because the open, unprotected turret top made it extremely vulnerable to artillery and mortar fire. The pulling was accomplished with both vehicles in reverse gear because the ridge was too narrow to have the luxury of turning around in the snow and ice. One man was killed and several wounded as they ran out there to hook cables and to guide the tank drivers as they backed in reverse some 180 yards to our lines.

When the tanks came back into our lines, I jumped up to pat the men on the back for a job well done. Just then, several 82mm enemy mortar rounds landed near us. I still recall the thump, whirr of metal, acrid smoke, and air pressure to this day! As luck would have it, I was hit in the face with several small mortar fragments and was knocked down with a severe head concussion. Blood even came out of my ears. No matter, I was one lucky dude! That ended it for me for about ten days as they moved me via the chain of evacuation to the U.S. Navy Hospital ship USS *Haven* located in Pusan Harbor for treatment. Besides another Purple Heart (second one), my battalion commanding officer chewed me out for being out where I had no business being. Oh well, it was an unforgettable day and a hell of a twenty-ninth birthday present! Furthermore, now I know our Lord was watching out for me!

///SGT. JOHN E. GARRIDO (U.S. ARMY)

I believe an analogy to the game of checkers well describes the deadly game of war that often existed between our tanks and enemy mortar or artillery rounds during the Korean War. It is true that the armor plate of the tank provided protection from small-arms fire or shrapnel from exploding shells, but it is also true that the enemy would fire the biggest guns at the tank in an effort to knock it out. This always created a dangerous situation for the tankers inside who where often within yards of being killed by these high explosive rounds hitting on the top of the tank where the armor plate, like the bottom, was the thinnest. At least this was true of the M4 Sherman tank of which I was a crewmember.

To compare the M4 Sherman tank to today's M1 Abrams main battle tank is like comparing the Model A Ford to today's cars, but in its day the Sherman did a good job and served this country well. It did, however, have less-than-desirable thickness in its armor, and this made it vulnerable to penetration from the top. This, of course, was especially dangerous for the crew inside of the turret when the tank came under indirect artillery or mortar fire. The North Koreans, for example, used 82mm and 120mm mortars that left a rather large crater when the round hit the ground.

To "bracket" in an artillery target is simply to establish the interval between the ranges of two rounds of artillery fire, as one over and the other short of the target, to find the correct range. In other words, if you fire at a target and the round falls short, you then estimate how far short the first round was from the target and elevate the distance by that much. If you should then hit above the target, you then would lower your range, so that in most cases the third round would strike the target. We sometimes used this method of range finding when firing our 76mm main-gun. We also used tracers from the coaxial .30-caliber machine gun, which was synchronized to the gun telescopic sight for shorter distances, followed by a main gun round if necessary. And, of course, range estimates from the tank commander. The gunners on the old tanks like the Sherman became experts at firing the cannon by using the telescopic sight, and most of the time hit the target with the first round. Today's tanks are equipped with a laser range finder and a computer that makes calculations and adjustments. All the gunner does is select the target.

As far as I know, all armies used the bracketing method in hopes that the third round would be on or near the target. This was especially true of indirect mortar or artillery fire, when it was at the direction of a forward observer who would estimate the range and bracket in the rounds. If you remembered this, you could guess which way to go to avoid being hit. It was like a game of checkers as you moved back and forth.

The large mortar rounds were lethal to infantry, but required a direct hit to damage a tank. We were fortunate that the enemy were not as expert at firing mortars as they might have been. On one occasion, I remember that the 4th Platoon parked its tanks in a rocky river bed close by a bridge, then dismounted for a break under the bridge. As we stood talking with others standing under the bridge, the NKPA started sending in rounds in an effort to hit the tanks parked in the riverbed with their hatches open. There was nothing we could do but watch as they attempted to bracket in on the tanks. I remember that for some reason we did not seek any other cover than what we had under the bridge, where we were standing without helmets. We were never issued tank helmets and most of the time we simply wore a fatigue hat inside the tank.

Suddenly, a round exploded in the riverbed, and a man close by me sank to the ground with a large piece of shrapnel sticking in the side of his head. His name is unknown to me at this time, but I remember him as a friendly, outgoing personality with a handsome face. He was the kind of person who, if you were making a bet, would bet he would always make it in anything he did. I am unsure if he survived, but I think not. Maybe someone remembers this incident? As suddenly as it started, the rounds ceased coming in, and none of the tanks were hit.

That incident took place in the Waegwan, South Korea area in August/September 1950, at a roadblock that we maintained on the road leading into Waegwan. I remember that the 5th Cavalry on the hills to our back were taking quite a pounding from enemy mortar fire. It was not unusual to see them carrying someone off the hill in a poncho because he had been wounded by mortar fire. One day the North Koreans decided that they wanted to knock out our tank with mortar fire, and I remember a round exploding in front of our tank close enough that I saw the crater that the round made in the hard soil. It was at least the size of a bushel basket, and dense black smoke and dust hampered our vision. We could not determine from what location the fire was coming because mortar fire unlike artillery makes no sound as it travels its course.

With only the narrow dirt roadway to move in, a quick decision was made to move the tank forward because the mortar round had landed in front of the tank. The checker game started as we moved the old Sherman forward and backward. We were fortunate that the game ended in a draw, and the incoming rounds soon ceased after just a few moves. If it had not been for the fact that someone knew about bracketing in on a target and moved the tank forward, we might have been hit by enemy fire. I am sure that such a large mortar round could have penetrated the top of the Sherman tank we were in. I am also sure that this is why we moved, because the driver stated his reason for moving the tank forward and backward. So, when I think of checkers now, I am reminded of the day that we played checkers with the enemy.

One of my most unforgettable experiences of the early days of the Korean War occurred near Waegwan, South Korea with its infamous hill

303, in August 1950, in a rice paddy, along the roadway adjacent to the Naktong River. This was part of the Pusan perimeter and the border of no man's land across the river. This is not a story about heroic deeds in warfare. In fact, it seems rather humorous to me now looking back on it, although at the time, it was not.

The little town of Waegwan saw its share of fighting and destruction from both sides. We would shoot it up each day, and then pull back our armor to a more secure area each night where we would usually be on 50 to 100 percent alert. In these early days of the war, most outfits were short of supplies and men, and you slept when you could.

On one August day, tanks of Company A, 70th Tank Battalion, attacked the town of Waegwan. It was during the battle that we lost the right track off our Sherman tank. In an effort to save the tank, a tow cable was hooked to it and another tank attempted to tow it back to our line, but the disabled tank slid over the side of the road into a rice paddy with tall grass. This rendered the tank and its guns inoperable because the tank was on its side.

Because it was getting late in the evening and we needed the proper equipment to retrieve the tank, it was decided that the tank would be left in the rice paddy overnight. It was also decided that the tank gunner, a man by the name of Gene Autry (not the cowboy), and I would stay with the disabled tank to protect it. I don't know why Gene and I were chosen. I guess we volunteered to stay. Anyway, the main thing that I remember about Gene was that he never wanted to get out of that tank turret unless he had to. He was a good gunner and a good man.

The sun soon set and night came on us as dark as black ink with no lights in the sky. In order to be as comfortable as we could be, Gene and I set down on the side of the tank with our backs against the side of the turret, armed only with .45s and hand grenades. As the long hours passed slowly by toward midnight, the sound of footsteps could be heard coming out of the darkness toward us, down the road. At that time, I felt Gene's elbow in my side as he asked, "John, do you hear that?" Before I could answer, Gene was in the road, and he yelled "Halt" at the same time he started to fire his .45-caliber automatic pistol into the darkness down the road toward the footsteps.

I also fired several rounds from my .45-auto, and then threw a grenade down the dark road. When the grenade went off it sounded like a whole platoon of men was running up the side of the hill. This was followed by an eerie silence for the rest of the night, as we hid in the tank unable to see through the tall grass. Dawn finally came, and we decided to investigate the situation. We were sure that we had had a narrow escape. We came out of our hiding place and walked down the road not knowing what we would find.

To our amazement, we found the carcass of an Ox in the ditch. We both surmised that when the grenade went off it scared the Ox so bad that it had a heart attack, and when it attempted to run up the side of the bank, it made the sound of many footsteps that we heard. Anyway, I could not find a scratch on the old bull.

When solders of the 5th Cavalry Regiment on the hills above us found out the reason for all the shooting, they teased us, especially Gene Autry (because of his name). We often heard them say, with a laugh, "Have you killed any bulls lately?"

That day we got our tank out of the rice paddy and continued with our part of the war. I will never forget the incident of the Ox, however, and that is no bull!

///SGT. ALLEN INHELDER (U.S. MARINE CORPS)

The United Nations (UN) police action forced the North Koreans back to the 38th parallel, the agreed upon division of North and South Korea after World War II. Instead of stopping there, the United States decided to take all of Korea. This would require capturing all the land north to the Manchurian border. This was to be achieved in the winter in rugged mountains with limited and poor supply line access. The Chinese entered the war with an overwhelming number of troops. The marines were on the eastern side of North Korea near the Chinese border when they were surrounded and had to fight their way out of the enemy encirclement to the sea.

The only escape route from the mountains to the sea evacuation site was little more than an enlarged oxen trail hewn into steep mountain slopes. This one-way road precisely followed every curve in the hillside. During the advance to the Manchurian border, bulldozers had widened some areas of the road that were not wide enough to accommodate a tank. Maneuvering the tanks up this narrow winding dirt/gravel road in the daylight was a difficult feat. This road was the only land supply road. We were then faced with driving our M26 tanks down the pass at night, which was a slippery, snow-packed, compacted-ice road—the result of being traversed by thousands of troops and vehicles that preceded our tanks.

The steel M26 tank treads were designed for dirt, not snow. The shallow tread protrusions would pack with snow, and the tank tracks would lose traction and slide easily on sloped surfaces. American tanks in World War II (Europe) had grousers that could be bolted to the treads with special track links. The high pressure points of the grousers pierced into the ice to prevent the tank from slipping. In the early stages of World War II, the Americans gave the Russians Sherman tanks until they could manufacture their own. The Russians quickly realized how poorly the Shermans performed on ice and snow and welded or bolted chains to the bottom of the treads. Lesson learned; Russian T34 tanks came equipped from the factory with grousers for traversing over ice and snow and could quickly be bolted on through the special holes in the track sections. Our M26 tank did not have grousers, and the tracks treads were not designed to accommodate this proven essential accessory for winter tank operation in the snow and ice.

Approximately two million Koreans fled to China during the forty-year Japanese occupation of their land. Most returned after World War II and were fluent in the Chinese language. These folks did not become refugees because they were afraid of the Chinese. The North Korean population became refugees only after some Chinese soldiers started to confiscate their food, and the UN forces implemented a scorched earth policy destroying their homes and buildings to prevent enemy occupation. We had a moral obligation to evacuate the civilians to prevent their starvation and death.

Our tank, B25, was positioned at the southern most edge of the Koto-ri basin next to the only road leading south to the Funchilin pass. The North Korean refugees (civilians) had an uncanny ability to avoid being caught in the fighting and had been entering the basin for several days. There was a steady stream of evacuees walking south, especially in the early in the morning of the scheduled U.S. Marine Corps evacuation.

Surviving in subzero temperatures required the consumption of lots of calories. We were told that we needed to eat five thousand calories a day. A plentiful supply of Tootsie rolls and gallon cans of strawberry preserves were air dropped into the basin. Sometimes the parachutes would drift and land on the enemy positions. I wondered what they did with the Tootsie rolls. The frozen Tootsie rolls were as hard as bars of steel and had to be thawed under our clothing; armpits thawed the candy fast. There were stories of marines breaking their teeth when trying to bite off a frozen section. Heating frozen ration cans in a fire was difficult. The outer area of food near the can surface would get burned and the inner area would still be frozen. Tank crews had it easy; they heated the cans in the cast-iron engine exhaust manifold on the back of the tank. The standard can size fit perfectly and warmed the food without burning. I learned to drink coffee at Koto-ri. It tasted bad but was warm and helped heat our bodies. Coffee was made by placing a helmet filled with water in a fire, then the coffee was put in a sock. The open end of the sock was tied and thrown in the helmet.

The population of Koto-ri was increasing as the marines fought their way back to the basin. The cold temperatures caused problems with body waste disposal. The frozen ground prevented digging below-ground latrines. The latrines at Koto-ri were above ground. I called them turd castles. The body waste would start freezing while in mid-air and formed pyramids. When the pyramid reached the seat, the latrine would be lifted and moved to a nearby location. Fortunately, the turd castles did not cause a health problems, as they were frozen solid.

We had been informed that tanks would be the last vehicles in the evacuation column, which was approximately ten miles long. This decision was a practical one and was based on the possibility of a tank breakdown that might have prevented the hundreds of wheeled vehicles from reaching the valley floor. We were issued rifles and carbines and told that if we had to abandon our tanks we were to join the infantry and continue by foot. This was not an appealing thought to a tanker. The crew hung their newly acquired weapons outside on the tank turret close to each hatch.

As darkness neared, the end of the column was in sight and the 2nd Platoon, Baker Company, tanks (B21–B25) assumed their position as rear guard. B25 assumed the last tank position with its 90mm gun facing to the rear. The cold made traversing the turret manually difficult. The electric traversing motor emitted strange sounds as it struggled to rotate the turret. On our way to the plateau, we could see many fires that were illuminating the sky in the Koto-ri basin. The fires were set by our troops, destroying the equipment and provisions that could not be transported by our vehicles.

Dusk turned to darkness; the crew was on full alert with eight eyes looking for signs of the enemy. The driver had his eyes fixed to the road ahead. We had an unobstructed 180-degree view to the rear. There was nothing between the Chinese and us. There were no refugees, not even stragglers. There was some movement in the hills to the left and right but no one directly behind. I assumed that the enemy had taken a needed break at the fires, warming themselves. We were told that there would be ground troops with us. Where were they? What ifs ran through my mind: What if our engine quit running? What if we lost a track? What if we ran off the road and could not climb back? Could we catch up with the tank was ahead of us? Being the last tank in the entire evacuation column without infantry support and the Chinese army in close proximity behind clarified the potential danger of our situation.

Our tank slid off the road several times on the way to the plateau area before the mountain descent. The maneuvers to climb back on to the road caused the tracks to scoop snow on to the topsides of the treads. The treads carried the snow up to the rear sprocket hubs and compacted it around the outside of the hubs. This snowball effect was causing the tracks to stretch and lift off the sprocket teeth. If the buildup continued, the tracks would slip off the tank rendering it inoperable. In order to keep up with the column, the crew equipped with large screwdrivers would reach between the upper and lower sections of the track and chip the snow (ice) off the sprocket hubs while the tank was moving. This was a dangerous procedure.

The M26 tank had a hot air heater that was not operable, as its radiator core froze and broke because of insufficient antifreeze. The tanks' thick, cast-steel walls acted as an insulated freezer. There were occasions at Koto-ri when the outside ambient air temperature was warmer than the air inside the tank. Historians describe the 1950 North Korean winter as "a one in one hundred years winter."

The crews' clothing was standard stateside issue and not intended for temperatures of -10 to -30 degrees that were encountered. Multiple layers of clothing helped. Grease spots on our pants and jackets provided a direct cold air path to the next layer of clothing. The crew did receive cold-weather rubber shoes. The shoes were not comfortable, and they were difficult to walk in. Sitting in the cramped crew tank positions with their shoes resting on cold steel caused a constant state of foot numbness. It was questionable whether these shoes provided better cold weather protection than our standard-issue shoes.

A tank commander in another platoon had brought a German shepherd with him from the states. He became a real nighttime guard duty companion at Wonsan. The shepherd was also suffering from the cold temperatures. In addition to his personal sleeping bag, the sergeant made special socks for him to reduce the risk of frostbite.

The column moved slowly, and it and was dark when we reached the plateau at the pass. We were told that B22 was to assume rear guard instead of us. B25 moved into second to last position. We had assumed that the tank commander Sergeant Dolby, who had received a Bronze Star at Wonsan, had more combat experience and skill under fire; we later learned, though, that B22 had a transmission oil leak and was placed last in case of a breakdown. Baker Company tanks started down the Funchilin Pass at 0100 hours, December 11, 1950, approximately ten hours after the start of the evacuation.

Our platoon proceeded slowly down the mountain pass for about two miles, and then stopped. After a much longer-than-usual wait with no forward movement of the column, our tank commander attempted to make radio contact with our platoon without success. Numerous books and publications explain that the poor radio reception was due to the many curves obstructing radio transmission. This may be technically correct, but it was not applicable to our situation. The tanks were about seventy-five feet or less apart, and we could see the tank behind and the one in front of us. It is important to note here that when the column stopped, each tank stayed in visual contact with the others, close enough to determine when the tank in front had stopped or started (line of sight). Today, the only reasonable conclusion for not being able to make radio contact at these close distances was that the tanks had been abandoned.

Sergeant Dolby (B22, last tank) approached our driver, Don Fox (Don's hatch was open), and asked us if we had radio contact with the platoon and if we knew the reason for the holdup? Don said no to both questions. Sergeant Dolby said that he was going forward to find the cause of the delay and asked to borrow our Thompson submachine gun. Don passed him the gun and several clips.

Our lieutenant's 2nd Platoon tank was three tanks forward of B25 and was less than 250 feet away; should have taken Sergeant Dolby no more than three or four minutes to reach B21 with a roundtrip walk of ten minutes. Our driver watched for his return. When he did not return, we thought that he had continued farther forward and that he would eventually return with instructions. This timeline further indicates that the 2nd Platoon tanks had already been abandoned. Other accounts indicate that the recon platoon was present when the abandon tank order was given. The crew became concerned after more than an hour passed and he did not return. While we were waiting for instructions, we did not observe "fleeing hoards of refuges" or marine infantry passing by our tank. Publications about this incident would have one believe that hoards of refugees were moving down the mountain pass behind the 2nd Platoon tanks in the middle of the night with infants, children, and old folks. These publications are pure fiction and fabricated by the recon platoon who was assigned at the plateau to defend the rear tanks. We did not encounter one refugee during our entire journey.

The cold winter silence was broken by the sound of mortar fire. Our crew at the time assumed that it was mortar fire or possibly friendly artillery fire that was shelling Koto-ri and the road to disrupt the enemy. The crew buttoned down the hatches. We received at least two hits that rocked our tank. The last hit occurred while traversing the turret in the direction of the ridge on the opposite side of the ravine. The turret could no longer be moved. After the barrage stopped, our tank commander told Frenchy Lemoine, our assistant driver, to go forward to get instructions. He returned a few minutes later and stated that the tanks were abandoned and there were no marines anywhere.

We should have realized that after the mortar attack ceased we would be receiving unwelcome visitors. The crew had been instructed (before Inchon) that in the event a tank is abandoned it must be rendered inoperative. Don Fox damaged the driver's switches and whatever else he could, and the gunner drained the 90mm recoil oil.

We exited our hatches to retrieve the rifles hanging from the turret only to find that they had been blown away. As the gunner was looking for the rifles on his side of the turret, he heard voices and saw Chinese climbing hand over hand up from the ravine below calling to him thinking that he was one of them. The crew looked toward the last tank (B22, lights off) as they jumped to the ground and saw and heard Chinese on and around the tank. As the crew dashed down the road from tank to tank, they were thinking, *Hey! Where did everyone go?* There were no dead or wounded marines, no dead or wounded Chinese, and no dead or wounded refugees. It was a frightening, eerie feeling: Had everyone but the enemy magically been lifted off the mountain but us? After we reached the last abandoned tank, the magnitude of the situation sank in. If we were ever to reach the sea, it would be achieved only by our own efforts.

Our young eyes quickly adjusted to the darkness. A tiny sliver of moonlight in its apogee was reflecting off the snow enabling the crew to see where they were going. One-quarter moon occurred on December 15 and a full moon on December 23. Being able to see where we were going meant that we could also be seen. The advantage of the dim light was that one could not recognize whether a human figure was a friend or foe. If you did not speak first, you had the advantage. Due to the mountain terrain and the need to catch up quickly with the rear echelon, the crew elected to make their escape by road rather than by ridge top or down to the bottom of the ravine two thousand feet below.

Having given our Thompson to Sergeant Dolby and the loss of our rifles left the crew with only their .45-caliber pistols with several clips each. Encountering the enemy head-on would be a losing battle. We quickly learned to speak in whispers and make as little noise as possible. I was impressed with the synergy of our crew. There were no complaints or arguments, just a dedicated single endeavor, our survival.

We crossed the north section of bridge and approached the concrete building that controlled the water flow to the hydroelectric plant below. To our surprise the south end of the bridge, which had been flown in from Japan and enabled the troop and vehicle evacuation, had been blown up. This left only a sheer, vertical concrete building wall on the left and the deep ravine on the right. There were no abandoned vehicles approaching the bridge area. The Chinese would have not blown the bridge after the evacuation column passed. The rear echelon of the evacuation column must have blown it up. The building did not have a floor and provided cover for only the four huge penstocks below. The numerous books that describe the engineers at the bridge blowing it up after the two tanks (Lett, Griffen) and recon crossed make no mention of "hoards of refugees." The timeline once again contradicts the recon platoon's statements of "hoards of refugees" encroaching the last tanks. The crew found a path on the upslope that circumvented the remainder of the bridge and building that led back on to the road south of the bridge.

When we reached B21 (before the bridge), we assumed that all the tanks had been disabled and did not know that it was operational. Had we driven that tank down the pass we would surely have driven it into the ravine not knowing that the bridge no longer existed. Finding that the bridge was blown with no sign of marines on either side further reinforced our belief that we had been left behind. Each negative factor that we encountered only reinforced our efforts for survival.

As the crew approached each curve, they would stop and observe if there was human activity. Voices were heard at the center of a long U-shaped curve. There could be no reason for marines to be there as there was now nothing to defend. This was an excellent enemy defensive position because of the long straight parallel legs of the U before the radius of the curve. There was no sign of activity on the curves below this one. The curve was in close proximity above hill 1081, which overlooked the concrete building and bridge location. The marines on this hill were to leave when Baker Company tanks had reached the road below this position. Through a miscommunication, the marines had left early. The crew decided to avoid the curve by sliding down the cliff to the bottom of the ravine. The snow-covered cliff was too steep to climb down and we found ourselves uncontrollably sliding down, smashing into rocks and bushes. We regrouped at the bottom. Everyone was okay, and we started our long and arduous hand over hand climb to the road. When the road was reached, we peeked over the edge, looked in both directions, and rested for a short while. The crew had bypassed the curve by a wide margin. Looking across the ravine, they could see five vertical dark lines that were plowed by their bodies and boots pushing away the snow.

The crew would observe each corner intently and continue to the next corner. There were several small shacks at one curve; all was quiet and we continued. As we approached one shack, a figure suddenly appeared and was speaking Chinese (Korean?). He recognized us as we rushed him and started shouting. He wore a Chinese quilted uniform and was not a refugee. One crewman put his hand over his mouth, but he continued to shout. We thought that he was calling for help. Another hit him over the head with his pistol. He started to cry and finally stopped after we gave him a cigarette. We did not want to call attention to our presence by a gunshot. Like it or not, we now had a prisoner. We had him walk about fifteen feet in front of us. Our thinking was that if the Chinese called out to him he would speak, leaving us only a few seconds to jump off the cliff into the ravine. Who in their right mind would attempt to pursue us down the ravine under these cold, dark, nighttime conditions?

After an all-night adrenaline rush, the crew finally made their way down the pass onto the flat land. Hazy, dim, dawn light had finally replaced the partial moonlight. There were signs of intense fighting everywhere, and we had still not caught up with the rear echelon. Had the troops boarded the ships already?

I must reiterate once again that we had not seen or passed one North Korean refugee after leaving our tank. There were no old folks or women with little children struggling to carry their belongings. The stories of hoards of refugees that had been infiltrated with Chinese endangering the tanks are simply not true. These stories evolved to justify the loss of the tanks and faulty rear guard protection.

Suddenly, in the distance, a large contingent of people appeared across the entire road. We could not tell if they were friend or foe. The crew started edging to the ditch on the side of the road when they heard "Who goes there?" We then realized that we had finally reached safety and shouted, "We're marines." Our excitement quickly turned to panic. If the rear guard had binoculars, they would see our prisoner, who was in front of us, and start shooting. We quickly placed the prisoner behind us and shouted that we had a prisoner with us. After the excitement of being with our fellow marines subsided, we turned our prisoner over and left to look for our company.

Both mentally and physically exhausted with aching bodies, the B25 crew had made it to relative safety. My feet and legs ached from walking and tripping all those miles in size eleven snow-packed shoes as the smaller sizes (size 8) had already passed out already at Koto-ri. The lesson here is that if the marines are passing out stuff, get in line early because there is usually not enough to go around. It is not clear how the crew continued to Hamhung—at least two crewmembers can't remember. Another believes that we finally caught up with the remainder of Baker Company tanks and continued on with them.

Baker Company tanks were up on the bank one hundred feet from the water's edge waiting for evacuation. An assistant driver, while exiting the hatch of his tank, stepped on his .30-caliber machine gun and accidentally fired off a round that was still in the chamber. Those of us who no longer had tanks were waiting at the water's edge to be evacuated by small boats to ships in the harbor. A single shot rang out and our driver, Don Fox, fell to the ground in severe pain; a bullet had ripped through his knee. The happiest day of my life (our escape) suddenly turned into the worst day of my life. After all our efforts to survive, it seemed unfair to have one of our crewmembers, who had been with the B25 since the Inchon landing, injured in this senseless way.

The United States requested that all the ships in the Sea of Japan assist in the evacuation. We were ferried to a small Canadian merchant ship named *Canadian Mail*. The captain, after seeing our filthy condition with disheveled dirty clothes covered with dark oil spots, asked what he could do for us. We asked him if we could take a hot shower, eat a meal with fresh food, and have a bunk to sleep in. The longest shower I have ever taken in my life was on that ship. Too tired to stand up, we sat and lay on the floor and just let the water pour over our bodies. The small ship's crew shared their clean clothes, sparing us from having to wear our old ones. Our first meal was beef stew with fresh ingredients. Either the food was too rich or we ate too much, because some of us threw up. I can't remember going to sleep or where I slept, but I remember the crew giving up some of their bunks. The Canadians were great folks, and I will never forget their kindness. Before the evacuation the captain was scheduled for docking in Japan. We were excited by the thought of some R&R there. No such luck; he was instructed to take us to Pusan, South Korea, where we received another M26 tank. Our new objective was to retake the land that had been lost by the Chinese intervention.

After reaching Hamhung, we were told that the four crewmembers of the last tank (B22) had not been accounted for. It was then that we realized they were probably still in their tank when the Chinese surrounded it as we were abandoning our tank. Years later, we learned that the crew had left the tank through the escape hatches under the tank and crawled into the ravine. Knowing that the enemy was on the road, they climbed down to the bottom of the ravine to make their way to the sea. They were captured the next day about twelve miles from the tanks in the flat lands near Chunghung. One of the crew died in a prison camp, and the other three were released several years later after the cease-fire agreement. Sergeant Dolby, the fifth crewmember of B22 who traveled past the abandoned tanks, was not allowed to return to his crew as there would be no rescue attempt. In a twist of fate, had their tank transmission not encountered problems, B25 would have been the last tank.

The seven tanks that had been abandoned in the mountain pass were destroyed the next day by air on December 12, 1950. Each M26 tank cost $81,000. This was a sad ending for our faithful friend (B25), which had carried us all the way from the Inchon landing to North Korea.

///LT. CHRIS BYRON (U.S. ARMY)

I served in the Korean War as a platoon leader and was a member of the 70th Tank Battalion, which was attached to the 1st Cavalry Division.

In Korea, because of the terrain, tank battalions and even tank companies didn't operate together as a unit. We were usually parceled out to an infantry unit. Quite often, it was just a platoon of tanks that was attached to an infantry battalion, and the platoon operated under the direction of the infantry battalion commander. Chances were that he didn't know anything about tanks. Even so, some of them were pretty good. One would say to me, "Tell me how you can help us in this mission that we have." Others were bullheaded and told you what to do. They thought they knew everything, like the one that I worked under quite a bit, Lt. Col. Paul Clifford. A good example would be on October 12, 1950.

Colonel Clifford commanded the 2nd Battalion of the 5th Cavalry Regiment. His battalion was given the mission of passing through the 8th Cavalry in a place called Songhyon-ni and attacking toward Kumchon, South Korea. On that morning, Colonel Clifford told me that he wanted me to lead an attack through a valley that contained heavy ground fog. Fog was not a common occurrence in Korea, but on that day, it was thick. I told the colonel that because of the heavy ground fog the gunners could not see through their telescopic sites; under those circumstances, it would be much better if the infantry lead the attack. His reply to me was, "If you can't see them, they can't see you." Of course, you know, they could hear us coming, and because of the size of the tanks, we would be seen first. Tanks in those days were not known for their stealth in storming enemy positions.

My protests to him were ignored, and I was ordered to proceed with his battle plan. In the plan of action, there was no room for the maneuver of tanks. To the west of the tortuous road leading north up a small mountain was high ground, not tremendously high, but hilly. Nevertheless, that high ground was impassible by tanks. In addition, I was told that there were friendly troops in that area. To the east of the road was a precipitous drop to a ravine. I don't ever remember seeing a guardrail on a mountain pass in Korea.

There was none here. So, in other words, the tanks and the troops, particularly the tanks, had to stay on the road. The troops could go up the hill if they wished. That was up to the battalion commander. Keep in mind, though, that because his information was that friendly troops occupied the high ground on the west of the road, it was not likely that his initial plan would direct the infantry to that area. There was no question that the tanks would be road-bound and could only proceed in a single file.

As was my usual custom, my tank was at the head of the column to lead the attack. I can recall the names of most of the people in my platoon. Sergeant Phillips was the commander of the second tank. Sergeant Culbertson was the commander of the third tank. I'm not sure who commanded the fourth tank, but my able and seasoned platoon sergeant, Wayne Smith, commanded the fifth tank. The infantry followed close behind. My radio contact with the infantry battalion commander was by way of a tank liaison officer, Lt. Edward "Corky" Corcoran.

At the appropriate time, I gave the order to advance through the dense fog in the road. We moved cautiously, expecting the worst and hoping for the best. Because of the limited visibility, I kept my turret hatch open. It was not long before we received heavy small-arms fire, forcing the infantry to halt after they had suffered many casualties.

Enemy troops, attempting to damage the tanks, began throwing hand grenades and satchel charges from the high banks overlooking the road. A fragment from a grenade entered the turret opening of my tank, striking me in the back. The wound was minor and didn't require hospitalization. Such a grenade or other explosive could cause minor damage to the tank, though, so at that point, I decided to close the turret of the tank. Before long, the fog lifted and we could see enemy troops on the high ground to our left. I reported our position and the situation to battalion headquarters through Corky, our liaison officer. Corky said to me, "If you are where I think you are, there should be friendly troops to your left."

My response was, "I don't know where you think I am, but all I can see to my left are men in brown uniforms pointing guns in your direction and advancing toward you. They sure don't look friendly." At the end of the day, I learned that we had broken through the defensive lines of the North Koreans and we had encountered a counterattack by a battalion of enemy troops.

We were urged to continue the attack, and as we rounded a bend in the road, there was an antitank gun in a defensive position pointing directly at us. My gunner, Sergeant Fred Sellers, destroyed it with one shot of the cannon. He was a superb gunner. He never missed. I hardly ever had to give him a fire command. I would just tell him what and where the target was, and chances were that he'd have the gun sight right on it and proceed to knock it out.

We continued to press the attack, and there were many infantry casualties resulting in bodies of American soldiers in the road. The tanks were not moving continuously, so when my tank was not in motion the bodies of some brave soldiers that had been killed landed in front of me. There was no room to maneuver around the bodies of those American soldiers. The road was too narrow; to the left of the road was a bank about ten feet high and to the right was a precipitous drop to the ravine.

We had some choices: dismount from the tanks to remove the bodies, remain in a static position until the infantry took the high ground to our left, attempt to go down the cliff to our right, or run over the bodies. The first option was not practical. Enemy troops on the high ground had been throwing hand grenades down upon us and had been firing at the infantry that accompanied us. There would be more bodies along the road. The second option, waiting until the infantry cleared the area, would stall the offense, would give the North Koreans a better opportunity to succeed in repelling us and pursuing their attack, and would be contrary to the principles of armored warfare. That choice would probably result in greater casualties. We had to be aggressive and move forward as quickly as possible. Although we were always fearful of getting close to the right edge of the road, the third option was never a choice that I would choose voluntarily. With great sadness that brings tears to my eyes whenever I think about it, I made the decision that resulted in the crushing of some American bodies.

Thus, we proceed forward. There were other bends in the road, and we encountered other antitank guns, which my gunner, Fred, also destroyed. I used to tell people that Fred made me look good and that certainly was true on that day.

With each encounter and each destruction, I would report the result to the battalion by way of Corky. At some point during our attack, Fred told me, "We're in deep trouble."

"Why?" I asked. He told me that the tank cannon could not be reloaded. I immediately called a halt to our forward progress just before a bend in the road. A high cliff and the bend in the road offered us protection from direct antitank fire.

"Well, what should we do, Fred?" I inquired.

"We can't go forward and we can't go backward," he said in his southern drawl. On this narrow road, no other tank could move around us to lead the assault. We had to correct the problem as soon as possible. The difficulty appeared to be that unburned powder in the breech of the gun was preventing a shell from being properly seated in the firing chamber.

Apparently, the rear echelon realized that we weren't moving forward, because Corky radioed to inquire about our lack of progress. I explained to him our difficulty. A few moments later, he stated that Colonel Clifford was upset that I wasn't moving forward and that he wanted me to press on, regardless of the consequences.

My response to Corky, no private communication over the airwaves, made a big hit with the men of my platoon, and indeed with others who heard it. It was, "Tell that stupid bastard that I'm not going around another bend in this road without a round in the chamber of the gun." A few years ago, Fred Sellers told me that I also said, "If he wants us to move forward, tell him to come up here and get things moving." There was no reply.

An infantry officer on Colonel Clifford's staff later told me that at battalion headquarters they had been listening to all my radio communications, which included reports of each time an enemy cannon had been destroyed. He stated to his fellow members on the staff, "He's doing all right. Why doesn't he (Colonel Clifford) leave him alone?"

In short order we were able to clear the breach of the cannon, then we loaded it. The advance continued with more antitank guns destroyed. I didn't count the number of guns that were destroyed on that day. I was just doing my job. The official account as reported in a research report of the Armored School states that we had destroyed ten antitank guns and an estimated 175 enemy infantry. Neither of those figures came from me, and I did not contribute to that report. Nobody asked me.

Although the enemy had used great skill in setting up their defenses in depth, their positions were overrun with slight damage to our tanks. The infantry, though, because of withering enemy fire, was not able to keep up with us. After we reached the summit of the hill, I looked down the other side to the valley to the north and could see that the North Koreans were retreating. We pursued them down the road and onto a flat plain.

There, the tanks behind me, automatically fanned out to the right and left to form a line. This was done without any command from me, and it was a good feeling that they knew what to do. They knew what was expected of them, and I was proud of them. After this maneuver was completed, I called a halt to await our infantry. In the meantime, we continued to fire at the retreating enemy troops, mainly with .30-caliber machine-gun fire. Each tank carried two .30-caliber machine guns and a .50-caliber machine gun that was used mainly for antiaircraft fire. The North Koreans didn't have any aircraft up in the air at that time.

In order to take full advantage of the enemy rout I got out of the tank turret and stood on the back deck of the tank to man the .50-caliber machine gun and fire at the retreating enemy. I was probably more gung-ho than I should have been.

We waited for about an hour for the infantry to catch up with us. As the infantry advanced through a cornfield on my right, they flushed out a North Korean soldier who was armed with a submachine gun. We used to call it a burp gun because it had a rapid rate of fire. He was no more than a hundred feet from me. He easily could have killed me while I was busily firing the machine gun, but probably was too terrified to try. In addition to the infantry, an army photographer who as on the scene apparently must have been impressed by what he heard on the radio and what he had seen because he asked me and my crew to pose for a picture together with our damaged tank in the cornfield. About a year later, an army captain who I had met at Fort Knox and was then in the public information bureau in Washington, D.C., ran across the photograph and sent me a copy.

In the meantime, Colonel Clifford finally arrived at the scene in his jeep, and having taken the same route as the tanks, had observed what we had accomplished. After he set up his battalion command post, I reported to him. I was wondering what I was going to say to him. He invited me into his tent to discuss what occurred. I expected a big reprimand for the language I had used. During our conversation, I alluded to my caustic radio transmission without stating the words that I had used, but he didn't want to hear it.

He said, "I'm recommending you for the Distinguished Service Cross." (Higher authority downgraded the award to the Silver Star.) Then he reached under his folding cot, removed a bottle of Ballantine's Scotch Whiskey, and offered me a drink. In fact, I had several drinks with him. He was obviously pretty happy with what my platoon had accomplished. From that day forward, we had a cordial relationship.

To give you an example, one time he sent me on an armored patrol that included infantry and a South Korean guide. We proceeded up a valley. As we approached a small village, we encountered some small-arms fire and sporadic rounds of mortar fire. We retaliated, and the situation stabilized. The South Korean guide pointed to a house on the side of a mountain and told me that it had been used as an observation post by the North Koreans. I directed cannon fire on that house, and it was destroyed. When we returned from our mission, I reported to Colonel Clifford. After I told him what the guide had told me, he asked, "What did you do about it?"

I looked him straight in the eye and replied, "Colonel, there's no longer a house on that mountain."

A big smile came upon his face, and he stated, "That's what I like about you. How many times did you fire?"

"Twice," was my answer.

He reached under his cot and produced a bottle of Ballantine's Scotch, saying, "Take two drinks." I dutifully complied without the slightest complaint, and I guessed that I should have told him that I fired more than twice.

On the day following the battle of October 12, 1950, I took over another tank because the minor damage to my tank had to be repaired. It's customary that the crew, with the exception of the tank commander if he is an officer, go to the rear area with the tank. The officer's duty is to take command of another tank until his tank is returned or he receives a replacement tank. One of the crewmembers had a camera and took some photographs of the destroyed enemy cannons and bodies of enemy troops. While the tank was in the repair area, the crew took it upon themselves to have a mount for a .30-caliber machine gun welded on the top front of the turret so that I could fire a machine gun without having to get out of the turret and expose my full body to target practice by the enemy. Well, that's about the story of that particular day.

I may have spoken disparagingly of Colonel Clifford, but really, he was a brave man. I saw him many times right up at the front, right next to my tank. All of a sudden, he would appear when there was a lot of fighting going on to give me some information and to see what was going on. So, I really had a high regard for him.

CHAPTER FOUR

VIETNAM WAR (1965–1975)

///LT. COL. JAMES WALKER (U.S. ARMY)

I had been working as the battalion support platoon leader since my arrival with the 1st Battalion, 69th Armor, 25th Infantry Division since early July 1967. I later learned that most of the junior officers new to the battalion were given a dose of the support platoon prior to being assigned out to line tank companies. The battalion commander, Lt. Col. Paul S. Williams Jr., was a demanding, results-oriented leader who cared deeply for his soldiers. I knew something was wrong when his usual grin was absent during the morning briefing.

He wasted no time in getting to the bad news and to the next chapter of my life. "Gentlemen, it deeply grieves me to tell you that Lt. David Nolan, 1st Platoon, A Company was killed this morning during a heavy fight with the Viet Cong near LZ (landing zone) Uplift."

I had met Dave Nolan only a couple of weeks before upon his return from his R&R. Company A had been attached to the 1st Cavalry Division in Binh Dinh province, long a stronghold of first the Viet Minh, then the Viet Cong (VC). The cav ranged throughout the province, literally dropping into many of these heretofore-untouched enemy sanctuaries with their new heliborne assaults, disrupting the VC's long-held sense of security and unhampered operations. Almost daily, Company A would get a call from a cav platoon or company in heavy contact with an unknown-sized VC force in a fortified village complex. The presence and masterful use of heavy, fortified bunkers and trenches constructed of mahogany or ironwood logs, earth, and even concrete by the VC greeted the cav in and around these villages. They would more often than not be pinned down in a maze of rice paddy dikes and hedgerows before they could even enter a village, much like the plight of allied troops in the hedgerow country of France following the Normandy invasion.

Dave Nolan had been killed by recoilless rifle fire during one of these actions while extricating a surrounded cav platoon. My boss, the battalion S4, Capt. Joe Allen, a soft-spoken southerner with an ever-present Cheshire cat grin, grimly informed me later in the day that I was to replace Dave Nolan. While apprehensive to say the least, I was getting my chance as a platoon leader with a proven, combat-hardened tank platoon.

The 1st Battalion, 69th Armor, was the first U.S. Army tank battalion to arrive in Vietnam in early 1966. Company A was into the first engagement with the VC a mere ninety minutes after its debarkation from LSTs (landing ship tanks) in Saigon harbor. Company B moved north in mid-1966 to the Central Highlands area around Pleiku with the 25th Division's 3rd Brigade and quickly earned high laurels for its decisive combat actions with a Presidential Unit Citation in August 1966 in one of its first major engagements with the North Vietnamese Army (NVA). The battalion and its component companies would serve with great distinction with the 4th Infantry Division until its stand down in

June 1970. It would retire from Vietnam as the most highly decorated tank battalion in army history.

The demands placed on the tank unit and individual tank crews during combat in Vietnam were diverse and intense. I could write volumes on this alone, but in reflection, my first firefight as platoon leader of the 1st Platoon, Company A, could not have demanded more of an officer or his men.

I had been with the platoon a mere two days. The platoon sergeant had just returned with my eleven tanks on a three-day mission with the cav on the beach. I barely had time to become acquainted with him when a call came in from the Brigade TOC (tactical operations center). A company of Sky Troopers had run into heavy VC resistance in a fortified village some five kilometers to the east. We were to saddle up, pick up two additional tanks from our company headquarters section, and proceed to a set of grid coordinates. We picked up the two HQ section tanks, no problem, and headed east on a trail notorious for land mines. Halfway to the objective we could see artillery bursts on and around a village. Several F4 Phantoms (fighter-bombers) from the air force base at Phu Cat unloaded a variety of HE and napalm into the same area. Quite a show, but we still had more than a mile to go.

Another quarter mile and we left the trail and moved to the northeast through intermittent rice paddies and hedgerows. Major challenge number one appeared in the form of a creek in which one of our tanks became deeply mired. It would not move—period! The tandem cable hookup of two towing tanks had little to no effect. The noise of battle grew increasingly louder as additional artillery assets joined the battle, and here we sat, stuck in the mud. One of my old soldiers, Sfc. Elbert Williams, a World War II and Korean War vet, suggested we pop the suction bubble beneath the tank with a pinch of C4 explosive. That would allow the towing vehicles to pull the mired tank free. It worked! We were on our way again after nearly an hour of time lost.

As we approached the village, we could see the cav troopers taking cover behind paddy dikes, trees, and in trench works taken from the VC. The village was nearly totally obscured by smoke with visibility no more than twenty-five meters. I informed the brigade commander of our arrival. His company commander on the ground found my tank a minute or so later. His company was spread out on line and had just entered the village when fire had broken out from all directions. The VC had let them pass by several hidden automatic weapons positions in the hedgerows and paddy dikes, nearly surrounding his men. A quick-thinking young officer rallied his platoon to the rear, destroying the positions and securing the company's rear. Now, the company commander needed to reenter the village to eliminate the resistance and recover his wounded and dead. That would be our job.

Despite the incredible pounding by artillery and air support, the VC continued to pour out a blistering volume of fire in every direction. The green and white tracers from the RPD machine guns and AK-47s were popping overhead and around us. However, the cool, collected manner of the cav commander was contagious. I guess that my adrenaline load had overcome my initial terror. I advised the cav commander to keep his men abreast and to the rear of the tanks in the assault line, and we'd all do just fine. We needed the flank and rear cover, and they needed a large, forced entry tool.

We entered the village in an inverted V formation with my tank in the center. We'd gone no more than fifty meters when a solid stream of green tracers found my turret. I dropped through the cupola hatch to try to find where the fire had come from. My 15 tank radioed that there was a big machine gun to my two o'clock. *Big* was an understatement as the green tracers, which seemed to float our way, looked as big as basketballs and were coming from a Russian 12.7mm (machine) gun. Swinging the turret in that direction, I found the source of the fire, an orange light beneath a hooch hut not forty meters away. My gunner put two high explosive delayed fuse rounds into the firing slit, silencing the fire.

In my excitement, I'd failed to see the trench immediately to our front, and I found it the hard way. As I ordered my driver to hit his left track and move to the right, we bellied up onto a log with one track over the trench now moving nowhere.

Off to my right flank, my 13 tank and Specialist First Class Williams were busy reducing a coconut log bunker with another HEP (high explosive plastic) round. The VC had dug their bunkers with the firing slits just above ground level making them nearly invisible. Though the HEP round did not silence it, the tank's driver simply put fifty-two tons of tank onto the bunker, crushing it and its hapless occupants beneath.

Next to him, my 12 and 14 tanks, along with the two attached tanks, were assisting the cav troopers with eliminating VC in the trenches criss-crossing the village and bunkers beneath many of the hooches. While my 15 tank moved to our front to help with a tow, I was busy on the radios, providing SITREPS (situation reports) to the cav command levels and talking with my tanks. Enemy rounds continued to ping off our tank from many directions, but thankfully, the fire from the rear had been silenced.

My loader and I dismounted the tank, unhooked the tow cables from the turret base, and cross-attached them to my 15 tank. We were off the log quickly and rejoined the war in earnest.

I moved the platoon ahead another forty meters or so into the village and again came under heavy automatic weapons fire. I fully understood what hairy shit this kind of fighting in a built-up area was. The infantry went to ground again while we continued forward another few meters to get the exact locations of the guns. Noticing a movement out of the corner of my eye, I had my driver make a hard right and swiveled the turret to the right just in time to see the muzzle of a 75mm recoilless rifle pointing right at me! I fired the main cannon (loaded with canister) at the same time the VC lit off the weapon. Lots of smoke and lots of noise as the tank lurched and stopped. I knew my driver was dead.

Jumping down onto the fender, a real dumb thing to do in a fight, I peered into the driver's hatch. Fred was counting battery caps (as we called the sudden drop of the driver's seat into the tank). He was quite alive but also quite shaken.

Nobody hurt, but the bad guy's big gun was destroyed; no piece of it or its crew was found larger than a shoe. (A canister round featured 2,200 one-half by one-half–inch tungsten pellets stacked atop one another, like a shotgun shell.) This was an ammunition type used for nearly three hundred years by artillery around the world.

Artillery was still falling into the village a mere 150 meters to our front, much too close for comfort for us or the cav troopers on the ground. A radio call moved the impact area another two hundred meters to the north of the village, hopefully reducing the enemy's options for retreat. My headphones crackled again with a request from one of my tank commanders to pull back and re-ammo; he was out of main-gun food. I told him to stay put with the grunts and expend his coax (coaxial machine gun) and .50-caliber ammo first.

Another strange sight appeared through the smoke and haze. Sitting placidly amid the chaos and danger, an elderly couple sat around a large cooking pot, mindlessly stirring its contents, seeming oblivious to the war around them. A mere twenty feet to their right, an RPD machine gun protruding from a slit beneath their hooch, snarled at us, its green tracers smacking into trees and our armor. I "hip shot" a HEP round into the base of the hooch, just below the flashing gun, instantly turning the hooch into so much pulp and splinters. The RPD was silen, and the old couple, fate unknown, was gone, the pot still boiling away where it stood.

Another request for ammo came through from tank 15; we were getting short in our main-gun supplies and 7.62mm for the coaxes was also dwindling. Another burst of tracers from my left nearly took my head off as I ducked into the cupola. Switching the radio push (term used synonymously with *frequency*) to brigade command, I requested an ammo resupply as soon as they could make it available.

My gunner, Sgt. Will Crump, hollered that he could see several VC running into a hooch off to our left carrying a machine gun and what appeared to be a 57mm recoilless rifle. I had my 15 tank remain in position, while my driver moved our tank head-on toward the suspect hooch. Again, the green tracers prompted our HEP response. The wall of the hooch literally turned to powder as the round impacted with the mud brick and stucco structure. Two VC literally cart-wheeled through the air, one landing a few feet in front of the tank. This guy had what remained of the 57mm recoilless in a death grip. The fire suddenly died down.

Then went another radio call requesting a SITREP and information from Colonel Karhose, the 2nd Brigade commander, and ammo to be on its way to us in zero five (five minutes) via a "hook" (slang for a CH47 Chinook heavy lift helicopter). The hook would simply drop the sling-loaded ammo at a point of our choosing to the south of the village. We always had several basic loads of ammo broken out of the boxes back at LZ Uplift available for immediate pick-up for just such occasions.

This transmission was followed by one that left me seething with anger and incredulous! Our commo (communication) sergeant back at the company HQ in Bong Son suddenly broke into the controlled chaos on the command frequency with a request for a list of the platoon's serial-numbered items. The comments from my tank commanders are unprintable. Did he think that we were having a picnic out here?

We halted at the northern edge of the village, VC fire now sporadic and limited. The brigade commander requested that we wheel about and run a sweep back through the village, checking all bunkers and hooches in the process. The cav troopers then moved on line with us back through the dissipating smoke and haze, significantly reducing potential flank and rear threats. The cav flushed several more VC, most nearly unconscious with shock from the effects of HEP and HE blasts. We similarly placed the dead and wounded cav soldiers on our back decks so the medics could prep them for the approaching medevac choppers.

We reached the south edge of the village and the clearing I had designated for our ammo drop and evacuation of the wounded. The hook could be seen approaching from the west with four UH1B-model Huey gunships as escorts. Leading them were two medevac ("Dust-off") choppers, which set down close to us.

The hook dropped its sling load between our tanks and backed off a bit to set down something unexpected. Eight cav soldiers from Uplift exited the Chinook and ran to our ammo point. The brigade commander had sent them to assist us in reloading our tanks. The cav again took care of us!

Major General John J. Tolson, Division Commander was airborne above the fight in his command and control bird as he always was when his troops were in contact. He set down some fifty meters from us, oblivious to any continued threat from the village. He asked for a SITREP, which the infantry company commander and I provided in turn, then he proceeded to mount each tank and personally thank my guys for their support of his Sky Troopers. We were all impressed by this man and his undisguised love for his soldiers and those in support.

We remained in a loose perimeter south of the village until just before dusk when we were ordered back to LZ Uplift. With the adrenaline wearing off, I had a chance to take stock of what we'd just been through and take a close look at our tanks. All bore the scars of close combat: pockmarked hulls and turrets from the heavy machine guns, road wheels chipped from bullet impacts, crew kit bags in the bustle racks turned to Swiss cheese, pings and holes inventoried for maintenance and to remember close calls.

Speaking of narrow escapes, I had had no idea how close I had come to having my proverbial ticket punched during my first fight! The incredible heat finally registered, and in the process of removing my fatigue jacket my heart stopped. There were five neat holes in my sleeves, cargo pockets, and shirttail not made by moths. I have that shirt to this day.

///COL. C. R. "CASEY" (U.S. MARINE CORPS)

During the Vietnam War, I commanded Alpha Company, 1st Tank Battalion, U.S. Marine Corps. Some of the most vivid memories I have of that time revolve around the early 1968 battle for the ancient South Vietnamese city of Hue, seized by units of the North Vietnamese Army (NVA) on the evening of January 31, 1968. My additional duty was armor officer for Task Force X-ray, the task force organized to retake Hue.

My company had gotten into Hue on February 12, 1968. During the twenty-six days of fighting that it took to recapture the city from the NVA, the company's tanks were engaged on a daily basis. We came in on U.S. Navy landing craft, up the Perfume River from the South China Sea. I had one platoon of five tanks in direct support of the 1st Battalion, 5th Marines, on the north bank of the river, which divided the old part of the city from the newer portion on the south bank. The rest of my company operated from the south bank of the river in direct support of 1st Battalion, 5th Marines, and 2nd Battalion, 5th Marines, with eleven M48A3 Patton tanks armed with 90mm main guns and two attached M67A2 flame-thrower tanks, known as flame tanks or "Zippos."

The flame tank was a modified version of the M48A3 Patton tank with its 90mm main gun replaced with a flame gun. Because there was no need for a loader, the crew on the flame tank consisted only of the vehicle commander and gunner in the turret and the driver in the front hull. In place of the loader, there was a large metal container for the storage of about 350 gallons of fuel.

To disguise the identity of the flame tank and the fact that it had no main gun, a dummy barrel, about the same length as the 90mm gun tube on the M48A3 Patton tank, attached to the vehicle's gun-shield. Hidden within the dummy barrel was the fuel nozzle for the flame gun, with spark plug igniters located just in front of the nozzle.

Due to the rush to get my company into Hue, we lacked the mixing and transfer pump needed to funnel the gasoline into the flame tank's turret-located fuel storage container. We also had nothing to stir the napalm that we added to the gasoline to thicken it before firing. This forced us to refuel both flame tanks by hand, a dangerous and time-consuming process.

Once the flame tank crewman topped off his vehicle's fuel storage tank, he took an old wooden stick and stirred the witch's brew together. All this took place while our own artillery fire into the enemy-occupied areas of Hue was creating large chunks of shrapnel, which bounced around us as we attempted to refuel the flame tanks. Once the vehicle's crewman got the mixture of gasoline and napalm thick enough, he could fire a good rod. A rod is the result after a flame tank fires. If thick enough, a rod can travel up to 150 yards.

During a pause between fighting the NVA in Hue, I came across one of my two flame tanks at the side of a street. To my great surprise, I found that the tank commander of the vehicle had created a little outdoor café on the rear engine deck of his vehicle, with a small round table and metal chairs surrounding it. He and the crew were nonchalantly sipping a bottle of French brandy and snacking on C-rations. Rather than attempting to hide the alcohol from me, he merely invited me to join his merry little get together. Having fought bravely under the most trying conditions, I could not say no to him and his crew and joined him along with my gunnery sergeant for a brief respite from the horrors of the war we were fighting.

Not too long after that, I came across a Catholic church in Hue. Upon entering the church, I discovered that the NVA had slaughtered most of the nuns who lived within. We found two of them still barely alive and tried to provide them some medical care; both, however, later died. Upon leaving the church, I found to my dismay that the crews of the two tanks outside the building were playing football with a human skull that they found among the rubble of the city. I quickly put a stop to that.

Another problem that I encountered in the retaking of Hue from the NVA was the large number of mines. As we drove down a street toward the Imperial Cemetery, a mine blew off one of the tracks of my lead tank. Because I didn't have a tank retriever with me, at the time, I pulled up behind the disabled tank, with the intention of towing it away to a safe place for repair. Sadly, upon doing so my tank struck a hidden mine and became disabled. I then radioed for help. I was promised a truck that was a wrecker as long as I didn't blow that one up. Well, sure as hell, as we backed that wrecker to my two disabled tanks, it hit a damned mine. So there we were with two dead tanks and a slightly worse for wear wheeled wrecker. We finally brought in a third tank and managed to drag all three vehicles back to a safe area and place them back into running condition.

On another occasion, I sent one of my M49 fuel trucks back to a refueling dump, with only a driver. After several hours elapsed and no truck or marine, I wanted to know what happened and proceeded to retrace his steps. I soon came upon the truck, but no marine. Curious as to what had happened to him, I began searching around the area for any clues. Upon looking into a nearby culvert, I found the young marine with one of those little Vietnamese girls doing what young men like to do. I promptly grabbed his boots and pulled him off the giggling girl. I told him that I was disappointed in him and to get to that fuel dump and back with a load of fuel ASAP.

Task Force X-ray declared Operation Hue City over on March 2, 1968.

///LT. COL. BOB JOHNSTON (U.S. MARINE CORPS)

I was commissioned a second lieutenant in the U.S. Marine Corps on January 20, 1966, after originally entering the service on May 23, 1963. I attended the Basic School at Quantico, Virginia, Class of 3/67 and Tank Officer School at Camp Pendleton, California.

During my time in South Vietnam, I was fortunate to have had two combat commands, as a tank platoon commander and later as a tank company commander. Some of the combat experiences I remember include numerous ambushes by the Viet Cong using RPG mortars and lots of small-arms fire.

While the thick armored hide on our Patton tanks made us immune to mortar fragments and small-arms fire, the RPG employed by the enemy could penetrate our thickest armor, which was on the front of the turret and measured up to a foot thick, with ease. The sloped armor on the front hull of the tank was a bit more than four inches thick.

Although not every RPG hit would knock out a Patton tank, some of our tanks suffered more than one penetration and continued to function. However, a strike to a tank's onboard ammunition could result in its complete destruction and a horrible death to its crew.

Another daily threat to our Patton tanks happened to be land mines. I now understand that they accounted for more than 70 percent of our vehicle losses during the Vietnam War. The enemy mines would occasionally blow the track and road wheels off our tanks. Due to the well-shaped hull armor of our vehicles, the crews seldom suffered any serious injuries from such unpleasant encounters. It just took a lot back-breaking hard work to put the tanks that struck mines back into running condition again.

Our constant encounters with enemy mines, however, began to develop within us a sixth sense about the location of possible enemy mines. In our endeavor to locate the enemy mines before running over them, we had help from a former NVA soldier who had defected to our side, bringing with him his expert training in laying mines, which helped us to identify their locations.

I thought highly of our Patton tanks, the M48A3 version to be more precise. It weighed about fifty-two tons, most of that weight steel armor. On some occasions, the weight of the Patton tanks proved a serious drawback, because the road and bridge infrastructure of South Vietnam did not support a vehicle of such size and weight. This really hit home to me on one occasion when one of our tanks came across an aging French-built bridge, rated for a maximum load of thirty tons. Rather than have the crew of the tank drive it across, I took it upon myself to do it. I can tell you that driving over that creaking old bridge, with that heavy tank, was not without some trepidation on my part, but, I did make it in one piece.

Our Patton tanks received power from a large twelve-cylinder, supercharged, air-cooled diesel engine that produced 750 horsepower. On level, paved ground, we could reach a top speed of thirty miles per hour. When going off-road, our speed sometimes dropped down to less than five miles per hour, particularity when busting our way through thick undergrowth. Despite our inability to keep up with the required daily maintenance on the tanks and a constant lack of spare parts, they proved extremely reliable under the most trying conditions.

The primary armament on the Patton tank was the turret-mounted M41 90mm gun, which featured a large muzzle brake on the end of the barrel. Unlike modern tanks fitted with smoothbore main guns, the 90mm main gun on the Patton tank was rifled. There was room for sixty-two rounds, averaging about forty pounds each, of main-gun ammunition in the Patton tanks, divided between the hull and turret. Unlike the Abrams tank, in which all the main ammunition is stored behind armored blast proof doors, in the Patton tank, it was unprotected.

In Vietnam the majority of main-gun rounds carried in the Patton tanks consisted of antipersonnel high explosive or white phosphorous "Willy Peter" rounds. One type featured more than one thousand steel pellets that, when fired, dispersed shortly after leaving the muzzle of the main gun in a shotgun-like pattern that could reach out to about three hundred yards. We referred to this as a canister round. The other type of canister round we fired contained four thousand small steel darts referred to as flechettes; this was called a beehive round. The beehive round had an adjustable fuse that allowed us to set the range at which it dispersed its deadly cargo. In addition to the two types of canister rounds, the high explosive round had a delayed action fuse that proved effective against bunkers.

The Patton tank also featured a coaxial .30-caliber machine gun fitted to fire alongside the main gun and an M2 .50-caliber machine gun mounted to fire from within the tank commander's cupola. Due to a lack of space within the tank commander's cupola, almost all of our tank crews in Vietnam mounted their .30-caliber machine guns on the top of the cupola for ease of use and access to more ammunition and in turn coaxially mounted the .50-caliber machine gun next to the 90mm main gun. We lightened the .50-caliber barrels by using a metal lathe and shaving off metal from the long barrel. This increased the cyclic rate of fire of the gun. Neither of these modifications were authorized, but both improved our weapons' performance. Our tanks normally carried into battle at least two thousands rounds of .50-caliber ammunition and at least ten thousand rounds of .30-caliber ammunition.

The Patton tanks were crewed by four men: a tank commander, gunner, and loader in the turret, while the driver sat in the vehicle's front hull. Of all the jobs on the tank, being the driver was the most fun, as the tank boasted power steering and an automatic transmission. The fun factor for the driver ended when we encountered enemy troops. During such times, the driver just sat in his seat, with his overhead hatch closed, while every weapon the enemy had aimed at the front of the tank. Unlike modern tanks, such as the Abrams, equipped with a sophisticated stabilization system that allows for extremely accurate fire on the move, the Patton tank had no such device fitted and had to fire from the halt. This, in turn, made us an easier target to acquire by the enemy.

The least favorite job on the Patton tank was always that of the gunner, who sat just in front and below the tank commander, on the right side of the main gun. Unlike everybody else, who had an overhead hatch to look out and take in some fresh air when not in combat, the gunner sat inside of the cramped, hot, humid, smelly interior of the tank, with his own view of the outside world restricted only to his weapon sighting devices. Only when in a firefight did the gunner find something to keep his mind off his discomfort. Using a power-operated traverse system, the gunner could turn the turret on his tank 360 degrees in just fifteen seconds. The elevation for the tank's main gun was also power operated. If the power-operated traverse and elevation system in the tank went down, the turret turned manually. The main gun also raised and lowered manually, if the need arose.

///WORLD WAR I (1914–1918)

TOP Showing off its grade-climbing ability is a British World War I heavy tank, these types of tank averaged a top speed on a level surface of less than 4 mph and had a maximum operational range of about thirty-five miles.
Patton Museum

BOTTOM During the last few months of World War I, when the fledging U.S. Army Tank Corps was first committed into action against the German army, they employed British heavy tanks as seen here with a rhomboidal shape and weighing in at about thirty tons. *Patton Museum*

TOP The French-designed and -built two-man Renault FT-17 light tanks, pictured here, which were used by the U.S. Army during World War I and weighed in at a little less than eight tons. They had a top speed on a level road of 5 mph. *Patton Museum*

BOTTOM On display at the U.S. Army's Ordnance Museum, located at Aberdeen Proving, Maryland, this is a British heavy tank used during World War I. Lacking any type of suspension system, they provided their eight-man crews a very rough ride off-road. *Michael Green*

TOP **Some of the crewmembers of an early model M4 series Sherman medium tank appear in this picture loading various items on their vehicle. The crew on all Sherman tanks consisted of five men, three in the turret and two in the front hull.** *Patton Museum*

BOTTOM **A U.S. Army M3 series medium tank, which weighed about thirty tons and had a six-man crew, is taking part in a World War II training exercise. There was a 37mm gun in the turret and a forward-firing 75mm gun in the front hull.** *Patton Museum*

TOP Belonging to the impressive collection of vehicles at the Patton Museum of Armor and Cavalry is this U.S. Army M5 series light tank. Armed with a 37mm main gun, the small seventeen-ton tank had a four-man crew, two in the turret and two in the front hull. *Michael Green*

BOTTOM Pictured taking part in a post–World War II training exercise in western Europe is a U.S. Army M26 Pershing heavy tank, later designated a medium tank, with a squad of infantry on its rear engine deck. The Pershing was a very late war replacement for the M4 Sherman tank series. *Patton Museum*

///KOREAN WAR (1950–1953)

The front of this U.S. Army M4 series Sherman tank in Korea features a very elaborate Tiger face paint scheme authorized for those tank crews serving in Operation Killer and Ripper, the UN counteroffensive that took place in early 1951. *Patton Museum*

TOP A major threat to both U.S. Army and Marine Corps tanks during the Korean War were antitank mines. An antitank mine has broken the track on an M26 Pershing tank seen in this picture. The Pershing proved underpowered and was replaced by the M46 Patton tank during the Korean War. *Patton Museum*

BOTTOM Coming off a U.S. Navy tank transport ship during the Korean War is a U.S. Marine Corps M46 Patton tank, with its turret turned to the rear and covered with supplies. The 90mm main gun on the M46 Patton tank was the same as that of the M26 Pershing tank. *Patton Museum*

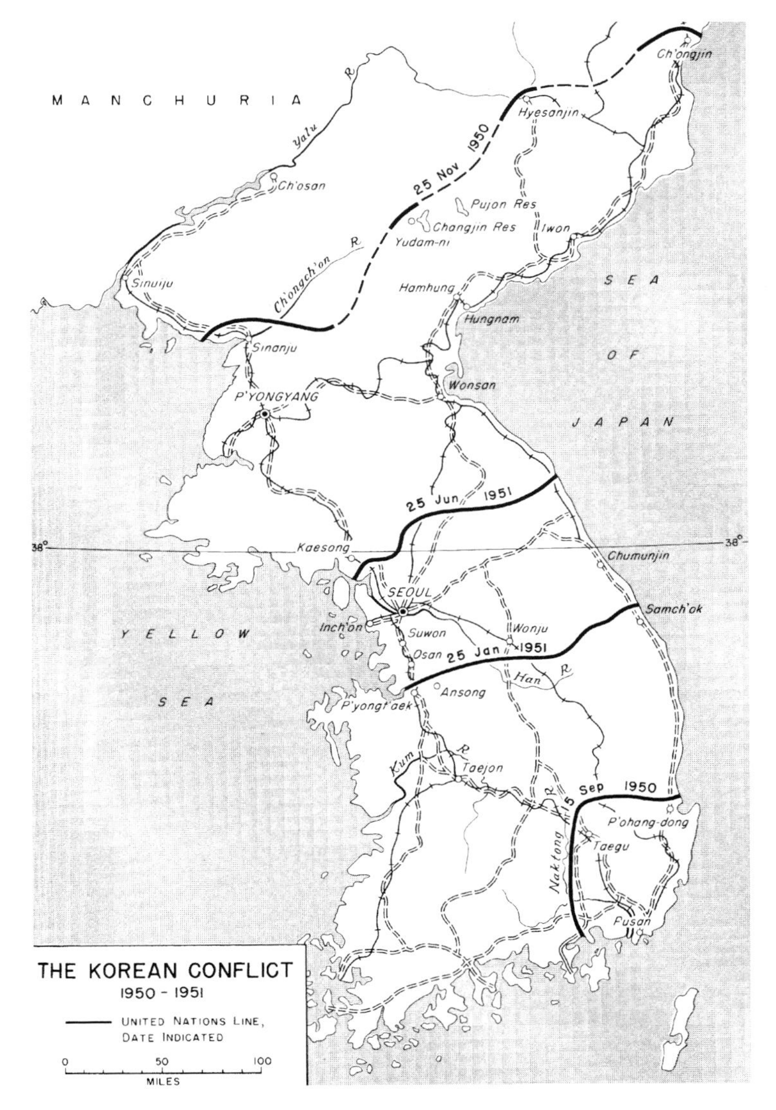

This map shows the various levels of advance and retreat of the American military ground forces during the Korean War. The 38th parallel was the original dividing line between North and South Korea. In November 1950 the Chinese army came to the aid of the North Koreans. *U.S. Army*

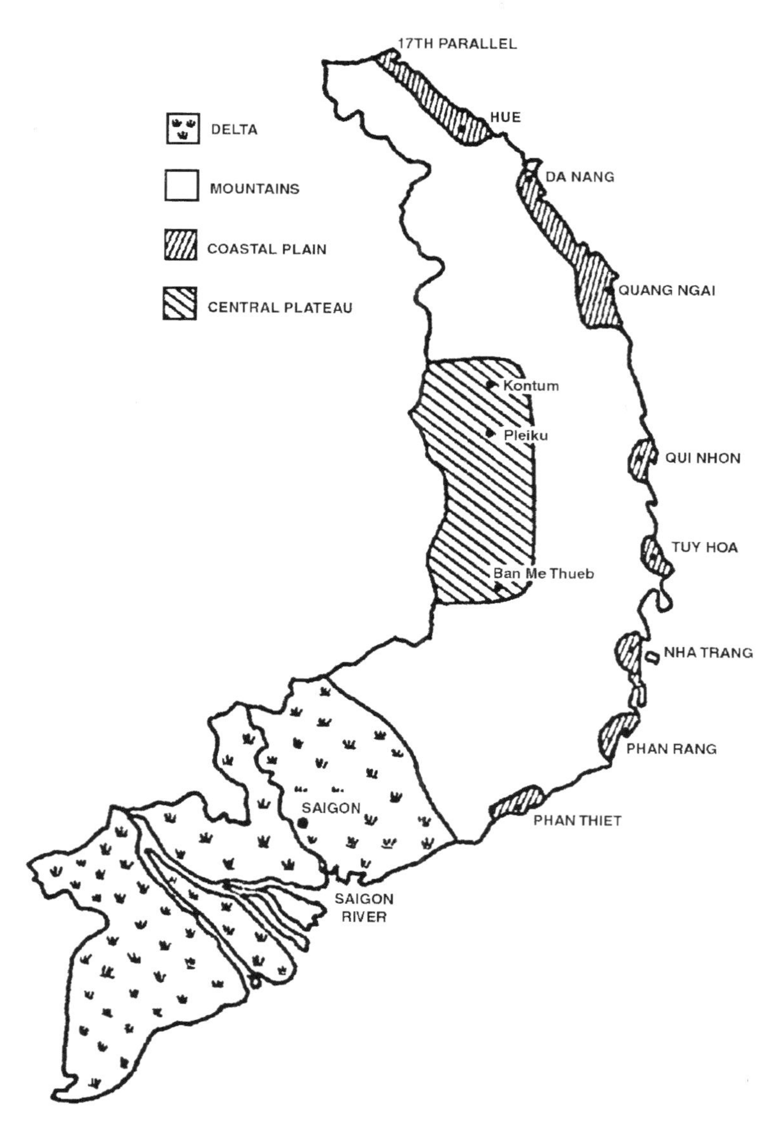

This map of South Vietnam shows how the former country was divided into four distinct terrain areas: the delta, the mountains, the coastal plain, and the central plateau, each with very different effects on vehicular mobility. Tanks could operate only in the delta, the coastal plain, and the central plateau. *U.S. Army*

TOP The boxlike structure just above the gun-shield of this M48A3 Patton tank in South Vietnam is a white light/infrared search light. Stored on the upper portions of the tank's front fenders are 7.62mm ammunition cans, while a very large .50-caliber ammunition can sits next to the vehicle commander. *Patton Museum*

BOTTOM The M67A2 flamethrower tank was a Marine Corps version of the standard M48A3 Patton, with its 90mm main gun replaced by a flame gun. The marines nicknamed them "flame tanks" and "Zippos." The maximum range of the flame gun was 250 yards. *Patton Museum*

TOP **Pausing during a break in a training exercise are two U.S. Army M60 tanks on the outskirts of a small West Germany town. The M60 featured a 105mm main gun and two machine guns and first showed up in western Europe in December 1960.** *Patton Museum*

BOTTOM **An impressive picture of a platoon of U.S. Army M60A1 tanks on the move. The tank commanders are using hand signals to alert one another to what maneuver to carry out. The M60A1 tank featured a new elongated turret compared to the rounded turret of the original M60 tank.** *Defense Visual Information Center*

TOP **Parked in the middle of small river is an early model M1 Abrams, armed with a 105mm main gun and two machine guns. The Abrams tank officially entered into U.S. Army service in February 1980, and was named after Gen. Creighton W. Abrams.** *Defense Visual Information Center*

BOTTOM **The U.S. Army never stopped improving the M1 Abrams tank. In December 1984, the army approved production of the M1A1 version of the M1 Abrams tank series. As seen in this picture, it boasted a larger and more powerful 120mm main gun.** *Defense Visual Information Center*

///OPERATION DESERT STORM (1991)

TOP A U.S. Army M1A1 tank rushes across the desert waste of Saudi Arabia as it heads toward the border of Iraq during Operation Desert Storm. U.S. Army and Marine Corps Abrams tanks received credit for destroying more than two thousand Iraqi tanks during the short conflict. *Defense Visual Information Center*

BOTTOM A destroyed Iraqi army T72 tank stands forlornly in the desert after the close of Operation Desert Storm. Although armed with an impressive 125mm main gun, the projectiles fired from the cannon could not penetrate the thick frontal armor on the American Abrams tank, even at point-blank range. *Defense Visual Information Center*

TOP The Iraqi army that fought in Operation Desert Storm employed a large number of BMP-1s. Pictured is a captured BMP-1 that belongs to the U.S. Army and is used as training aid. Soviet-designed and -built, the vehicle has a crew of three and carries eight infantrymen. *Defense Visual Information Center*

BOTTOM A captured Iraqi army MT-LB tractor used as an armored personnel carrier sits in an equipment yard after Operation Desert Storm. Thinly armored and armed with only a 7.62mm machine gun in a small turret located at the front of the vehicle, it proved easy prey to American armored fighting vehicles. *Defense Visual Information Center*

///OPERATION IRAQI FREEDOM (2003–PRESENT)

TOP **While many American Abrams tanks suffered varying degrees of damage during the initial invasion of Iraq in 2003, due to hostile fire, only a handful suffered abandonment to the enemy after being disabled. The picture shows one of those tanks after being hit by American fire to deny it to the enemy.** *Defense Visual Information Center*

BOTTOM **The business end of the 120mm main gun that makes the M1A1 Abrams tank such a fearsome opponent to all those who confront it in Iraq. The crew of the tank pictured has attached tow bars to the front hull of the vehicle to make the process of vehicle recovery quicker.** *Defense Visual Information Center*

TOP **A U.S. Marine Corps M1A1 Abrams tank rears up as it climbs a roadway embankment during the initial stages of Operation Iraqi Freedom. All of the Abrams series tanks receive power from a 1,500-horsepower gas turbine that can propel it to a top speed of about 40 mph.** *Defense Visual Information Center*

BOTTOM **A U.S. Marine Corps M1A1 Abrams tank shows one of the many modifications made to the tank in response to the type of close-range urban fighting that often occurs in Iraq. The tank's loader now has a transparent armor gun-shield for his 7.62mm machine gun.** *Defense Visual Information Center*

TOP **Standing watch during the fighting for the Iraqi city of Fallujah is a U.S. Marine Corps M1A1 Abrams tank. Besides carrying forty rounds of main-gun ammunition, the tank carries nine-hundred rounds of .50-caliber machine-gun ammunition and ten-thousand rounds of 7.62mm machine-gun ammunition.** *Defense Visual Information Center*

BOTTOM **Traveling at high speed over an Iraqi roadway is a U.S. Marine Corps M1A1 Abrams tank. The light green–tipped funnels on either side of the tank's turret are smoke grenade launchers. Visible just behind the tank commander is a plastic lawn chair.** *Defense Visual Information Center*

The M48A3 Patton tank was extremely versatile and repeatedly demonstrated with good success its firepower, armor protection, mobility, and shock effects—important characteristics while in support of marine infantry. On one such occasion, I led a heavy section of three tanks to relieve a platoon of marine infantry that had been caught in a horseshoe ambush by the Viet Cong. The ambush occurred along the banks of the Song Cau Do River south of Da Nang at a point where the river's channel had formed an arc horseshoe around the pinned down marines' position. The Company B, 1st Marines, were pinned down in the middle of this arc by .51-caliber machine-gun fire, AK-47 and small-arms fire, as well as mortars and RPG rockets being fired from the opposite side of the river all along the arc. Upon arrival, our tanks immediately became targets for the enemy gunners. The .51-caliber rounds fired at us sounded like sledgehammer blows on the outside of the turret. We positioned our tanks between the beleaguered infantry and the enemy firing positions allowing the evacuation of our dead and wounded while providing point-blank direct fire support with our 90mm main gun and the coaxially mounted machine guns. Several RPGs were also fired at our tanks during this ambush, which deflected before exploding without causing any major damage.

The enemy was so solidly dug in on the other side of the river that they continued to return fire. I then called in an air strike from F-8 Crusaders that were circling above like giant birds of prey. The first bombing runs of the F-8s were according to proper procedure and made parallel to my tank's position. Still the enemy fire continued. The next bombing runs were made in an unorthodox manner vertical to my position and directly overhead. I remember vividly to this day watching from the vision book on my tank commander's cupola the five-hundred-pound bombs that had been released seemingly coming straight at my tank. I was in awe. It seemed like it was happening in slow motion. My tank commander's hatch was open, and when the bombs burst on their targets 150 feet away, all the air in the tank seemed to be sucked out of it. My hair stood straight up, and I couldn't hear a thing for an hour afterward.

I was stunned as were my men. With these bomb blasts, the ambush ended and we received a "well done" from the infantry company commander, the only commendation that means anything to combat marines.

Hue City has come to be known as one of the great battles in the history of the U.S. Marine Corps. Again, tanks played a major part in that crushing military defeat of the North Vietnamese Army. During that battle I was assigned as executive officer of Company A, 1st Tank Battalion. Captain C. R. Casey, the company commander, had deployed our tanks in support of infantry from the 1st and 5th Marine regiments. Hue City was combat in a built-up area. Our M48 tanks and our M62A flame tanks provided direct fire support as marines retook the city from North Vietnamese regulars. During the battle, our troops even used tear gas to great advantage to root out enemy positions. We set up our company command post at the MACV compound near the Perfume River, which was also headquarters to Colonel Hughes, the Task Force X-ray commander. While there I hand-mixed napalm for the flame tanks with Captain Casey because we lacked the proper equipment and a pump to do the job.

We also had a platoon of Ontos assigned to our company while in Hue City, which proved to be ideally suited for this combat in an urban area. The Ontos was developed by the U.S. Army for use as a lightweight antitank weapon against Soviet forces in Europe. The marines had it in their inventory, and it provided a tremendous firepower punch with six 106mm recoilless rifles mounted on top of its lightweight tracked chassis. The Ontos could wipe out a city block with one blast of all six recoilless rifles. This was called an "auto double" discharge.

We lost a brave marine at Hue City, Staff Sergeant Novack, killed by a sniper while in support of South Vietnamese troops. I was disappointed in the overall combat performance or lack thereof by South Vietnamese troops. Our press releases sought to impress the world with the dedication of these troops in their "brave struggle" against communism. My experience led me to a different conclusion. When I first arrived at Hue City, I was able to trade a carton of Salem cigarettes to a terrified South Vietnamese soldier for his M1 carbine. The poor fellow had already thrown away his uniform, and I needed a weapon with more range than my .45-caliber sidearm.

Tank armor is made of homogenous steel. The continuous generations of marine tankers are like steel, each united, interconnected, and bound by a unique, transcending bond and esprit de corps. To have been part of it all has been my life's proudest achievement.

///CHIEF WARRANT OFFICER II JAMES CARROLL (U.S. MARINE CORPS)

I served in Vietnam between 1967 and 1968, which was around the time of the Tet Offensive. It had erupted in early 1968 and was still underway, or at least the remnants of it were. I was up north with Company A, 1st Marine Tank Battalion. I had a platoon of five tanks and was attached to the army's 101st Airborne Division, the Screaming Eagles, because they didn't have any tanks. My company commander was Capt. C. R. Casey.

In May 1968, Captain Casey got a request for tanks to support a sweep operation outside the famous city of Hue, Vietnam, because we were only a few miles outside of it. I linked up with an army captain and planned on going out on a three-day sweep with his company to see if we could locate some of the North Vietnamese units that had not yet left the area.

The fighting in the city of Hue, which had been quite fierce, had already cooled down. I didn't take part in that. I got up there right after that. We knew that the North Vietnamese units were operating in the area. But, of course, they would hit and run, so we would try to find them during the day, and then at night sometimes they'd come out and take shots at us to show us that they were still there and to give us a signal that they had not evacuated.

During one day of our three-day sweeps around Hue, we saw some Vietnamese moving around as a group, so we rather expected there might be some activity that night. Sure enough, we set up the tanks and the infantry in a wagon train circle with our backs to a river estuary. We believed that we were safe in the rear unless the enemy swam across the estuary. Because we didn't have the sophisticated thermal imaging sights that modern tanks have, we generally settled down at night and put out sentries. In this case, the army infantrymen were a little bit out in front in our tank by a few yards.

We took turns staying awake on the tank, and after my turn had come and gone, I laid down on the back of the tank on the boards above the engine. It was warm there in Vietnam, and that was the most comfortable place to be. My driver was asleep under the tank on the ground; at about three in the morning, the North Vietnamese came out of where they were holding up and fired a couple of RPGs. The comment here is that RPGs were a popular weapon way back; this was 1968 and we are still hearing about RPGs today.

Anyway, they took a couple of shots in our position, and one of the shots hit short of my tank, exploded, and pieces of metal flew up and struck me in one hand and arm as well as in my back. Although bleeding, I was not seriously injured and jumped off my tank to return fire at the enemy.

When the firing stopped and the enemy pulled back, we all began checking on one another. We couldn't find the driver and were worried that he may have been killed. However, it turned out that he had gone to sleep under the tank, in his poncho. A small piece of metal entered his temple on the side of his head, so he was unconscious, but he did survive.

In the meantime, the army captain had called in a medevac helicopter. I was helped into the helicopter with the other more seriously wounded. Because the helicopter crew wanted to leave the area as quickly as possible, they failed to close the large side doors on the craft. They also forgot to put a safety belt on me. This was a problem, because I was sitting next to one of the open doors, with one bad arm. This meant that I couldn't do the safety belt on my own. I quickly figured out that if the helicopter pilot banked the wrong way during our flight to the triage unit I was going to be doing a freefall without a parachute. I panicked and took my good arm and jammed it up into the overhead pipes and cables of the helicopter fuselage, then hung on for dear life for the entire flight. Fortunately, for me, the pilot never banked his helicopter during our flight. Of course, the guys who were seriously wounded had been strapped in their stretchers into the helicopter.

When we got to the triage unit, I thought, *Wow, I survived that one*. It was one of those million-dollar wounds and I suffered no after-effects. I didn't have to go back into the field because I was only a week away from my rotation date back to the states, which was Memorial Day of 1968.

///MAJ. DON F. SNOW (U.S. ARMY)

It all started as the command and control helicopter in which I was riding prepared to settle on the refueling pad at Blackhorse Base Camp near Xuan Loc, South Vietnam. My earphones crackled with a report from the commander of a tank company operating a few miles away. "Three-zero, this is four-six. My lead vehicle has hit a mine. I need a dust-off for one seriously wounded. Urgent!"

I spoke into the lip mike. "Let's get going to four-six's location. We'll make the dust-off." Then on the command net, "Three-zero, this is three. I'll make the dust-off. Call six and give him a report. Break. Four-six, this is three. I'll be at the location in zero five. Have your man by the road where I can pick him up."

"This is four-six. Roger. Out."

Minutes later after taking off, we dropped into the heavily wooded valley through which the tank commander had been moving. Just as the herringboned column came into sight, the radio jumped into action again. "Three-two, this is four-six. Is that you cutting across the field?" No answer. "Three-two, Three-two, this is six-four. Over." Still no answer. I thought I might be able to get him from the air. "Three-two, this is three. Over." Nothing.

I could see where the mine had blown an eight-foot hole in the ground under the lead tank, which had been three-two. The fifty-two-ton vehicle had made a right turn and was heading across the fields at twenty-five miles per hour. There was no time to contact the stricken tank with a wounded man on the ground. As the chopper circled and started down to make the pickup, another report came from the company commander. "Three, this is four-six. That guy you're going to pick up is the driver of three-two, and the rest of the crew jumped when the mine blew. That damn tank is going by itself. Break. One-six, follow that tank. It's cutting a big circle."

The chopper was just touching down when I looked back to see if we were clear. I saw two soldiers running toward the runaway tank as it headed straight for our helicopter. I also saw a small yellow dog sitting on the gun-shield. He smiled at me and seemed proud to be the sole rider on the tank.

"Take off. Take off! Take off!" I shouted to the pilot through my mike; no response. (I later learned his intercom had failed.) I looked back. Both men, in Keystone Kop fashion, had caught the runaway and were scrambling aboard. One jumped into the driver's compartment and waved frantically at us to move.

I looked forward. A small group of men had picked up the wounded man, started toward the chopper, then set the stretcher down and begun jumping, waving, and yelling at us. I again looked back and saw the tank closing fast. The would-be driver was standing on the left fender, using every known hand signal trying to get us out of the way. The other man had jumped off. My would-be savior gave up and stepped off, turning back only to toss the little dog outward.

About this time, my pilot looked back and saw tracks, hull, and turret within fifteen meters. We were airborne in seconds. In fact, less than two minutes had passed since we had landed. As we lifted off, another tank backed out of the way, the wounded man was moved forward, and three-two bounced across the road to begin the second lap of what might become the longest unmanned thrust in the history of warfare. It had made one circle about a kilometer wide and looked as if it would do bigger and better things on the next round.

As we made our own circle in our C&C (command and control) ship, I noticed an armored personnel carrier moving away from the pack in pursuit of three-two. The M113 closed the gap as the driver spurred his steel mount toward the runaway. As he drew alongside, two men jumped to the driverless tank and wrestled with its controls a short time, then jumped back to the APC (armored personnel carrier). Their breathless report came over the headphones. "Four-six, this is one-zero. The controls are blown to hell and the fuel shutoffs are shot. Guess we'll just follow this thing for the next two hundred miles while it runs out of diesel."

Again, we touched down, and four soldiers carried the wounded driver to our chopper. The man's shirt and trousers had been blown off. He looked pretty bad, with little purple marks left by tiny particles of shrapnel visible on his chest and abdomen. We sped the man to a medical aid station in less than three minutes and returned to the "action" area.

The tank had run wild for three laps and finally had come to rest in a ditch too steep for it to climb. Four-six had his column back in order, and all that remained was to drag the wayward tank into the base camp.

When the company returned to the base camp, I went to see the company commander and found him in the shower. We mumbled about "that damn tank" and I told him I was sorry about the driver. "Are you kidding me?" he asked. "That guy is over at the club drinking beers that his buddies are buying him." The holes I had seen in him were not holes at all, and aside from being a little shaken, he was in good shape.

As I left, the little yellow dog was laying in front of the orderly room. He also was in fine shape and smiled at me again as I passed. I'd swear I saw him wink.

///COL. PETER D. WELLS (U.S. ARMY)

My Vietnam War combat experience began in 1968 with my assignment as platoon leader of the 2nd Platoon, A Troop, 3rd Squadron, 4th Cavalry. The wooded area in which we operated consisted of heavy undergrowth and provided excellent cover for NVA and VC activity.

During the dry season, which generally ran from January through July, the rice paddies were divided by one- to two-foot dikes and were hard as concrete. They flooded during the rainy season. Armored vehicles could pretty much go anywhere they wanted to during the dry season, except into those areas close to low-lying streams, but were pretty much road-bound during the rainy season. There were some hardtop roads, but most were macadam surfaced, and many were simply dirt tracks, with the dust being heavy during the dry season. Most villages grew along roads or at intersections, but there were also villages linked only by dirt tracks; most of those isolated villages near the heavy woods tended to be support facilities for the NVA or VC.

When I joined A Troop, it was doing mounted patrols called reconnaissance in force, or RIFs, along the approaches to the Cambodian border. These patrols would involve moving in troop formations, which normally consisted of a wedge or a column through the rubber plantations, woods, or rice paddies during the day and splitting up into night defensive positions at night along the border approaches. During these missions, the platoons often worked with South Vietnamese Civilian Irregular Defense Forces (CIDG) led by U.S. Army Special Forces personnel. There was little respect between the two forces because the American soldiers assumed that the VC had infiltrated the CIDG and were passing information on the disposition of American forces to the NVA and VC. There was also the worry that they might actually betray the American forces during a firefight, which resulted in occasional fistfights between members of the two forces.

In 1968, a divisional cavalry squadron consisted of three identically organized ground troops, an air troop, and a headquarters and headquarters troop. The line troops each had three platoons consisting of three M48A3 Patton tanks and five M113 armored personnel carriers modified into ACAVs (armored cavalry assault vehicles) armed with a cupola-mounted M2 .50-caliber machine gun and two shield-protected M60 7.62mm machine guns on either side of the rear cargo hatch. Also part of each troop was another M113 carrying an infantry squad of twelve men and another version of the same vehicle designed to carry a 4.2-inch mortar. We tended to call the various versions of the M113 we used "tracks." The troop also had vehicle-mounted ground surveillance radar and a full complement of wheeled support vehicles.

The air cavalry troop consisted of three basic platoons: They were a gun platoon (the red platoon) equipped with AH1 Cobra gunships, a scout platoon (the white platoon) equipped with OH6A observation helicopters, and an aero-rifle platoon (the blue platoon) in UH1 Iroquois helicopters (Hueys). The scouts and guns operated in teams known as pink teams (red and white mixed) while the aero-rifles were the blues. The headquarters and headquarters troop included all of the support and command and control elements, and it included two M113s configured as flamethrowers, which were seldom used.

My troop stayed in Tay Ninh along the South Vietnamese and Cambodian border for the month of December, and on New Year's Day 1969, the entire squadron road-marched to the lower Boi Loi woods. No one in the division had been in the Boi Lois since the end of the dry season in June 1968, and the division was interested in what kind of enemy activity was going on in that area. As the three troops drove their vehicles the twenty-five or so miles from Tay Ninh to the Boi Lois, Lt. Col. Robert McGowan decided that he would do a preliminary reconnaissance of the area. He mounted his M113 ACAV and joined my platoon. The eleven tracked vehicles then traversed the entire lower Boi Loi woods before rejoining A Troop that night in a night defensive position.

During this sweep, the platoon saw many signs of extensive NVA and VC activity in the woods and found out that the woods contained numerous B-52 bomb craters covered with a thin mat of branches and dirt to resemble a large tiger trap. The platoon discovered them when some of the tracked vehicles nosed over through the thin mats and plunged down into twelve-foot craters. The crews would then have to hook up tow cables and pull the stricken vehicles back out.

Fortunately, there were no mines and there were no covering fires from watching enemy troops. In fact, the platoon met absolutely no resistance during this lightly armed reconnaissance.

The next morning the squadron sent B Troop directly back to the area covered by my platoon while sending A and C Troops into different sectors. B Troop met immediate stiff resistance and began a fight that lasted through the day and into the night. C Troop also got into a fight, but a smaller one that lasted only several hours. A Troop met no resistance that day. For three days following the B Troop fight, the squadron found no active resistance. On the fourth day, the 1st Platoon of A Troop under 1st Lt. John Moore ran into an ambush and had to fight its way clear and then hold until C Troop was moved to provide support. I do not know why the squadron did not send the rest of A Troop, but the 1st Platoon won the Presidential Unit Citation for their fight that day.

For the next two weeks, the squadron patrolled the lower Boi Loi woods without meeting any further resistance. They did, however, find weapons, supplies, and vacated camps. On January 19, 1969, the entire squadron moved to the upper Boi Loi woods and entered that unexplored area on three separate axes moving from west to east. As each troop neared the river marking the eastern boundary of the Boi Loi woods and the northern boundary of the lower Boi Lois as the river flowed to the east after flowing south, all three ran into battalion-sized NVA forces that had been camped along the river. A Troop moved right through the camp firing at everything that moved. Once the troop got through the camp, it set up a position providing for 360-degree security and began to fight the NVA battalion it had just disturbed. Captain Melvin Moss received a wound in the buttocks while standing on his track and directing fires. The fight went on for the rest of the day, but the firing began to slacken at dusk. The experiences of all three troops were the same, so the squadron commander moved B and C Troops south to join with A Troop to form a strong squadron-sized night defensive position in the woods along the edge of the river. The night passed with no further action by the NVA, and the squadron moved back to the lower Boi Loi woods at dawn. Another unit was committed to the upper Boi Lois.

On February 2, 1969, C Troop found a large NVA force between Cu Chi and Tay Ninh and engaged them. The force proved to be too strong and Lieutenant Colonel McGowan committed all three ground troops. My 2nd Platoon was in the center of the A Troop line, which was in the center of the squadron line. After buttoning up and calling in close air support and artillery to even the odds, one trooper stuck his hand out the top of his ACAV jokingly asking for a million-dollar wound, only to lose the hand to a large piece of flying shrapnel.

Just before dusk, the squadron moved forward on line firing into the NVA position. The two flank troops bogged down quickly leaving A Troop in the center still moving forward. Then the 1st and 3rd Platoons of A Troop bogged down. The 2nd Platoon, however, assaulted the NVA positions and actually penetrated the lines before being called back by the captain in charge.

As the platoon backed up and maintained a strong base of fire on the enemy positions, the intercom in my track went out. I then climbed onto the roof of my track and crouched next to the driver's hatch to guide him because he could not see to the rear of the vehicle. Shortly after that, my track hit a land mine near the middle of the left track, right below were I was standing. I went straight up and then came back down. In the process, I struck the rear of the open cargo hatch with my lower back. I then plunged headfirst onto the ammunition cans in the bottom of the track, loosing consciousness immediately. I came to on a stretcher in the emergency room of the 12th Evacuation Hospital in Cu Chi with a tag pinned to my bed covers stating that I had a broken back and should be sent on to Japan for additional care. Because I could move both my feet and legs, I doubted this diagnosis and flagged down the first doctor who came by to check the tag and confirm my injury. As it turned out, my back was severely sprained and not broken. I did, however, have a chipped vertebra. I received a Bronze Star for Valor and a Purple Heart for my actions during the engagement that put me into the hospital.

I returned to duty with my unit later in February 1969. That same month saw the introduction of the M551 Sheridan armored reconnaissance airborne assault vehicle, as a replacement for the Patton tanks. The Sheridan was a seventeen-ton tanklike vehicle armed with a 152mm main gun that doubled as an antitank missile launcher. The antitank missile system components did not arrive with our new tanks because they were classified technology and an unneeded capability in that part of the world. They also mounted an M2 .50-caliber machine gun in an electrically controlled cupola for the tank commander. Our unit's tankers were not happy about turning in their well-armored, fifty-two-ton Patton tanks for the thinly armored Sheridan. They felt naked and exposed in the field on the new, light tank. When the first one hit an antitank mine, the hull ruptured, the vehicle caught fire, and then it burned to a pile of slag; this incident further undercut the soldiers' confidence in the Sheridan.

While the tankers were out training on the new vehicles, the squadron troops fought several fights near the Cambodian border in an area known as the Parrot's Beak. One troop (C, I think) got into a major fight with heavy casualties. A Troop (and the 2nd Platoon) went on only day patrols into that area and incurred only mine casualties. The infantry track (28) hit a command-detonated mine while leading the platoon back from one of those patrols. The driver and the TC (track commander) were both medevacked, as was one dismount, the driver because of the initial detonation under the left front track, and the TC because he was blown out the top of the vehicle. The dismount was struck in the head by the cargo hatch, which snapped closed on detonation. This was not an uncommon incident, but the casualty rate was higher than normal because of the size of the mine, apparently and U.S. Air Force bomb that had failed to go off when dropped. During this period, the platoon medevacked a large number of civilians who had stepped on mines or who had been hurt when their livestock stepped on mines. At one point, we were forced to kill a water buffalo that had stepped on a mine and lost one of its legs. M16s (rifles) had no apparent effect, and it required several rounds from a .50-caliber machine gun to put the animal out of its misery.

In March 1969, I received the assignment as the unit's pay officer, which required me to fly back to a base camp the night before payday to pick up the payroll first thing the next morning. I would then fly back to the field, pay the troops in military payment certificates, and then return to the base camp in order to turn in any excess money, spend another night in the rear, and then return to the field. The flight back to base camp went well, and I then headed for the squadron officer's club to spend a pleasant evening talking to the squadron officers who stayed in the rear, drinking. At 11 p.m, I wandered back to the officer's billets to hit the sack. Around 2 a.m., I awoke to the sound of bullets going through the hooch above my bunk. I rolled onto the floor and picked up my rifle and ammo, struggled into my unlaced boots, and crawled out the door to figure out what was going on.

The squadron billets were located across the perimeter road from the base camp fence line. The defense of that fence line fell upon the base camp–stationed soldiers, such as the engineers, the ordnance personnel, and the quartermasters. The 65th Engineer Battalion guarded the cavalry sector. Just across the road from the fence line was a parking lot where our returned Patton tanks sat in storage. These tanks saved our butts. The NVA attackers who had penetrated the base camp defenses had killed a large number of the engineers either in their bunkers or along the road as they tried to reinforce their beleaguered defensive positions. When they encountered the parked Patton tanks in the storage yard, they thought the tanks were operational and spent a long time firing at them with RPGs. This gave the squadron soldiers in the base camp time to react.

When I came running out of my hooch, the first sergeant had already rallied the troop base camp soldiers. Their barracks were right behind the tanks and the officer's hooch, maybe one hundred meters farther back. The executive officer and I hooked up with the first sergeant and set up a defensive line along the base of the orderly room and the officer's hooch. As the NVA finally penetrated the tank line in the parking lot, they began to throw hand grenades into the troop barracks and engage the residents with rifle fire. When they came through the line of billets, the dug-in A Troop troopers took them under fire. After a spirited fight, with no significant A Troop casualties, the NVA withdrew from the area. Several headquarters troop soldiers were severely wounded during the fight in their section, because there were no tanks in that area to decoy the NVA efforts. The S4 (logistics) NCO won a Silver Star for gallantry in action for his part in this fight.

Elsewhere in the squadron area, the headquarters troop came under intense attack, because there were no tanks between them and the perimeter road. B and C Troops came out okay, as did A Troop because the parked and stored tanks delayed the NVA. Elsewhere in the division, soldiers were less lucky. The NVA penetrated the airfield and blew up about ten CH-47s (helicopters) on the field and killed a large number of the engineers in their billets as they came through the wire and crossed the road. One of the infantry battalions cleaned up the last of the NVA about 10 a.m. the next morning near the PX in the center of the base camp.

When I finally brought the pay out to the field, I found that my unit had enjoyed a pleasant evening with absolutely no contact. Several nights later, however, the troop had their first real test of the new M551s in combat. The troop spent the day patrolling the dry rice paddies and lightly forested areas along the alternate supply route to Tay Ninh. When the evening came, the troop pulled into a large open field and set up a standard night defensive position. Each platoon occupied one-third of the perimeter with the platoon leader's track in the center of the perimeter sector and the platoon mortar track in the center of the defensive formation. Each track erected a section of chain-link fence propped up against six-foot engineer stakes (pointed sections of angled steel) about ten feet in front of the tracks. These were rolled up during the day and carried along the front of the ACAVs and on the rear of the M551s and were intended to detonate the RPGs fired at the vehicles at night.

The crew of each vehicle also dug a bunker midway between its vehicle and the one to its right and dismounted an M60 machine gun to put into the bunker. These were generally chest deep with three rows of sandbags on each end to support a piece of perforated steel plating (normally used to build airfields with) that was about six feet by three feet long with three layers of sandbags on top to provide overhead cover. Generally, sand bags were piled three feet high behind the bunker, as well, to protect against indirect fires. The idea was to provide a place for crewmembers to fire grazing fire against attacking NVA or VC at night because the vehicle-mounted machine guns fired down from the tops of tracks (plunging fire) and so were less effective against attacking infantry at night.

About 10 p.m., B25, the Sheridan belonging to Staff Sergeant Bender, the 2nd Platoon platoon sergeant, observed through the night vision sight a group of about six people crawling out of the wood line about 250 meters away and hiding behind a clump of bushes about 150 meters away from his vehicle. He called me, and I in turn notified the troop commander, who quietly alerted the entire perimeter and told the 2nd Platoon to hold their fire and watch the group. The crews quietly manned all their machine guns (kept loaded) and the bunkers and watched through their starlight scopes. More people emerged from the woods and spread out in a semicircle around both sides of the troop. These NVA/VC (unknown at this point) were centered on the middle of the 2nd Platoon but working to encircle the entire perimeter.

When the troop commander realized what was going on, he told the entire troop to be prepared to fire on his command. When the 1st and 3rd Platoons both reported that the encircling troops were moving about halfway into their respective sectors, he gave the command to fire. Staff Sergeant Bender's Sheridan was aimed at the initial command group, and his opening shot was a beehive round containing ten thousand two-inch darts in the 152mm projectile that obliterated that group. As all the weapons of the troop opened up, the enemy was caught fully exposed. The troop commander also called in 155mm artillery on the area beyond where the NVA emerged. The NVA did not appear to have fired a single shot.

It was over in just a minute, and all platoons reported no movement to their fronts. When day broke, the platoons sent patrols to their fronts and found more than ninety dead NVA from the 95th Regiment, all lying where they had been shot. There were additional blood trails and evidence that some survivors had escaped the carnage. This one engagement improved the soldiers' opinions of the new Sheridan—good night vision and exceptional firepower.

A troop spent most of March patrolling through the Boi Loi woods. A typical day would start with a visual recon by the troop commander in an OH-6A helicopter. Normally, one or more platoon leaders would accompany him. They would look for tracks or indications of NVA or VC (very little of the latter) activity. If they saw some indications, the troop would focus on that area. If not, the troop would go look to see what could be seen in their area. The troop commander was a stickler for training and discipline, so we would move in formations appropriate to the terrain, frequently changing the formation and shifting the platoon locations within the formations so that we could do that quickly and without confusion. The standard formation was the troop wedge, with either a single platoon in a wedge in the lead with the other platoons in parallel columns behind the leading wedge, or two platoons in a wedge, one forming each wing, with the third platoon in double column behind the wedge. Rarely would the terrain be open enough to allow a full troop wedge with one platoon forming the wedge and each of the other two extending the wings; they might have done that once or twice. They practiced moving from the wedge into a troop line and practiced refusing the flanks on the move.

No discussion of field duty in Vietnam would be complete without some mention of fire ants. These one-inch-long red ants lived in trees where they built nests in the forks of branches. When disturbed, they swarmed to attack, and their bites contained enough toxins to generate a fiery burning sensation. Armored vehicles traveling through the woods with radio antennas erect frequently dislodged entire nests of these pests onto the heads and shoulders of the soldiers riding on the vehicles. The resulting bites were so painful that the soldiers would stop everything as they frantically tried to knock off the biting insects. Firefights occasionally stopped when both sides encountered the insects. When soldiers discovered the insect nests before they dislodged them, they routinely sprayed them with lighter fluid and torched the nests for pleasure.

On March 25, A Troop got into a heavy firefight with an NVA battalion. The troop had been working near FSB (fire support base) Patton on the back road to Dau Tiang when we were alerted that the normal resupply convoy had been ambushed between us and Cu Chi. The troop packed up and immediately moved in column down the road to the ambush site. The convoy had kept moving with the vehicles that had been hit, moved, or shoved off to the side of the road, this being the normal procedure. We drove past a number of destroyed or damaged trucks that had been moved off the road and deployed with my 2nd Platoon in the lead. My platoon moved up to the first tree line with dismounts down and between or just in front of the tracks. As they reached the tree line, the scouts signaled that there were people in the next tree line over. The radios in the command track stopped working, and firing broke out over at the right flank of the platoon. I hopped to the ground to go find out what was going on. Staff Sergeant Jake Roth, the track commander of the command track, hopped down as well and tossed me an M16 rifle with a pouch of magazines and a claymore mine, telling me that it wasn't safe to either go alone or go with just a pistol. As we started to the right along the tree line, an NVA soldier raised the cover of a spider hole in that same tree line and drew a bead on me. Jake shot him and threw a grenade down the spider hole. We then moved along the tree line looking for more spider holes. We found five more, shooting the occupants and grenading the holes.

The firing from the far tree line increased, and when the two of us got to the right flank of the platoon, we found a group of about four other platoon members and a medic crouched on the friendly side of the tree line and looking out into the field. They could hear screaming coming from a depression about twenty-five meters into the field. The squad leader explained that one of the new soldiers had moved too far out as a dismount and had been shot in the initial exchange of fires, and he was lying in the depression wounded. I had the two nearest tracks lay down a base of fire, and then I, the medic, Jake, and two of the others dashed out to the depression, firing our rifles as we went. We continued to fire while the medic treated the wounded soldier (hit in the leg) and put him in the stretcher. Jake and I and one other soldier stayed in the depression firing to cover the medic and another soldier as they carried the wounded man back to the safety of the platoon position. They we all dashed back safely to the rest of the platoon.

I used one of the track radios to update the troop commander (already unhappy about not being able to talk to me during the engagement). We received instructions to back the platoon away from the tree line while the troop commander brought in air strikes and artillery. The troop would redeploy ninety degrees to the side and attack on line as soon as the fire support stopped. This we did and re-established radio communications at the same time.

As soon as the jets left and the artillery stopped, the three platoons assaulted the NVA position with our vehicles. The firing was intense, especially once we had overrun the position because we were then taking fire from 360 degrees. A bullet shattered the radio microphone that I was holding. There was a loud continuous scream over the radio followed by a frightened soldier yelling words to the effect that "he's hit, he's dead—oh my God." I looked over at Staff Sergeant Bender's Sheridan and saw him lying on the turret halfway out of his hatch with his loader trying to work on him. The driver then reported that Bender had been hit and they could not stop the bleeding. Jake Roth immediately jumped from the track and dashed across to B25, under fire all the way. He climbed up, pulled Bender off the vehicle, put him on his shoulder, and dashed back to B20, still under fire. I had the tailgate door open when he got there, and the medic began to work on him to try to stop the bleeding. He had been hit in the groin, clearly in an artery. While the medic worked, I called for a medevac helicopter. Because this was a fairly heavy fight, there was a medevac on station, but it would not come in for a pickup because the area was hot. Overhearing my radio call, one of the OH-6A aero-scouts called and asked if the platoon could move him out of the wood line so he could land. Vehicle 20 backed out of the woods (under fire), and the pilot brought his helicopter in near the track (also under fire). The crew of twenty moved Staff Sergeant Bender into the helicopter while the medic tried to keep the artery clamped and the pilot lifted off safely. Unfortunately, Staff Sergeant Bender bled out on the way to the hospital. Both Staff Sergeant Roth and I received Silver Stars for our actions that day.

Following the medevac of Bender, B20 went back into the woods and rejoined A Troop as it swept through the NVA position, eliminating all resistance as the sun dropped. There were about ninety-five NVAs on the ground, none surrendered or were captured, but there were indications of others escaping, some leaving blood trails. A Troop lost two men killed and about twelve wounded during the engagement.

Three days after this engagement, A Troop was called on to sweep the back road from Cu Chi to Tay Ninh for the daily convoy. The lead element was a heavy pink team from D Troop (two scout helicopters and two Cobra gunships). They reported evidence of some activity in a position that had been occupied by RVN (Republic of Vietnam) Rangers but abandoned the day before. A Troop deployed with the 2nd Platoon in the lead along the convoy line of march. As it approached the area of suspected activity, I deployed the platoon off the road and moved toward the objective in a line perpendicular to the road. At a range of about fifty meters, the NVA fired a barrage of RPGs at the approaching platoon and opened fire with small arms and machine gun. Track 21 was hit multiple times and caught fire. The track commander, Sgt. Mike Pogie, manned the .50-caliber returning fire while his crew abandoned the burning track.

As he leapt from the back of the burning track, he was struck numerous times by small-arms fire and killed. His crew was also cut down on the ground, all killed.

The platoon pushed forward to rescue the downed crewman (not knowing they were all dead) but could not displace the NVA. After recovering two of the bodies, the platoon fell back to call in air strikes and artillery on the NVA position. The remainder of the troop arrived and deployed on the flank of the 2nd Platoon. Under cover of artillery and air strikes and with supporting fire from two of the Sheridans, tracks 20 and 22 and myself dashed forward to the burning track 21, hoping to find any surviving soldiers. The crews dismounted and pushed past the burning track, where they found Sergeant Pogie and another dead crewman (the fourth and last) and began to load them into track 22. Hearing a noise, Sergeant Roth moved into a nearby gully with an M60 machine gun and discovered an NVA squad moving toward the two tracks. He opened fire and killed them all. Roth and I then covered the withdrawal of the two tracks. Sergeant Pogie received a Distinguished Service Cross for his actions, and Roth received a Bronze Star for Valor.

When the two tracks returned to the troop lines, the entire troop began to assault the position on line with the air strikes, and artillery fire shifted to the rear in an attempt to cut off the NVA retreat. After the cavalry had moved several hundred meters into the wood line and were out of sight of the road, a platoon of M42 Dusters, armed with a pair of 40mm cannons and based on the M41 light tank, arrived at the site. They traversed their guns toward the sound of the battle and began to fire directly into the rear of the troop. Fortunately, the troop commander managed to get the 40mm fires lifted even as he adjusted fire along the path of the NVA withdrawal. The unit was awarded the Valorous Unit Citation for its performance during the period from January 1 to March 31, 1969, as well as the unit citation of the Vietnamese Cross of Gallantry with Palm.

April saw a series of patrols in troop or platoon size through the area between Cu Chi and Tay Ninh. Generally, the troop would depart the night defensive position shortly after daylight and perform an area reconnaissance of a section of woods and rice paddy defined by the squadron staff the night before. They would seldom see any enemy but would frequently find evidence of their presence, occasionally finding recently evacuated bunker lines or tunnel complexes. When the troop or platoon found such a complex, they would secure the area, dismount, and examine the positions one by one to ensure that they were, in fact, evacuated and that they had found any potential intelligence information. Occasionally, they would find tunnel complexes and would get volunteers to strip down to trousers and crawl into the tunnels with a .45 pistol and a flashlight to see what could be found. They never encountered any VC or NVA on these excursions, but they were frightening nonetheless. Each officer conducted at least one such exploration to set the example. When we had finished investigating the positions, we always did our best to destroy the positions with C4 explosives or by neutral steering the tracked vehicles over the bunkers.

Here is an example of one of the April actions: Around the middle of the month, we pulled into a large open field to set up a night position. There had been a number of indicators that there were NVA or VC about, and we pulled in early with lots of daylight left. We occupied our normal defensive positions with the RPG screens up, the bunkers dug, and the machine guns dismounted to the bunkers. The troop commander then got us all together to explain what he expected to do if we were hit that night, then we went back to our positions. As soon as it got dark, we remounted the machine guns. After midnight we detected movement in the woods along the 1st Platoon sector and went to full alert. Suddenly, the NVA poured it on, primarily against the 1st Platoon. At the troop commander's order, the 2nd and 3rd Platoons pulled out of position and began to move in column away from the 1st Platoon. Once we began to move, the 1st Platoon began to back away from the NVA on line while continuing to fire.

The NVA followed, leaving the woods. About halfway down the field, perhaps five hundred meters, the 1st Platoon stopped backing. The artillery flares came in above the NVA, the 2nd and 3rd Platoons peeled off from their movement column to come on line on each side of the 1st Platoon, and we all began to drive back toward the NVA with all weapons blazing. The NVA were in the open, illuminated by the flares, and most died. There were about forty-five of them when we reoccupied our original positions.

About every third night, the troop would spend the night occupying and securing the fire support base occupied by the 155mm self-propelled artillery battery that routinely supported the squadron in its area of operations. We became so used to the comforting sound of 155mm explosions in support of our activities that when we were forced to use 105mm support when outside the range of our supporting artillery, we were shocked at how small the bursting radius of the 105mm rounds was when compared with the 155mm or even the troop's own 4.2-inch mortars. In any event, the troop would occupy the fire support base and send out patrols through the immediate area at once after dark to detect any potential threatening activity, and then put listening posts out to extend the range of our senses. The soldiers all learned to sleep through the constant boom of the powerful guns during the night (though newbies found it disconcerting). Here are a series of anecdotes illustrating this type of activity.

One evening after the troop had been away from the fire support base for a couple of weeks, they returned and followed the normal routine. The evening patrols found nothing of particular note, and the soldiers settled down to the evening routine of posting guards in the cupolas of the tracked vehicles and manning the machine-gun bunkers built into the defenses. One of the listening posts detected movement and alerted the 2nd Platoon sector. I reported it to the TOC and focused the night observation devices of the platoon on the area in question. Soon the platoon detected a man crawling out into the open field. He settled into a sitting position and hefted what was apparently an RPG. When the scout vehicle observing through a night sight mounted on his .50-caliber machine gun noted that he had a clear sight picture, and that the man was in range, I gave the order to fire, simultaneously notifying the troop TOC what he was doing to ensure that no one else overreacted. The scout fired, and the man collapsed in place. After coordinating with the other platoons, I sent a patrol out to check out the position. They brought back a body and an RPG. About that time, the artillery major in command of the FSB came raging into the platoon area. He was mad because this VC apparently came out every night and fired an RPG round over the perimeter and then crawled away. He had never hit anything but the dump. The major was mad because he thought that the VC might now send someone who was more accurate! Needless to say, no one in my unit bought into his argument.

On another evening, the troop arrived at the fire support base and began to set up in their sector when there was a rifle shot. When I arrived at the location, I found the driver of one of the Sheridan vehicles standing over a dead dog that had a dead duck in its mouth. The driver had made a pet of a duck he had found on a sweep. He kept it on the front deck of the Sheridan as they drove around all day, and it hung around with the crew at night. It had no particular purpose other than more company. When they pulled into position, he had let the duck loose to wander. The dog had immediately attacked the duck and killed it. The driver then shot the dog. Soon after the shot, the artillery major (yep, the same one) arrived at the scene at a dead run. When he saw the dog, he again flew into a rage; it was a stray dog that he had made his pet! It took awhile for the troop commander to cool down because he had to convince the artilleryman that killing a dog was not a serious offense.

There were two other interesting events in April. The 2nd Platoon discovered a baby mongoose one day while on patrol and adopted it as a mascot. It was a friendly animal and would ride around all day on the top of track 20. In the evenings, it would dash from track to track snacking at each stop. It would also crawl up the pant legs of soldiers and sit on their shoulders as they walked around. Unfortunately, it grew larger, became wilder, and eventually took up residence within the firebase where it remained friendly but kept pretty much to itself. Of course, the platoon named it "Riki" for Kipling's own *Riki Tiki Tavi*.

In May 1969, I received a promotion to captain and took command of B Troop, my squadron. On the morning of June 25, 1969, C Troop got into a large fight in a small village on the southern edge of Tay Ninh province. B Troop was on a RIF farther south and not initially involved. As the morning progressed, it became apparent that C Troop had bitten off a lot more than they had expected and that the NVA were strongly dug in and were defending tenaciously. Intelligence reports had indicated the probability of a large-scale NVA offensive throughout the III Corp Area and this appeared to be it. The squadron commander directed me to move my B Troop north, stopping at a Vietnamese Regional Forces (RF) compound to pick up additional dismounts and move to the village in question.

Late in the morning, my B Troop arrived at the RF compound. I was surprised to see that all of the RF soldiers were wearing full uniforms, including boots and helmets, and seemed to be well disciplined. They formed up with bayonets fixed to their M16s. The RF company commander reported to me, along with an interpreter, and mentioned that they were of the Cao Dai sect, a Buddhist sect that put great emphasis on discipline and prided itself in its military ability. Tay Ninh was the center of this sect and included a magnificent temple.

I moved B Troop west of the RF compound, meeting up with elements of C Troop on the east side of the village. The squadron commander met with Capt. Gary Carlson, commander of C Troop, and myself and organized the assault. C Troop would move on the south side of the road, and my B Troop would move on the north side of the road. Air recon indicated that there was no civilian activity inside the village, though they could not tell what was inside the hooches.

As soon as the troops got within RPG range of the village, they all came under fire from RPGs and machine guns, and both troops began to receive casualties. The two troops moved through the village along the long east/west axis paralleling the main road and got perhaps one-fifth of the way through when the resistance became incredibly intense. C Troop took the worst of the fire. I began to pivot my B Troop at the junction with C Troop to swing in from the north so that the two troops began to form an "L" with C Troop, arranged south of the road on a north/south line, with my B Troop deployed north of the road along a southeast/northwest line. Captain Carlson was talking on the radio when he screamed and the mike went dead. Several minutes later, his vehicle commander, a young buck sergeant, came on the net to say, in a calm voice, that Captain Carlson had just been hit in the throat with an RPG and was dead. In fact, all the people on the track were wounded. I felt a deep chill when he heard this and zipped up my flak jacket. Lieutenant Colonel McGowan began to talk directly to the young buck sergeant who acted as the go between, maintaining control of C Troop. By this time, all of the officers in C Troop had been wounded and only one remained on the field.

With C Troop stopped and acting as a base of fire, my B Troop completed its pivot, then began to assault through the village take heavy fire. A rifle grenade hit me in the chest, knocking me back into my seat but not detonating, because the NVA soldier who had fired at me had forgotten to pull the arming pin before he fired it. My B Troop backed off fifty meters and brought in napalm on the village, and then began assaulted the village again. As they closed on the huts, they were running parallel to small bamboo hedges radiating out from the village. These hedges concealed spider holes occupied by NVA soldiers; the RF dismounts plunged directly into them with their bayonets, routing out and killing the NVA. I looked to my right, past the FO (forward observer), and saw an NVA soldier come out of his hole and take aim at someone else with his weapon. I drew my .45 pistol and fired four rounds rapidly, just past the FO's head, hitting the NVA soldier and knocking him down, scaring the FO badly. About that time, B25 took a direct hit from what appeared to be a recoilless rifle and burst into flames—all the crew successfully evacuated. As the troop moved forward, resistance got stronger.

Suddenly, there was an explosion directly in front of me. An RPG had hit the front antenna of the track and exploded. It hit the interpreter in the arm and took it off. The splash hit me in the face, chest, and left forearm, breaking my arm, then hit the FO in the chest and neck with a minor splash. The medic hopped onto the command track and began to work on the interpreter. My arm went numb and caused me to drop my hand mike. Other than that, I was otherwise okay for the moment. The track commander called for a second medic, who climbed on the track and fixed a sling for my numb arm, and then applied bandages to my bleeding wounds. Everything in my flak jacket pockets was shredded. The entire troop came to a halt because similar events were happening up and down the line. I dismounted to talk to the engaged platoon leaders and got the troop moving again.

As B and C Troops moved through the village, all resistance ceased. As it turned dark, B and C Troops combined into a single unit and began to assess the results. The position had been carried, but every single officer in both troops and many of the NCOs were wounded. C Troop had four or five dead and B Troop had two dead with one Sheridan burned to the ground. I remained in the field overnight, taking Darvon every hour or so. Lieutenant Colonel McGowan landed and spent the night on the ground with the combined troops, as well. In the morning, the troops moved through the village to assess the results and found about thirty bodies and evidence of more having been evacuated. In some of the hooches, they found dead civilians. Later that morning, I was medevacked back to the 12th Evacuation Hospital in Cu Chi for treatment. I stayed in the rear for about a week before returning to duty.

While in the rear, I witnessed Lieutenant Colonel McGowan offering another captain command of C Troop to replace Captain Carlson. The captain refused three times. Also witnessing this was Capt. Don Appler, who had just arrived from the states for his second tour; he immediately volunteered, and Lieutenant Colonel McGowan sent him to the field. I received my second Bronze Star for Valor and a Vietnamese Cross of Gallantry as well as my third Purple Heart for this action.

During July 1969, the division's inspector general showed up at Cu Chi to conduct the annual inspection. The troop was in the field, so they first checked all of the records in the base camp and found no serious problems. They then insisted that they had to check weapons and vehicles for maintenance. Because the troop was in the field, the XO (executive officer) loaded them onto a helicopter and hauled them out to where the troop was in a firefight. As they flew over the firefight, he asked which vehicle they wanted to inspect first. The team opined that the vehicles seemed to be working just fine and the weapons did, too, so no further inspection was required. They returned to Cu Chi and gave B Troop a clean bill of health.

In early August 1969, I jumped off the top of my command track and my left knee collapsed, spilling me onto my back. The apparently minor wound I suffered in early June had proved not so minor. A trip to the 25th Medical Battalion Hospital showed that a piece of hand grenade fragment had worked its way into the knee joint and was floating through the entire joint. It would occasionally touch a nerve, causing the knee to collapse. This meant the end of my field time in Vietnam, because I was no longer medically fit for such duty. I retired from the army twenty-six years later.

///LT. COL. GENE BERBAUM (U.S. MARINE CORPS)

My most challenging job as a marine officer in my twenty-plus years of active duty began in the Republic of Vietnam in 1969. I was assigned to the 1st Tank Battalion, 1st Marine Division, located south of Da Nang in I Corps. I was assigned to relieve another major as the battalion S4 officer, logistics. The job required me to be responsible for all the logistical needs for a tank battalion and the attached units, which included an infantry platoon and an antitank Ontos platoon (tracked vehicle with six recoilless rifles). Both platoons were attached due to the fact that we had the mission of running the Southern Defense Sector of the 1st Marine Division Headquarters in Da Nang. This position sounds easy enough, but it required every waking hour of my time and all of the conniving I could muster to get the job done.

To understand the complexity of the position, an explanation is required as to the makeup of the battalion and how it was deployed in support of the infantry division in Vietnam. The battalion was broken down into three gun companies containing seventeen M48A3 tanks and one M51 tank retriever. Each company was broken down into three gun platoons each having five M48 tanks. The company headquarters had two gun tanks and the retriever. The companies were normally assigned to support one infantry regiment as an attachment, but the responsibility for logistical support remained with the tank battalion. The regiment normally assigned one platoon of tanks to support each of their three battalions at the disposal of the infantry battalion commander. The tank company commander and his headquarters section remained with the infantry battalion commander as his armor advisor. This arrangement dictated that the assets of our battalion were spread out in at least nine different combat locations within roughly two hundred square miles. Each of the nine platoons required the support of the 1st Tank Battalion. This included fuel, ammunition, repair parts, third-echelon maintenance, and all other classes of supplies.

In order to provide this assistance as the S4, I had the help of many special sections and platoons. They consisted of a maintenance platoon, commanded by a captain; a motor transport platoon of more than thirty-five vehicles, commanded by a first lieutenant; a communication platoon, commanded by a captain; a supply section, commanded by a captain; a medical section, commanded by a naval doctor lieutenant; and an engineering section, commanded by a warrant officer. We also had a food preparation and cooks section under a gunnery sergeant. The infantry units had little in the area of motor transport and had to rely on support from the division motor transport battalion as an on-call requirement. This put the responsibility directly back on our battalion.

The combat situation required that the enemy be engaged in a piecemeal fashion throughout the tactical area of responsibility. They had to be located, isolated, and destroyed as the situation arose. The enemy chose to attack in numbers only when they thought they had surprise and number superiority to their advantage, or at night.

Having tank assets and personnel spread out in so many locations made supporting them a nightmare. The roads were always mined and subject to ambushes, which added to the complexity of the mission. I can't emphasize enough the courage of our engineers in the daily minesweeps of the roads and the pure bravery of all of those vehicle drivers who risked their lives daily to support our marines.

I recall one recovery mission I was sent on by the division G4 office. We were directed to go out to an area called Charlie Ridge deep in "Indian Country." It seems a platoon of tanks from the 5th Tank Battalion, while supporting a battalion from the 28th Marines, had managed to sink all five tanks in mud up to and over the sponson boxes. They had been there more than two days and could not get out. The infantry battalion commander, who I knew personally, was livid as he had to leave his troops there to protect the tanks and Charlie (slang name for the Viet Cong) had begun to find the range for harassing fire.

The only tank retriever available belonged to our battalion. Fortunately, I was able to borrow an LVTP5 (landing vehicle tracked personnel–5) retriever from force logistics command (FLC). We set out on this mission with the two retrievers and the two battalion headquarters tanks. Upon arrival, we saw all five tanks almost buried in what we learned later was an old Vietnamese graveyard, with no hopes of getting out. After a full day of rigging and pulling we got out only one tank. In the meantime, we stuck and unstuck all of our own equipment at one time or another. The situation seemed hopeless. That night I contacted the division G4 and assured him that we could not succeed unless they could supply us with some heavy timber or logs to use as tonnage. The next morning an army "Jolly Green Giant" (CH-47 Chinook) helicopter appeared over the hill slinging a huge bundle of eight-by-eight-by-eight-by-fifteen-inch beams and delivered them on the spot. Once we had the lumber, we were able to build ramps and finally extract all of the vehicles from that mess. I don't know the fate of that platoon commander, but I am sure it could have not been good. Mission complete. "Over."

Another recovery mission that sticks in my mind was when a tank from Company B was returning to the company and 5th Marines containment area at a place called Phu Loc Six after supporting the Korean marines in Hoi Ann and hit a command-detonated mine as it finished fording a river. There were marines riding on the outside of the tank; one lost both his legs and the others were seriously injured as well. The driver managed to pull the damaged tank clear of the water before the tank died. The crew set up a base of fire and called for a medevac. The tank was left in place.

The next morning we had to go back in and retrieve the tank from enemy country. The operation was set up utilizing two gun tanks, an M51 retriever, and two LVTP5s outfitted with line charges and launchers to clear any more mines, which were sure to be there. The rescue column was ready. The area was pounded by artillery for more than an hour before commencing the operation. I had opted to take the place of one of the M48 crewman positions to relieve a short-timer, rather than riding the M51. The artillery was lifted, and we proceeded to the objective. All went well until we were in sight of the tank. There were several Vietnamese visible who appeared to be working in the rice paddies. Wrong. They were neutralized. The LVTs were brought up and each one launched its line charge toward our recovery route, causing several secondary explosions. When we made it to the tank, we could not believe our eyes. The bad guys had taken all of the 90mm ammo out of the tank and arranged the shells by type on the sand along with the machine guns and ammo, maps, and binoculars. Had we not gotten there when we did this stash would have been used against marines in future battles. The tank was recovered, repaired back at battalion, and back in combat in a week. Throughout the year, there were many similar recovery operations.

Another major challenge was getting necessary supplies and repair parts. On many occasions, the normal supply channels had to be circumvented by devious methods such as scrounging and the barter system. All sources were utilized; the U.S. Army Depot, the U.S. Air Force at Da Nang Air Base, the Seabee battalion, and sometimes even the South Vietnamese Army. All supplies in the marine system came through FLC (force logistic command) which was commanded by a marine general. This was a huge complex hidden safely out of danger on Red Beach in Da Nang. This unit was too large to be effective and often was not.

During this time, we experienced a rash of suspension system damage involving left torsion bars. All requests were put on back order, not in stock. Not believing this, my logistics chief, Gunnery Sergeant Biers, and I went the fifteen miles to FLC to check. We were given permission to go to a specific warehouse to look for parts. Driving through this huge building, we spotted torsion bars on shelves about fifteen feet high—we had a winner. We got a forklift and loaded a dozen or more in our vehicle. When we were asked to sign for them, I told them they were not in stock so I couldn't sign. We ended up getting five tanks off deadline and back into action. This is just an example of the supply problems.

On one of my recon missions to FLC, I came across a shiny new M48A3 tank sitting in the ready equipment float. I contacted the officer in charge of the float and requested a direct exchange for one of our code H (out of service) vehicles. The purpose of this float, I was told by the major in charge, was to keep all assets in the float, because the inspector general was due soon and they wanted to have a decent-looking display. In a combat situation, nothing could be dumber. The following Saturday I informed my maintenance officer to have a code H tank hooked onto our retriever by 0600 Sunday and to have a tank crew with him.

We went on Sunday because we knew that FLC troops did not work then. We got into the complex, dropped off our code H vehicle, performed an LTI (limited technical inspection) on the new tank, loaded the machine guns, and were headed back to our battalion before lunch. Within two days, that tank was fifty miles south of Da Nang at a combat base called LZ Ross, which was surrounded by the enemy. During the first week, the position was attacked and tanks saved the day.

I received a call from a colonel in the division G4 office, who I personally knew, asking me if I stole a tank from FLC, knowing full well I had. The sentry had recorded the serial number and tactical markings on my jeep. I was busted. I told him it was a direct exchange, and he asked me if I had the paperwork; well, of course I didn't. He told me the division commanding general and the general at FLC were looking for my head, and I replied I would love to explain why it was a necessity to have to steal a tank to support marines in combat. I never heard another word about it; I was, however, reassigned shortly to the division G4 office and made the division material management officer. That is called payback.

I served in that job for three months before I was assigned to be commanding officer of the 1st Tank Battalion. I later brought my battalion out of Vietnam and relocated to Camp Pendleton, California.

///LT. JOHN POINDEXTER (U.S. ARMY)

Grabbing my Coke, hot by now, from Seege, I walked down the M577s (command version of the M113 APC) ramp and slumped into a canvas chair in the tent extension attached to the vehicle's rear. The tent cover was invaluable in the miserable five-month rainy season. Its value in the equally miserable seven-month dry season was questionable. A couple of field mechanics and mortar crewmen stood outside, trying to decide whether a delicious meal of C-rations and dust was worth the effort.

"Flange two-nine, this is Racer two-nine." George Hobson came up on the battalion net again. "I'm getting down toward the last of my smoke grenades and a few magazines per man. Over."

"This is Flange two-nine. Roger. We've got some more air for you now, so get ready to mark your position." Flange two-nine, Lieutenant Colonel Conrad sounded reassuring as he continued to do all he could, but those grouped around the radios in the M577 had listened to the traffic on the command frequencies for much of the morning. Charlie Company had about eight hours left.

Racer two-nine's voice, cracking under the strain of a four-hour firefight against severe odds, betrayed the despondency of a man who had exhausted his limited options and was merely awaiting the final outcome to be thrust upon him. Lying on his back with a painful face wound amid the bullet and shrapnel-scarred trees, George stared into the unclouded sky at the aircraft circling symmetrically overhead. He could read a map and he knew the size of the enemy force. It had to be clear to him that he faced the North Vietnamese, not the Viet Cong, and that they would not run away from the bombs and the gunships.

"Well, what are we going to do? It's about four-and-a-half klicks (kilometers), maybe five from us to George." Jim Armer laid his plastic-coated sectional map on a five-gallon water can next to his chair in the tent extension and smiled. We were now face to face with the subject that had brought our never-robust pace of conversation to a near standstill for the past hour. Except for the busy radios, there was silence under the canvas. Outside, an engine fired up, probably to heat a few cans of C-rations.

"Four hours for the whole trip, maybe more," our new and still overweight first sergeant ventured. The shrinkage of waistlines was directly proportional to the number of weeks in the jungle. "The busting looks pretty bad, but at least there aren't any big streams between Charlie Company and us. It'll mean a night operation coming back, and the men are just about shot after last night."

The sergeant in charge of the landmine-damaged ACAV (armored cavalry assault vehicle) marooned inside our perimeter, with many more months in country than our first sergeant, was obviously preparing to unburden himself. At least our small part of South Vietnam was free, admission to the M577 was not restricted, and everyone was entitled to an opinion. "There's a good chance of an ambush on the way with all the enemy around here. Do you want to volunteer, sir?" He spat as he laid down the challenge.

"No." Jim recoiled from the TC's question, which had but one sensible response in Vietnam. "But if I was with those guys, I'd sure want somebody to get me out." Because his men rode where we drove, Jim's planning inputs tended to be suggestive rather than determinative. The company commander of our infantry detachment sat patiently next to his map, a sturdy young man in a sweaty olive undershirt, wearing glasses and slowly corroding steel dog tags.

I worked through the logic yet again. It was unlikely that the infantry-oriented senior officers overhead imagined that Alpha Troop could traverse the impossible forest terrain to Charlie Company in time to be effective. On the other hand, someone in the command structure might decide later in the afternoon that it was necessary to try, resulting in an unduly perilous night mission for the troop. And, of course, the resourceful Lieutenant Colonel Conrad might have a last-ditch plan that employed Team A reasonably. But would it not be best to stand up right now and carry out this unsought task our way?

The rawest newbie sitting around listening to the intermittent conversation could tell that to be involved at all would probably cost lives, perhaps even his own. It was not entirely paranoid to suspect that the NVA considered the troublesome Team A to be the real objective and was setting us up. Still there were almost one hundred Americans trapped and already dying up there. The sweat ran freely.

After some moments, the right answer, the only answer, could no longer be avoided. "Seege," I sighed.

"Sir?" The chief RTO (radio telephone operator) sat as if he expected to be slapped but was resigned to the blow.

"Call flange control and tell Conrad that Team A is prepared to react."

"Roger. What else?" There had to be more, of course. It was never so straightforward.

"Tell one-six and three-six to pick up their grunts and move back here ASAP. Two-six is to continue busting a trail north. Don't say north, just tell him to continue as rapidly as possible in his current direction after picking up his people." Mike would know we were joining him when we arrived, and we did not need to inform the North Vietnamese monitoring our frequencies. The men under the canvas, their tension now dispelled by the immediacy of action, scattered into the sun to prepare their vehicles and collect their gear; Team A would start on its mission before Lieutenant Colonel Conrad ordered us to move. Jim smiled for the last time that day, relishing our macabre little game of military one-upmanship.

Within fifteen minutes, the 1st and 3rd Platoons had returned to the night defensive position and had married with the command section, consisting of A66 and the medic and artillery forward observers' ACAVs. As soon as the expected instructions arrived from a preoccupied Lieutenant Colonel Conrad, we were on the move north to join the still-rolling 2nd Platoon. At the night defensive position, only the M577 with Seege's radiomen, the depleted mortar section, the recovery vehicle, and one disabled track remained. We left two squads of infantry for their protection, but we took the crewmen from the inoperative ACAV to fill vacancies in their platoon. Thus, the first big risk of the mission was a dangerously thin night defensive position that hadn't been moved in two days. No choice.

Closing on the 2nd Platoon, the troop quickly reorganized into jungle reconnaissance array and pushed toward the encircled Charlie Company. Each cavalry troop had its own set of formations designed to deal with particular tactical situations. In thick brush and forest, we reconned in three columns. The left and right columns each consisted of one platoon with the platoon leader's ACAV immediately behind his lead tank and the balance of the unit following at five-meter intervals.

The last platoon squared off the rear of the formation and was usually deployed as the maneuver element in small engagements. The center column contained the troop headquarters, led by a Sheridan tank from one of the line platoons with A66 second. Positioning the troop and platoon command tracks so far forward was illogical but unavoidable because the American soldier is willing to be led but is reluctant to be directed.

As we snaked through the multicanopied jungle, more than two hundred cavalry and infantrymen perched atop twenty-seven metal boxes, each man keenly aware of the inevitability of battle and the possibility that an ambush could erupt at any moment. For these men, unlike their horse cavalry antecedents, there was no heart-pounding charge across an open field in an all-or-nothing gamble. In Vietnam, victory went not to the bold but to those who best withstood the tension and committed the fewest mistakes. We were opposed by masters in the art of patience, whom we had to seek out on their terms and on their own ground. Every advantage of temperament and terrain was theirs.

Among American soldiers, the crew of A66 was fairly typical. Topper, the left machine-gunner, had an open, trusting face and a thick shock of hair barely concealed under his helmet. He was a fairly recent replacement and too green to brood over dangers that he could visualize only dimly. His buddy on the right M60, also being broken in, was similarly naive. Both would soon be more wary.

On the other hand, our driver, Marty, was well seasoned but so steady under fire that it was clear to me he did not fully appreciate the seriousness of his situation. During one battle, he was observed reading an issue of the limp pornography included in the publications shipped to the troops in the field. He seemed undistracted by the .50-caliber machine gun pumping away just over his head and the M60 working over his left shoulder. About one inch of aluminum plate separated him from incoming frontal fire, and a layer of sandbags below his seat provided some protection from landmines.

Sergeant Dennis Jaybusch, the track commander, was a tall, gangly fellow with a light blond mustache and all the grace of an adolescent giraffe.

When handling the radio, his soft, conscientious voice reliably backed me up on the invisible network that was our sole lifeline to the world. It was becoming obvious that Dennis was just about through, though. He'd been exposed in his cupola behind the .50-caliber for too long and now merely plodded through the remaining few weeks before his rotation date.

Peering intently into the thick underbrush, the closely packed infantry and armored crewmen on A66 and the other tracks attempted to spot the camouflaged enemy before they heard the incoming. The lead tanks, always working with a 152mm canister round in the chamber in hopes of an early shot, squirmed around large trees and smashed smaller ones as the underbrush flattened into a path. The loaders on the jungle-busting Sheridans had the difficult and dangerous assignment of riding outside on the rear decks to brush fallen branches and debris away from the engine air intakes.

Each vehicle followed in the path of its predecessor to avoid detonating randomly placed mines. Sweat soaked into the bulky flak jackets and caused ink to run on forgotten letters in dirty pockets. The humidity was so high under the foliage that it was almost possible to watch rust form on the well-oiled machine guns.

For the first hour, the troop made exceptionally good progress, covering perhaps one hundred meters of the dense forest every five minutes. At this rate, however, the lead Sheridans overheated their powerplants, which were too light for the brutal work of busting jungle. We rotated the leads every thirty minutes as the retiring tank crews pulled over to the side of the route, swung their turrets off-center, and removed their radiator caps. Careful handling prevented anyone from being scalded by the resulting geysers of steam.

Crashing forward, we wrenched a path from the unwilling jungle with about as much stealth as a parade down Main Street. But not a single vehicle threw a track from the road wheels despite the logs, stumps, and eroding bomb craters that we traversed. Not one engine, drive, or mechanical system malfunctioned from misuse or poor maintenance.

Had a single vehicle gone down, an infantry platoon would have had to remain with it until the repair was completed or the vehicle was dragged back to the night defensive position. In a jungle where enemy battalions roamed about, this was an unthinkable risk.

As the troop progressed, the gravity of the mission penetrated deeply into the consciousness of those crewmen who had not gathered around the M577's radios during the morning. Within the first hour of the march, as details spread among the last to be informed, gunners loosened the protective towels around the operating mechanisms of their weapons. Crews removed a few of the more accessible ammunition cans from stowage on the floors of the ACAVs and spaced them about on upper decks, mainly to place them within easy reach but also in a human attempt to pile bulk between the crew and incoming fire.

Crews took extra machine guns from internal racks and placed them in convenient positions atop the ACAVs: no M60 gunner was ever seen trying to replace an overheated barrel or damaged firing mechanism during a firefight. Men passed around pistols and rifles, even though no one favored hand weapons over the heavy machine guns. In battle, there is a perverse satisfaction in the feel and sound of the large automatic weapons. It is almost as if the enemy can be frightened by the noise alone. Almost.

Over the radio, George again reported that his ammunition and pyrotechnics were nearly exhausted. When the last of Charlie Company's smoke grenades were expended, the forward air controller overhead would have to place air strikes from memory in the failing light. Lieutenant Colonel Conrad or his S3, Maj. Charles Blanchard, would direct the artillery in the same risky manner. At that point, the danger to the infantry increased astronomically, but the alternative was a stand-up ground assault by the unharried enemy. With compasses and melting grease pencils, the more experienced of the platoon leaders and I bent over our map cases. Jim Armer talked nonstop on his PRC-25 (radio) on the rolling rear deck of A66. The hours passed.

Driving hard, A18 in the rear of the 1st Platoon column began to pour more than its usual volume of smoke from the engine compartment. This was our most wornout Sheridan, and the overheated insulation appeared to be burning from its wiring harness. The tank's crew kept it plugging along through the unorthodox, yet seemingly effective, technique of dumping five-gallon cans of water directly into the engine compartment. A18 finally got an opportunity to cool off when we penetrated an old B-52 bomb strike area, and the drivers slowed down to thread a path through the closely spaced craters.

"Rider two-nine, this is Racer two-nine. I've saved one smoke. We'll pop it when we've got you in sight." For the first moment since the early morning, George's voice echoed a tentative note of hope. The sounds of Team A's splintering trees and racing engines must have penetrated the remaining distance to his position—and to the North Vietnamese lines, as well.

"This is Rider two-nine, Roger. Out." No reason to disguise our intentions now. "Flange two-nine, this is Rider two-nine. I'm putting out smoke on my point. Can you give me a spot relative to Racer?" The exact angle of our approach was critical, as we had to arrive at Charlie Company's southeast flank, the vicinity of the lightest reported contact. But, even if our navigation had created no tactical problems, the NVA commander might attempt to generate one for us by inserting a few squads among the American units during the approach. A spontaneous firefight could result in the lead tanks wiping out the exposed Charlie Company as well as the NVA.

"This is Flange two-nine, Roger. Wait. I'll come around and take a look." Lieutenant Colonel Conrad's tone against the background of whirling helicopter rotors expressed no satisfaction, as was entirely appropriate, with Team A's timely arrival.

"This is Flange two-nine, identify green. Make a half-turn to your left, writer, and come around to a heading of three-one-zero. You've got about two hundred meters to go. I'll put a little air on in the next few minutes."

"Thanks, two-nine. Out," now, for the three platoons. "One-six, two-six, three-six, this is six. Elevate all weapons until we find the grunts. Nothing heavier than an M16; do not fire directly forward under any circumstances. That's where the grunts are. Acknowledge!" If a trap had been prepared, it would be sprung now, when we might be entering a minefield surrounding the enemy base. One of our most fundamental strengths, maneuver, was restricted, and our flanks were exposed as the drivers cautiously picked a path through the craters marking another chewed-up B-52 strike area.

The officers stowed their maps and compasses, and everyone cinched their flak jackets tighter. Crews crouched behind steel gun-shields, fingering the trigger guards of their puny-feeling rifles. The infantry lay as flat as their bulky equipment allowed on the exposed rear decks of the ACAVs, eager to jump overboard and bury themselves in the inviting bomb craters at the first shot.

Tension transformed into noticeable anxiety. Eyes refused to remain fixed for more than a moment. Anyone with even the most trivial task immersed himself in it. Hands not clutching a weapon were busy at nothing. Soft drinks appeared from the intestines of the tracks and were poured lukewarm down tightened throats. Quickly emptied cans bounced over the side, marking, as always, our progress across the face of South Vietnam.

Yet incomprehensively, there was no fire from the brush rimming the far side of the bombed-out area. Had the air strikes masked our arrival? Had the NVA radio operator who was assigned to monitor our traffic been injured or misunderstood our intention? Was the ambush in the wrong place or had the NVA commander simply made a mistake, randomness, again?

Suddenly a spluttering smoke grenade arced out of a clump of brush ahead. "Racer two-nine, this is Writer, identify yellow."

"Racer two-nine, affirmative, affirmative," George was elated.

Reentering the sheltering vegetation on the far side of the forgotten air strike, the lead moved only a few meters before three-six came up on the horn. "Ah, six, looks like we've got some of our guys out front here. They're beat up all right."

The men of Charlie Company huddled apathetically behind scarred trees and in depressions scooped out under the brush. Few stood as the troop crashed through their position, forcing our drivers to move carefully to avoid running over survivors. The dead were a group of partly covered forms in the midst of a larger pool of wounded grunts.

Breaking from the reconnaissance formation, the medic track pulled up to the shore of the casualty collection area. After jockeying around to point their frontal armor toward the enemy, the medics dropped the rear ramp into the stained brush. Specialist 4th Class Felthager and his two assistants went to work, using the medical supplies in their ACAV to supplement the meager resources of Charlie Company. Urgent wounds had to be handled immediately because there would be more from A Team soon.

Jim and I unhooked ourselves from our communications gear and jumped the six feet to the ground as George dragged himself over to A66. While the troop was waved past the infantry command post in three columns, George briefed us from behind his lopsided face.

"Very strong, at least a battalion here, lots of RPGs. Very well controlled. Sure glad to see you guys," he said between bloated lips. His bandoleers and harness hung down empty of ammunition and grenades. "The main part of the complex is just north of my position here. But it's a semicircle shape, and we walked right into the hollow part this morning. Never had a chance, head-on and flank fire is bad, especially from the west. Lightest where you came in, only about half the company is still effective. Whatever you do," he squinted at the lines of armor and infantry moving through, as his walking wounded struggled in, "don't waste too much time on the dinks (derogatory term for Vietnamese). My guys need help bad."

At this late hour, saddled with the Charlie Company injured, we could follow only one course of action: an assault directly into the center of the enemy bunker complex. There was no daylight remaining for a careful probe around the exterior of the enemy configuration for the weak element. No time to execute an attack on more than one axis and, without our sister units from the 1st Squadron, no opportunity to envelop the NVA battalion and eradicate it entirely—just a brutal, unoriginal shot straight ahead, which the enemy commander would expect, and we probably were outnumbered two to one.

If the North Vietnamese were subdued quickly, I intended to release one of the platoons to bust a landing zone nearby and evacuate the wounded. Were this to be accomplished, Lieutenant Colonel Conrad probably would use the same LZ (landing zone) to insert a couple of infantry companies with instructions to try to surround the enemy position, thereby leading to an all-night action. Speed was essential.

Behind the hundreds of tons of metal, ammunition, fuel, and flesh that was the troop assault line, the spent men of Charlie Company slumped down to secure the casualty collection point. Alpha Company gladly dismounted to assume its customary position behind the tracks. The grunts and the tightly spaced vehicles faced north toward the Cambodian border a few kilometers ahead. The well-led 1st Platoon occupied the dangerous left flank facing the greatest concentration of enemy activity. The less-experienced 3rd Platoon leader held the center of the line with A66 in close proximity to his right. The 2nd Platoon extended eastward through the least threatening terrain all the way to the bomb strike zone. A18, now unquenchably smoking, was abandoned in the rear of the 1st Platoon, a crippling loss.

Blue max gunships ineffectually expended their loads on east to west sweeps just forward of the troop line as we prepared for the battle about to be joined. The principal value of the tactical air was to distract the NVA and to keep their heads down within the bunkers. Only rarely did the helicopter ordnance destroy the carefully constructed underground fortifications. Occasionally, when rockets detonated in the trees, they caused friendly casualties.

Up and down the line sounded the sharp clatter of men jacking back their .50-calibers and rearranging ammunition cans. Here and there, a final soft drink passed around and the container, as usual, wound up overboard. The grunts dropped their excess equipment into the weeds, scattered out while adjusting their bulging ammunition bandoleers and pockets stuffed with grenades, and waited silently.

All was still.

"Commence fire!"

Twenty-five .50-caliber machine guns, forty M60s, and five main tank guns blasted into action. The vegetation began to disintegrate, and a few nearby bunkers became visible. The more skilled gunners began to work their rounds from two or three feet in front of the forward slope of their tracks out to almost horizontal deflection and then back in close. From bitter experience, they knew the fatal damage that could be done by an enemy rifleman lying in a concealed hole only a few feet away. The sharp rattle of the automatic friends felt like ice picks on our eardrums, and concussions from the tanks' main guns a few feet away threatened to tear the smoky skin from our faces.

After bolstering our courage through the full demonstration of the troop's firepower, we began our advance. Twenty-five tracks in a long single line pressed forward into the unknown, firing at will into a jungle that yielded its secrets so grudgingly. After the first ten meters, the volume of fire picked up again. Excessively, the gunners were expending too high a share of their basic load in the early stages of the fight. A disastrous shortage of ammunition inevitably would ensue!

"Cease fire! Cease fire. Let's see what's going on," I radioed urgently. "Acknowledge!" The hallmark of a disciplined unit is its fire control, and we usually had been able to stop shooting within a few moments of the command. Today, however, nervousness must have been especially widespread as the rate of fire slackened only slightly. After perhaps five seconds, without warning, a long burst of AK-47 fire walked up the tank turret of A27 and glanced off its gun-shield.

The line re-erupted into a wall of flame and smoke. It was now obvious that the troop's rate of fire reduction had been paced by a corresponding increase in incoming. Staff Sergeant Pasquel "Gus" Gutierrez, the track commander of A27, knew that crouching down for protection from the enemy fire would increase the likelihood that more would follow. Instead, he grabbed the TC's override and violently traversed his turret to the left. As soon as he judged the gun tube to be more or less correctly oriented, he let loose with the main gun and cleared a considerable swath of jungle. While his loader slammed another round into the breech and A27's gunner fired an M16 from the left hatch, Gus lobbed grenades out front. Swinging around to the right, he blew away more brush, clearing a bunk roof near A66.

"One-six, two-six, three-six, casualty reports. Over." There was a short delay.

The radio hummed as the 1st Platoon leader shoved the transmission switch on his CVC (combat vehicle crewman) helmet forward. "I've got two hurt on one-two. They're on their way over to the medics. The grunts are carrying them." Willie McNew was already taking a beating to the left. Another static punctuated delay.

"This is two-six, only one man lightly hurt." Gutierrez had performed. Long delay.

"Three-six, seems to be two hurt for sure and, I believe, one KIA."

On and on, a meter at a time, the platoon leaders urged their men forward, always struggling to remain as nearly on line as possible to afford all vehicles an unrestricted field of fire. Rolling over logs and around craters and trees, we advanced another five, ten, twenty meters. But, recognizing the increasing momentum of the attack, the NVA fought back with courage and determination. The RPGs began to hit with telling force on vehicles and in the trees.

In order to aim, however, the enemy soldiers had to expose at least their heads and shoulders, and we exacted our price. Nonetheless, by 1800, with about an hour of full daylight remaining, the situation had become grim. We had made too little forward progress through the thick jungle to consider establishing a night defensive position and clearing an

LZ. The Charlie Company casualties were still suffering, and the medics reported that we had incurred many new ones. The race to darkness continued with little time remaining to break the numerous, entrenched enemy or to begin the journey home.

"Six, this is one-six. I'm taking heavy fire from the left! What do you want me to do?" McNew was excited, a rare event.

"This is six. Orient you're outside ACAV to the left. Keep stringing them out as we move up. Let me know when you're down to your last track. Over."

"Wilco. That won't be very long. Out." Willie's report meant that we were flanked on the left and, although the echelon formation he was assuming should protect him in the short run, the distance that the troop could advance was now mathematically fixed. The hornet's nest had begun to close about our wrist as our fist thrust toward its center.

"Rider, this is Racer two-nine. By the way, we've had dinks behind us for some time. Don't stop; we can hold." The NVA commander had apparently launched a counterstroke aimed at the casualty collection point, our weakest link. Even if George could hold them back—and he must or we would have to break off our attack—the trap was closed and we were surrounded.

Jim Armer picked his way through the tangled undergrowth to A66 on line. As he clumsily stumbled forward, encumbered by his bulging ammunition pouches and assorted grenades, canteens, pistol, and first aid kit, he didn't exactly resemble John Wayne on the silver screen. Severed by a stray rifle round, a branch dropped from the trees overhead and settled gracefully near him as he clambered onto the rear of our track.

"The RPGs are playing hell with us! I've got eight hurt now," he shouted directly into my ear under the CVC helmet. "I'm moving up tighter behind the tracks." His face had miniature channels on each side of his nose where the sweat had worked away at the grime on the way to his chin. Like everyone else, his eyes were pink from the harsh smoke and the exhaust fumes.

"Okay. How's it look?" I shouted back at him as he stood on one of the fender projections extending from the rear of the ACAV.

"No sweat," came the all purpose response. *What an incongruity*, I thought, as I admired his aplomb. "Most of their stuff is high now. We're hurting 'em bad." Jim lowered himself carefully to the ground and waddled back toward his men to reposition them and to direct their fire.

Meter by meter, the advance continued. Some of the weapons in the vehicles were silent now, their gunners dragged away through the brush and debris to the toiling medics. Occasionally, one of the infantrymen crawled up through the clutter of the battlefield to an ACAV and manned an idle machine gun, a heroic act for an untrained grunt.

Fifty meters now, and as the all-too-few minutes until darkness melted away, the enemy fire showed no signs of slackening. The NVA were proving to be just as efficient as we were in recycling patched-up but still-functional soldiers to replace the newly wounded on the line. Or else, unlike us, the enemy commander controlled tactically unlimited reserves that he could throw into the firestorm.

Our gunners on A66 seemed to take their first large-scale firefight in stride, especially Topper, who bent over his M60 and fired skillfully into the more suspicious of the surrounding brush. Not yet twenty years old, he was, by now, almost certainly a killer of men. We had consumed most of the upper layer of the two levels of ammunition carefully arranged on the floor of A66, and our path was littered with empty olive ammo cans and brass cartridge cases. One M60 had been replaced, and Dennis had expended a pint of lubricating oil, pouring it directly on the almost glowing .50-caliber barrel. His Adam's apple worked up and down furiously as he screamed for another can of .50 to be passed up. Gunners, even mature track commanders like Dennis, and especially those approaching their rotation date, rarely felt secure unless the thumb-activated trigger was depressed.

Inevitably, some leaders were more forceful than others were. On this courageous day, whenever there was momentary lag in the advance, Sgt.

1st Class Robert Foreman thrust his Sheridan tank forward. Each time his platoon loyally followed. Again and again, Sergeant Foreman, our most senior African American NCO, led the way when it seemed that further progress was blocked. Each effort required that his crew expose the thinner side armor of their tank to head-on fire and then defend their exposed position until the lighter tracks, including A66 on his immediate right, could pick routes forward to cover his flanks.

Regardless of the exertions of Foreman and others, however, it was becoming obvious that there were just too many North Vietnamese and not enough of us. I reached for the radio frequency control box lying just behind the .50-caliber cupola and switched over to the battalion command net to discuss a situation that was now almost hopeless and growing costly beyond reason. Just as my mouth opened, a sense-destroying explosion enveloped me, and I was hurled unconscious to the ammo- and weapon-strewn floor of the ACAV.

Utter blackness, deep and comforting. Sometime later, shades of gray and hazy images but no sound beyond the ever-present ringing of my ears. How long I lie there I don't know, but at last and grudgingly, I began to function at some threshold level of awareness.

My first incoherent thought was that Sergeant Foreman, just to our left, had traversed his turret too far and blown us away. Nonsense. Then my eyes began to focus and I saw a pile of expended cartridge cases where my nose ended on the ACAV's floor. With a bit more reluctant concentration, Topper's fatigue sleeve came into range where it peeled away from his crimson arm. Straining to rotate my eyes, I slowly brought into focus the right gunner peering out from his lacerated face.

I apprehensively flexed each limb of my body in sequence, much like switching on lights room by room. All of me turned except for my left forearm. This seemed more than reasonable because my hand was a mess. My neck throbbed like a bass drum when I attempted to turn it, and blood dripped on my flak jacket from somewhere. Dennis was nowhere to be seen.

Struggling to stand, Topper began to yell, not particularly noisily but with conviction. He hoisted himself out of the fighting compartment onto the rear deck, rolled over, and fell into the brush with a thud. Holding his dangling arm to his side, he ran in a limping but resolute manner toward the medics.

The right gunner rallied, grasped his M60, and began to fire furiously, although it was unlikely that he could see much from behind his sliced-up face. After a few rounds, he shot away one of the radio aerials, shrugged, and followed Topper to the rear. Dennis was still among the missing. The invincible A66 was, like me, a helpless spectator.

Smoke curling out of the turret and a scarred gun-shield on Sergeant Foreman's Sheridan explained our helpless condition. An RPG had landed squarely in the center of his machine gun's shield, punching a hole through it and exploding his upper body. A brave man, operating in a racially ambivalent time and place, had repeatedly risked his life on our behalf, and finally had lost.

The rocket that had disintegrated Foreman and immobilized A66 also had knocked out the ACAV on his far side and sprayed shrapnel among the grunts nearby. With three tracks and the adjacent infantry silent, the center of the line was in grave jeopardy. Soon the alert enemy would pour fire through the gaping hole created by the unfortunate rocket. The incoming would fall not only upon our vehicles, but also upon the unprotected infantry, the injured Charlie Company, and the casualty collection point directly behind us.

These images drifted listlessly through my mind to merge with some immensely distant recollection of duty and personal obligation to the men. There was no seasoned second-in-command among the cavalry platoon leaders who would be able to handle three company-sized units in a desperate battle, the two infantry captains on the field knew little about armor, and the senior officers circling overhead could do nothing for us on the ground.

Senselessly ignoring the still-functional M60s, I stood up to full height near the left gun-shield, groggily drew my dependable .45, and aimed the ineffectual pistol at the area from which the RPG had come. I squeezed off one round into the green fog, and then another and another. The shots filled the dead space, their effect unknown. Yet, for the moment, no more rockets shattered the pistol-punctuated silence. The magazine emptied. I stood, awaiting the inevitable.

Jim Armer, comprehending our desperate situation, unexpectedly ran from his position in the underbrush to Sergeant Foreman's tank. He struggled onto its rear deck and leaned over the turret, grasped the bloody .50-caliber machine gun handles, and began hosing down the jungle. Jim had fired only a few rounds when Dennis' head bobbed up unsteadily from his cupola. He blinked his bulging eyes, pointed to his neck, and asked wordlessly in the reviving din what was wrong. With blood leaking from the back of his neck, he didn't look too fit, but my dreamy smile reassured him and he leaned into the .50. Now two machine guns clattered.

Jim soon ran out of ammunition in the tray or jammed his weapon. Not knowing how to solve either problem, he fired several magazines from his rifle, and then jumped down from the tank. He probably moved some of his grunts up to replace the newly wounded and re-establish a base of friendly fire in the center of the line. By this time, Dennis and I, mostly by instinct, had the guns in our track going, and the ACAV on the other side of Foreman's Sheridan got back into the fight. A66's bandaged gunners returned a little later and relieved us of our frantic, three-armed exertions. Gutierrez cleared the area in contention with his main gun.

It seemed almost as though the attack on Sergeant Foreman had been the tactical climax. An unaccustomed silence began to spread, along with the deepening shadows, across the battlefield. Our ammunition supply approached a level that could not long sustain the troop, and replenishment remained impossible. Enemy flanking forces to the left effectively contained our advance, and we still had no way to evacuate casualties.

The only rational course of action was to attempt to disengage and fight our way back to the previous night's defensive position.

Of course, we had been surrounded at last report, so the success of a withdrawal was problematic. My comprehension of our perilous situation slowly floated toward full consciousness as I found myself on the radio requesting permission to withdraw and, apparently, helping to direct the air strikes.

Field mechanics and crews swarmed over those tracks that had taken hits, attempting to restart them. Others were towed off line so that repairs could take place away from the continuing sporadic fire. Exercising good field judgment, the mechanics cannibalized essential parts from two vehicles that obviously were finished. One of these was A34, a shattered wreck wedged, immobile, between two trees.

I instructed Bob Henderson, the 3rd Platoon leader, to strip the hulk of its armament, ammunition, and valuable parts. He dismounted to supervise men swarming around the permanently lodged track as they wrenched equipment free from mountings, dragged it the few feet to a waiting ACAV, and heaved it aboard. The carcass would be left for the aircraft to destroy after our departure, a mission at which they might be more successful than they had been in their attempts to demolish enemy bunkers.

As we began the slow disengagement, incoming fire slackened further, and I was able to disconnect from the life-sustaining radios and climb down carefully from the faithful A66. After prudently cleaning myself up enough to be presentable, I picked a path over to Bob and his toiling men. My route crossed a forest junkyard through which a herd of bulldozers seemed to have run amok. Shattered trees, scarred ground, crushed bunkers and trenches, discarded ammunition cans, and assorted junk lay everywhere. In the midst of the disorder, the inexperienced lieutenant did a speedy job on A34, standing next to the collapsed rear ramp and pointing out items he wanted pried loose. Standing still, however, was an error. Just as I scuttled up to him in that crablike posture we quickly learned, Bob's face assumed a perplexed expression and he sank to the ground.

Kneeling at his side while the men continued to slash at the carcass of the A34, I rolled up the jungle fatigue trousers through which he was bleeding.

Several lacerations, none spewing blood, meant that he had picked up only some shrapnel. No problem, if the rate of leakage didn't increase before his blood clotted.

"I'm okay, sir. We should be done in about five." Insisting on rising under his own power, although unsteadily, Bob hobbled to the far side of A34. The more experienced of his men had been working there all along.

During a sunset invisible through the towering trees, we finally started all vehicles except for the abandoned A34 and A18, which was rigged for towing. The bruised line of armor backed across the battlefield, which had been so costly to gain, frontal slopes and weaponry always oriented in the direction of the now-silent enemy. Not surprisingly, there were few NVA casualties visible on the field as we inched away. The enemy commander had executed an orderly and effective withdrawal within a well-prepared defensive position that was far larger than any I had previously experienced.

"Flange two-nine, this is Rider two-nine," I reported. "I'm ready to move out the advance element now. Can we get any light for the trip?" Overhead aircraft or artillery flare illumination would be necessary within minutes unless we fancied the suicidal technique of turning on our headlights for the return journey, assuming any headlights had survived the firefight.

"Rider two-nine, wilco, out."

"Two-six, this is six. Listen up. Move your tracks out on the route we came in on. If you see anything at all suspicious, shoot it up big time. Be careful. They're out there. When you get through and after you've moved about three hundred meters, all the way back past that bombed out area, toss some smoke and contact me. Also, I've been hit. I'm okay"—just like Bob Henderson—"but if you don't hear me on the horn for a while, you're in charge."

"This is two-six. I'll get through. On the way." Mike Healey, with the least bloodied platoon, could best deal with the ambush likely to await us down the trail. Driving straight into it, he might be able to smash his way through and clear the path for the rest of us. There was the scant possibility of busting a new trail through the jungle after dark.

The casualties were distributed among the remaining tracks as quickly as their pain allowed. Insufficient time remained for the medics to segregate the dead from the wounded, and both were crowded haphazardly on the vehicles nearest the aid station. Alpha and Charlie companies' soldiers swarmed aboard, rending the cavalry vehicles' weapons inoperable and covering the ammunition stacked on the ACAV's floors.

"Rider, this is Racer. We're all loaded up."

"Six, this is one-six. I'm ready to go."

"Six, this is three-six. Me too."

From the rear deck of A66, Jim grabbed my flak jacket and nodded. He was ready to pull out also.

"One-six, this is six. I'm afraid you're last. Make a lot of racket when the rest of us move, and throw some smoke out for the choppers. Give us a couple of minutes, and then come out as fast as you can. Good luck."

"This is one-six. No sweat."

The tracks began their ponderous exit from the field. We were completely at the mercy of the NVA if the 2nd Platoon could not break out. Had the expected mines been planted and trees felled across our exit route? Was the killing zone covered with automatic weapons and grenadiers? The minutes passed as the burdened troop pursued the 2nd Platoon. No firing echoed down the trail after Mike's initial bursts when his tracks first pulled out.

"Rider, this is Flange two-nine. I've got your rear in sight, also the point. But where're you? Get out some smoke so we can cover you, huh?" A note of irritation intruded into the battalion commander's voice.

"This is Rider. Wilco." I switched over to the intercom. "Hey, Dennis, did you get that? How about throwing a few?" Without turning, probably because his neck wouldn't pivot, Dennis unhooked two of our last smoke grenades from a strap securing them to the side of his cupola armor. He dropped the two fizzing olive soup cans over the side. With a gentle pop lost in the roar of the engines, the artillery forward observer's track behind us was wreathed in yellow tendrils of smoke.

Acknowledging our signal, Conrad made reassuring sounds over the radio.

"Six, this is two-six. You won't believe this! It's clear here. Repeat, clear all the way out." Mike's voice expressed joy first and then relief. If he'd fully understood the risk his platoon had just run, the sequence might have been reversed.

"Roger . . ." Was it possible that the enemy commander hadn't thought to impede our withdrawal? Were his forces insufficient to defend the bunker complex and hold us in the trap simultaneously? Was he hurt too badly to pursue? Or had he begun to move out toward Cambodia while we were preparing to return southward? Randomness too complex to contemplate just now.

But the 1st Platoon was in the barrel again! Willie McNew reported that a recoilless rifle had opened up on him. One round slammed into the deserted turret of A18 under tow, and McNew dropped the line to return fire with his main gun.

"Six, this is one-six. You've got a choice. Old 18's back there and it's going to cost plenty to go back and get it. It's stripped and there ain't nothing left on it. Can we leave it?"

The canny McNew was probably lying about completely stripping A18. There had not been time. But he was unquestionably correct about the probable cost of retrieving the hulk. Required decision: Did the 1st Squadron's tradition of salvaging every vehicle justify risking the 1st Platoon? And how would we react if the 1st Platoon and its cargo of infantry and casualties were surrounded while trying to retrieve A18? Decisions were still difficult to make. I hesitated.

"All right, one-six. Dump it," no need to instruct the 1st Platoon to hurry. The sounds of the racing engine in the background while Willie was on the air told me that they hadn't paused after their brief firefight. It occurred to me that our rear element might have encountered the anticipated ambush in a formative stage after we had slipped through the noose.

Overhead, Lieutenant Colonel Conrad and his staff, with some help from me, directed the air cover on our flanks and attempted to destroy the two vehicles left on the field. Down among the trees, it was growing difficult to see and the drivers soon would have to halt if aerial illumination were not forthcoming. But the 1st and 3rd Platoons did use what little sunlight was left to close on the lead element.

"Flange two-nine, this is Rider. Have we got any light yet?"

"Not yet, Rider, how many minutes can you move without illumination?"

"This is Rider. Not long. Let's see if our mortars can shoot some for us. We'll keep you advised." It would never do to shoot down the battalion commander with an errant illumination round. "Roger. Out."

With four kilometers of jungle to traverse, we were dead in the water unless, and only unless, the remnant of the troop's shattered mortar section back at the night defensive position came through. Undoubtedly, they had at least a few parachute flare rounds remaining in the one undamaged mortar track salvaged from the flames the night before by the desperate driver. Whether the mortar crew could compute, arm, and fire a mission after the previous night's debacle I didn't know.

"Rider control, this is six. Did you monitor?" Seege was sure to be on all frequencies back at the night defensive position, and I was too tired to repeat all those words again. I assumed the night defensive position was still there because we hadn't heard about it or from it all afternoon.

"Roger," Seege answered at once on the troop frequency. "He's right here."

The raspy voice of Sergeant Smolich, the mortar section chief, came up. "Where are you, six?"

"We're a little less than a quarter of the way home and hurting. Can you shoot us some light?" It was impossible to read a map so as to provide our current location by checkpoint. Besides, the map case was buried somewhere in the bowels of A66.

"Yeah, we can, six. Sure."

"Okay, do it ASAP. Post the air data from there." I flipped to the higher command frequency.

"Flange two-nine, this is Rider. Better to get some altitude. They'll call in the air data, but your guess is as good as anyone's where they'll shoot."

"I'll take care of things up here, Rider." Godlike confidence.

The swaying interior of A66 was a dark jumble of bodies, most of them quiet, but a few making noises that no one wished to notice. The upper deck of the track was covered with infantrymen, as crowded as a lifeboat at sea and just as defenseless. Only our constant companions in the jungle, discomfort and pain, kept me alert, and on the radio; morphine, so temptingly available from the medics, was never an option.

"This is two-six. We can't see a thing up front, six. Do you want me to hold up?" Seconds passed, then in slow motion the back of Dennis' steel cupola hatch seemed somehow lighter. Within moments, it was possible to distinguish the individual casualties lying below my legs in the shadows of the fighting compartment. The men littering the upper deck of A66 stared overhead, their opened mouths expressing amazement at this unexpected miracle.

"This is six. Drop two hundred and fire for effect. Keep one up as long as it lasts. Drop one hundred every three minutes or so and stay on top of Flange control for that light ship. Outstanding."

"Thanks. We've got about an hour of stuff, six. Out." Nothing further was required between us.

But the welcome illumination also revealed the desperation of our condition. Dennis and the worn-out gunners slumped over their gun-shields. The grunts looked worse. Only the less thoroughly beaten down Marty was in motion as he manhandled A66 down the dim alleyway through the jungle. One thrown vehicular track on A66 or any other vehicle on the narrow trail, and the whole operation would grind to a halt.

If there exists a merciful providence for the helpless, then we must have qualified, for we passed through the jungle unmolested. With little warning, the troop broke into the relative safety of the clearing surrounding the night defensive position. Jim and I stared at each other aboard A66. He shook his head. I couldn't understand how we had done it either. For a few moments, we sat together quietly, then Alpha Company began to move into the wood line to secure our position. Jim lowered himself wordlessly to the ground and, linked by the umbilical cord of the communications handset leading to his radioman, was swallowed up in the dusty gloom.

The ACAVs discharged their grisly cargoes as each vehicle exited from the last of the forest. As long as the supply of stretchers lasted, the injured were placed upon them. After that, medics pressed ponchos into service. The dead were segregated to one side. More than an hour of dusty relays would be necessary before the medevacs were finished.

In the faint light provided by the aerial illumination, the haggard crews returned their vehicles to the well-worn defensive perimeter and set about cleaning their filthy tracks, replenishing basic loads and breaking down weapons, another testimonial to self-imposed discipline and good sense. There may even have been something to eat.

In its turn, A66 dropped its rear ramp near the choppers as the medical personnel rushed over to haul away our casualties. The troop executive officer, 1st Lt. Paul Baerman, appeared to have the evacuation well in hand, so I removed my CVC helmet and, without thinking, shoved myself over the side of the track. The mortar section chief caught me before my legs completely collapsed and set me back upon my feet. Guided only by habit, I began to walk unsteadily through the maze of struggling medics in the direction of the M577. About halfway there, Conrad emerged from the shadows. As we approached each other, he held out his arms and wrapped them around me.

Charlie Company was home.

CHAPTER FIVE

COLD WAR (1947–1991)

///MAJ. JAMES D. BROWN (U.S. ARMY)

For most Americans, the Cold War conjures up visions of air force bomber crews sitting strip alert beside B-52s armed with live thermonuclear weapons. It could also be of navy crews drinking endless cups of coffee while they cruised silently beneath the waves in "boomers" full of ballistic missiles, any one of which could deliver more destructive power than had been unleashed in all of World War II. For most, however, Elvis Presley starring in the movie *G.I. Blues* colors their visions of the army during the Cold War. Elvis' days seemed to have been spent in crisp khakis, and his nights occupied with singing impromptu songs in the *gasthausen* of post-war Germany. I was later assigned to the same tank battalion in which the real-life Elvis served, and my recollections of service in the U.S. Army diverge a bit.

These are recollections of a war in which no shots were fired, no battles fought, no territory gained. Although few writers will find it worthy of a book or a movie script, it is nonetheless a story of hard work and devotion to duty that saw America through the perilous post–World War II era.

The story of my journey as a tanker begins in ROTC summer camp at Fort Lewis, Washington. With Vietnam nearly at its peak, all the army's eyes were on unconventional warfare in Asia, and the highest aspiration of most cadets was to become a steely-eyed, flat-bellied military machine wearing the insignia of an Airborne Ranger Special Forces soldier. So it was on one hot dusty morning that I found myself part of a cadet infantry company in a forced approach march down a dusty tank trail. We were carrying everything we would need for a three-day tactical problem to include M14 rifles and a limited supply of blank ammo. I was six feet, four inches tall and 190 pounds, which meant in the eyes of my cadet platoon leader that I wouldn't find it that much tougher to carry the M1919A6 Browning .30-caliber machine gun in addition to my rifle. He would have been right, except for three minor facts; the trusty World War II relic weighed about forty pounds; it was made of stamped steel parts whose edges cut into your neck and shoulder as you carried it, and even worse, the thing didn't even have a blank adapter or ammo, so you didn't even get the satisfaction of firing the thing once the action started.

Part of the approach march led us down a dusty tank trail. The dust had the consistency of cake flour and was ankle deep, so even our foot-slogging passage stirred up eye-stinging clouds. We were overtaken by a platoon of National Guard M48 tanks, en route to support our attack. The tanks stirred up dust much more efficiently than our boots, and as an additional bonus, we got to suck up some diesel fumes along with significant quantities of the state of Washington. As one tank passed, a metallic cylinder tossed from it landed in the dust between me and the next man ahead. My first thought was, *Great, a tear gas grenade to add to the training realism. Now we get to do this in a protective mask.* Before I could reach down for my NBC (nuclear-biological-chemical) mask, the sun glinted off the cylinder to reveal an empty can of Olympia beer, still enrobed in glistening beads of condensation. I looked up to see the tank commander who had thrown it reaching back into a cooler for another. Time stands still at such moments, and even through the haze of forty-odd years, I recall the scene as clearly as if it were yesterday. In addition to the cooler, the tank's bustle rack also contained a folding beach chair, a barbecue grill, and a sack of charcoal briquettes.

At that moment, I was bathed in an intense white light and received an epiphany as real as that experienced by St. Paul on the road to Damascus. A voice came from above saying, "Jim, I have sent you this sign to show that I have chosen you to be a tanker." I fervently replied, "Thy will be done," and never regretted it through the rest of my army career.

I requested armor as my first branch choice, and on commissioning day pinned on my lieutenant's bars and a set of armor branch insignia. First Sergeant Ralph Bosellet, the top NCO of the ROTC unit, was waiting after the commissioning ceremony. It was the custom of the day for newly minted officers to give a dollar to the first NCO who saluted them. I therefore had a silver dollar ready in my pocket as I approached him. After the ceremonial exchange, he told me, "Congratulations on becoming a tanker, and congratulations on your initial assignment to Germany. You're going to love it there."

After the armor officer basic course, I headed for an assignment to the 3rd Armored Division in Germany. It wasn't long before I discovered that First Sergeant Bosellet had either seen too many Elvis Presley movies, or he had an extremely subtle sense of humor. The title *G.I. Blues* took on an ironic savor as the reality of the army's situation in Cold War Europe sank in. Budgets had been cut back to pay for Vietnam, so everything from fuel to repair parts was hard to come by. My battalion was fortunate to have a paved motor pool, when others less fortunate did their maintenance in the mud. The barracks in which we lived went up before electricity and indoor plumbing, and the resulting hodge-podge of utilities was unreliable. The thick stone walls of the battalion classroom still had built-in mangers for the horses that were its original occupants.

Both officers and NCOs were being promoted rapidly, as Vietnam casualties and low re-enlistment rates created vacancies. Consequently, most leaders (myself not excepted) were inexperienced. One of my ROTC instructors was a major with five years of service. I made captain after two years of service. Selected high achievers in advanced individual training were sent directly to NCO academies; honor graduates of the so-called "Shake 'n Bake" schools were promoted to staff sergeants with a little more than a year of service. The senior NCOs, those who had achieved their rank before Vietnam, were truly the backbone of the army. They dealt with officers and junior NCOs who were learning their jobs on the fly, with bare-boned resource levels and a largely reluctant body of conscript soldiers.

By far the worst problem facing both officers and NCOs was that the social ills of America in the 1960s were reflected in the predominantly draftee troops. This generation had been raised on bumper stickers that read "Question Authority" and "Don't Trust Anyone over Thirty." Draftees served a two-year enlistment. The first four months or so were basic training and advanced individual training, and an individual was ineligible for assignment to Vietnam if he had less than thirteen months left on his enlistment. That left a window of scarcely seven months of productive time, during which a soldier was subject to reassignment to Vietnam. Every last soldier kept a mental calendar of how many days remained during his window of eligibility. Once Vietnam was no longer a possibility, most started a short-timer calendar, which counted their days remaining in the army. Nowadays, when civilian friends ask me whether I think the army will go back to the draft, they get a heartfelt laugh.

Although the troops listened to Country Joe and the Fish, Joan Baez, and Crosby, Stills, Nash & Young singing about how great it would be if everybody just loved one another and there would then be no more wars, the Russians were tuned to a different frequency. The 8th Guards Combined Arms Army sat across the Iron Curtain from us, and they were definitely not part of the Woodstock Generation. At best, we could hope to be outnumbered by only eight to one. That meant that our battalion needed to kill the better part of a Soviet tank division in order to survive. These were the days when the United States did not enjoy absolute air superiority and our motor pools were only about a ten-minute flight from the border in a Russian fighter-bomber. Had World War III started as a conventional ground combat without warning, the Russian bombers would have gotten to our motor pools before we did. We pretended that we would have advanced warning, and so ran through endless alerts intended to allow us to get into our wartime dispersal areas. We pretty much knew, however, that any real move of American forces during a time of heightened tension would have resulted in a road-clogging exodus of the German population. If there ever was a truer example of the definition of the army as "the unqualified leading the unwilling to accomplish the unnecessary," it was the U.S. Army in Europe during the Cold War.

My personal wake-up call came at a predawn formation when I received the guide-on signifying command of Alpha Company, 3rd Battalion, 32nd Armor from the battalion commander, Lt. Col. William Jewell. After nineteen months of commissioned service, I found myself ankle deep on a snowy parade ground with the weight of the world (specifically seventeen tanks and eighty soldiers) on my shoulders. It wasn't that others hadn't borne heavier responsibilities, it was that I hadn't enough experience to prepare for this one. Because the army gave one the chance to "be all that you can be" long before that was a recruiting slogan, I took the guide-on as a twenty-three-year-old first lieutenant and resolved to make good the faith that Lieutenant Colonel Jewell had vested in me. The responsibility really hit home later when I overheard 1st Sgt. Hubert V. Hall begin a meeting of the platoon sergeants with "The Old Man expects . . ." For a moment, I thought he was referring to the battalion commander, but was caught with a chill when I realized that this loyal NCO, who was old enough to be my father, was referring to me. In the many years since, I have learned that you do your best when the motivation is to not let down your brothers in arms.

A few months later, Alpha Company was out in the local training area for a dry-fire gunnery training session. The training ran all day and all the next night, with crews sleeping when they could and the officers and NCOs not sleeping at all. We received our normal resupply at the end of the daylight portion and waited for the twilight to settle in for night training. I was looking over the map of the training area and noticed a dashed line with the German word *mauer* (wall) snaking an irregular trace through the woods. I followed the trace and found a symbol labeled *Romisher tor* (Roman tower). The northern frontier of the Roman Empire had once run through the *Taunus* mountains, and there is a restored Roman fort about thirty kilometers away, so it made sense that this might have been the Roman equivalent of the Iron Curtain. I told the XO and first sergeant that I was going on a recon and would be back before the start of night training.

I stopped the jeep and dismounted where the trace ran across the road. My driver was more interested in sleep than in Roman towers, so he remained with the vehicle. In the gathering gloom, the bare-limbed trees and matted wet leaves made it difficult to find the wall, but I soon found myself walking atop a ridge of dirt only a little more than a foot high and not much wider. The ridge led to the promised tower, an unrestored two-story structure. While the tower roof and the timbers of the second floor had long since decayed away, the walls stood essentially undamaged by nearly two millennia of weather. I stood just outside the tower on the wall, wondering what it would have felt like to be a Centurion, standing astride the wall with one foot in Rome and the other in the land of the barbarians. The parallels to my situation in the twentieth-century U.S. Army in Europe came into focus. Surely, my distant predecessor must have wondered what he was doing in a far-flung and forgotten edge of civilization, keeping barbarians from the gates while his friends were back in Rome enjoying the fruits of security and paying little attention to his sacrifices on their behalf. The bluish caste of twilight painted an almost surreal scene and set the stage for the second epiphany of my life.

The realization struck me that he must have done it out of a sense of . . . duty! Outside the pale of glamour, wealth, and material comforts, true soldiers do it out of a sense of duty! Few men are privileged to be conscious of the moment in which the courses of their lives are set, but at that moment, I ceased being merely "in the army," as one might describe my current occupation, and became a soldier.

Not all of my early experiences as a Cold Warrior were somber and weighty. All soldiers manage to find humor in adversity. Once such example is a sector recon we conducted one Saturday morning. We routinely worked six-day weeks when in garrison, with Saturdays devoted to working on any dead-lined tanks and inspections. On this occasion, the battalion had been left in care of the NCOs while the officers went on a quarterly reconnaissance of our wartime dispersal areas. Ours was near the Fulda Gap, and it was considered inadvisable to draw attention to ourselves by conducting the recon with a large force. Despite having our unit designation boldly stenciled on our bumpers, as a concession to operational security, we took only jeeps and did not travel in convoy. The battalion commander, Lieutenant Colonel Jewell, remained behind to attend the brigade commander's weekly meeting, with plans to join us in sector after the meeting.

The company commanders had agreed to rendezvous at a *gasthaus* on the *hauptstrasse* (main road, but not an *autobahn*) to conduct a "coordination meeting" prior to the arrival of the boss. We had all seen the sector several times before, so we reasoned that there was more benefit to be had from a map recon than from driving around muddy forest roads. Accordingly, when I arrived at the *gasthaus*, I directed my driver to park around back. We ran a radio remote by wire through the back window of the *gasthaus* and sat around the table enjoying the light and warmth, as well as the luxury, of a flat table without rain or wind blowing across it. The German *kaffee mit brotchen* (coffee with rolls) didn't hurt our productivity either. The speaker of the remote set came alive with a call from six (call sign of the battalion commander) to one-six (call sign of the headquarters company commander, Junior Barnes).

"One-six, this is six. What is your location?"

Thinking Lieutenant Colonel Jewell was probably just getting out of the meeting back at the *kaserne*, and therefore about forty-five minutes away, Junior Barnes fudged his location slightly when he encrypted the coordinates of the prospective battalion CP in his reply. There was a slight pause while Lieutenant Colonel Jewell decrypted the coordinates and plotted them on his map.

"One-six, this is six. I'm at those coordinates now, and I don't see you anywhere."

While the rest of us performed a reasonable facsimile of a flock of chickens being flushed out of a coop by a fox, Junior Barnes replied, "Six, this is one-six. I'm not at my present location at this time. ETA at my present location is zero five minutes. Out."

This would have been hilarious at the time, but as the Alpha Company commander (call sign two-six), I knew before the radio crackled what the next call would be: "Two-six, this is six. What is your location?"

"Six, this is two-six. I'm not at my present location, either, but I'm closer than one-six is. ETA is zero four minutes. Out."

We all thought Jewell to be a hard SOB at the time, but he had the wisdom to figure that neither three-six nor four-six was likely to be at their present locations, either, so the conversation ended. No word was ever mentioned of this, save that in future situations where someone was not in the right place at the right time, members of 3/32 Armor were likely to hear a sheepishly murmured "I'm not at my present location at this time. Out."

The Cold War is a memory for most soldiers now serving. More people can name the Beatles than can name the Soviet premier of the era. The Soviet Union collapsed not under force of arms, but under its own weight, and the Russians are no longer our enemy. Most of the M60 tanks we kept honed to a razor's edge in anticipation of combat in Central Europe are now fish reefs or (ironically) razor blades. There are still a few of them around, though, as well as a few people who remember that the Cold War was the longest continuous military struggle in American history.

When I visit Jacques Littlefield's tank collection, there's a tank there with the same bumper number as the one that carried me and my bride from our wedding in the Friedberg post chapel to our reception. When I see these old tanks, I see not just the rubber and steel, but the crews who worked so hard to keep them ready. Men, who can rightly claim to have won the Cold War, offer as evidence of their victory only the fact that there was no war.

///MAJ. JAMES M. WARFORD (U.S. ARMY)

My relationship with tanks began when I was six years old, when I received a remote-controlled toy tank for Christmas. No one knew it at the time, but it was love at first sight. Some kids like trains, some like cars; I loved tanks. This love affair continued through my grade school years and followed me into high school. It was there that I realized the army was my destiny, and some research led me to the army ROTC. Upon graduation from college, I received a commission as a second lieutenant. Off I went to the armor school at Fort Knox, Kentucky, for the armor officer basic course. It was there that I had my first real experience with tanks and knew I had chosen the right path for my life. Every morning at 6 a.m., approximately thirty tanks used to support the training activates of the armor school would rumble directly past my bachelor officer's quarters bedroom window; it was music to my ears.

After graduation from the armor officer basic course, I went on to become a tank platoon leader in West Germany, with a platoon of six M60 tanks of two different versions. Although it was a good unit with good soldiers, we were unaware of the challenges facing us from across the East German border. In a situation similar to what faced American tank crews in World WarII, the Soviets, like the Germans decades earlier, had developed and fielded tanks that were superior to our own. The Soviet T64A premium tank mounted a 125mm smoothbore main gun, which made our 105mm main gun seem small by comparison. In addition, the new Soviet tank boasted superior mobility and armor protection compared to our M60 tanks.

The composite armor on the T64A premium tank made it virtually impenetrable to our 105mm main guns, and the M392A2 and M728 armor-piercing discarding sabot (APDS) ammunition we carried. Unfortunately, those higher up the chain of command rarely acknowledged this fact. To make matters even worse, the armor-piercing fin stabilized discarding sabot (APFSDS) ammunition fired by the T-64A's 125mm main gun would easily penetrate the conventional armor protecting my M60 tanks.

Like the Soviet army, the U.S. Army continued to improve its tanks, and in 1981, my platoon received a brand new version of the M60 tank, designated the M60A3 TTS. The letters TTS stood for tank thermal sight. Besides the thermal sight for the gunner, it also came with a laser rangefinder. While these new features did much to improve the lethality of the M60A3 TTS tank over the earlier versions of the same tank, we still lacked a main gun and ammunition that could deal with the problem of the T64A Premium's superior armor protection. This became an even more serious issue, when in 1981, the Soviets fielded a newer version of the T64 tank, designated the T64B Premium tank. It brought with it, among other improvements, significantly improved armor protection over that protecting the T64A Premium tank.

To deal with this problem of heavily armored Soviet tanks, American tank crews got the more capable M735 and M774 APFSDS ammunition as we continued to react to continued Soviet tank innovations and improvements. These U.S. Army improvements, however, still fell short, and the T64A Premium tank along with its stable mate the T64B Premium tank continued to reign supreme. Finally, in 1983, the U.S. Army fielded the new M833 APFSDS ammunition that gave the 105mm-armed M60A3 TTS and new M1 Abrams tanks the ability to defeat the armor of the T64A and T64B Premium tanks. Had the "balloon gone up" and the Cold War turned hot in the years between the forward deployment of the Soviet T64A Premium tank in September 1976, and the fielding of the M833 APFSDS round in 1983, the Soviets would have had an advantage on the battlefield that may have been unrecoverable.

I returned to West Germany for my second tour overseas in September 1985, as the commander of an M1 Abrams–equipped tank company. In my eyes, the situation couldn't have been better; I had the best soldiers in the world, manning the best tanks in the world. If our mission was to help receive the remainder of III Corps as they deployed in preparation for war against the Warsaw Pact or to attack east to break through Soviet and East German forces, to relieve a surrounded West Berlin, I was confident and ready to go hunting for Bear (a nickname for the Soviet army).

I first saw the M1 Abrams while firing tank gunnery at Grafenwöhr with my platoon of M60A3 (TTS) tanks. The M1s came from the famous 11th Armored Cavalry Regiment (ACR), and they were simply awesome. The inevitable comparison between these two tanks only confirmed what we had been hearing all along. The M60A3 (TTS), with the huge exception of the tank thermal sight and laser rangefinder–fed fire control system, was in many ways, a modernized World War II tank. In all the years since World War II, the design characteristics of U.S. tanks truly hadn't changed much. This unfortunate situation changed with the design, development, and deployment of the M1 Abrams.

As the Cold War dragged on, the capabilities of the M1 and the impact it had on how the U.S. Army would fight its wars simply became legend. In it's first REFORGER (REturn of FORces to GERmany) appearance in West Germany, the M1 rightly earned the nickname Whispering Death because the tank's 1,500-horsepower AVCO Lycoming AGT-1500 gas turbine engine was quiet enough to allow U.S. armored forces to sneak up on surprised opposing force defenders. The M1 actually gave U.S. Army commanders the ability to think outside the box. In one case, the M1s high road speed persuaded one tank battalion commander to consider modifying his unit's combat plan to include his M1 tanks, literally jumping over the many canals that characterized his defensive sector. While this plan never happened, the fact that it was even considered speaks volumes about what this new tank brought to the battlefield.

///COL. JOHN BLUMENSON (U.S. ARMY)

From 1986 to 1990, I served as an armor officer in West Germany. For eighteen of those months, I was the commander of Company D, 3rd Battalion, 35th Armored Regiment of the 3rd Brigade and the 1st Armored Division. The 1st Armored Division at that time was centered around the city of Nuremburg, and we defended the approaches from Czechoslovakia into West Germany.

A tank company at the time consisted of three tank platoons, each of four M1A1 Abrams tanks, so I had twelve tanks broken down into three platoons. Each platoon was commanded by a lieutenant with NCOs and enlisted soldiers to fill out the tanks. I also had a tank for myself plus another one for my executive officer, a lieutenant.

The major functions a tanker must always carry out are to be able to move, to shoot, and to communicate. Our communications equipment always had to be working; we had to know various codes. Even though we had encryption devices on the tanks at that time, as they do today, they were earlier generations and we could talk freely. But still we used call signs and brevity to reduce our electronic communication signals.

We trained hard in our gunnery skills, the shooting part. An American tank crew on average would fire, I would guess, between 150 to 200 main gun rounds per year in gunnery-training exercises. We went to an intensive, scored training exercise once every six months and fired thousands of rounds of machine-gun ammunition from our 7.62 machine guns and our .50-caliber guns as well.

We also did maneuver exercises in Hohenfels, Germany, which was a large training area. These were evaluated, as well, force on force; they were tough, extreme exercises, and the army did its best to prepare us for combat and the hardships associated with that training.

Going back to the gunnery, as we were prepared to fire all these main gun rounds, each crew would spend up to forty hours prior to firing in what was called the unit conduct of fire trainer, or UCOFT. This was a computerized turret simulator, and we went through hundreds of engagements;

different types of scenarios firing at multiple tanks, single tank, aircraft, dismounted troops, trucks, armored personnel carriers, and on and on. We were evaluated on how we did on our fire commands, on the techniques we were employing, and it could get stressful inside those turret trainers.

Additionally, they also had networks of vehicle simulators where a platoon could actually maneuver. Now, this was in the late 1980s, mind you, so the technology was limited compared to a simple video game or PlayStation of today. Still, I would say that in 1988, our simulators and the computer graphics we had were probably as good as late 1990s video games; so it was good.

We focused heavily on our shooting skills in day and at night and weather was never an issue for us, because of the thermal sights on the tanks. We could see through just about anything—day, night, cold, hot, dust. So, I've talked about the communications, I've talked about shooting, and the next part was the maneuvering.

We trained for maneuvering, but that was also a key part in our general defensive position (GDP) mission; that's why we were there. We were there to defend the integrity of the West German border. Our positions were located in an area that was one kilometer from the Czech border. We were facing east, obviously, and to our north approximately forty kilometers was the East German border. Bavaria, for those who might not be familiar with the geography, was a large bulge along the Czech border. To our north was actually East Germany, so we had our primary adversary coming from the east, the Czech and Soviet forces, and to our north we had to be worry that we might be flanked by East German and Soviet forces, if war broke out.

We were confident in our systems, our equipment, and our crew training. I once read a quote from a Soviet officer when I was in graduate school, which would have been 1991. He said, "The difference between American tankers and Soviet tankers is that when American tankers go to the field, they practice their war-fighting skills. When Soviet tankers go to the field, we pick potatoes." So, we did not go to the field to do anything other than train to fight. Again, our crews fired lots of ammunition in training, and I think it's safe to say we would have done considerable damage to any forces that would have breached the border.

That said, our numbers were limited: we had the 1st Armored Division, the 3rd Armored Division, the 3rd Infantry Division, the 2nd Armored Cavalry Regiment, the 11th Armored Cavalry Regiment, the 8th Infantry Division, part of the 2nd Armored Division, and part of the 1st Infantry Division. We also had separate corps artillery regiments, logistics, and medical—the whole nine yards. About two hundred thousand troops, I recall, were stationed over there.

We also did missions called border augmentation missions, which were generally eight weeks in duration where we would occupy and patrol along the Czech border. In my particular company's case, our mission was to serve as a trip wire against any breaches of Warsaw Pact forces or to protect any one fleeing those countries. If they came across the border and we were able to sequester them, we'd provide them protection from pursuing police or military forces.

Going back to our general defensive position missions, again I'm confident that we would have inflicted a large number of casualties on enemy forces. However, that said, being up on the front line right at the border, our chances of long-term survival were not real good. We expected to fight in a dirty environment, meaning chemical, nuclear, and biological. The forces behind us were part of my own organic battalion and brigade in the division and German army forces, as well. We often forget that the German army had an equal number of tanks and personnel carriers. If we had to pass back through our lines, we were certain that we would have suffered some friendly fire incidents if, in fact, we were able to get out from where we were.

We had an opportunity after the Wall came down and the borders opened up in 1990 to go into Czechoslovakia and visit, and then drive back on the main freeway or autobahn through my own defensive positions. I can tell you that we had some decent defensive positions.

It just reinforces the fact that we could have inflicted serious damage to the Warsaw Pact countries.

As far as life during the Cold War in Germany, we had our tanks uploaded with the main-gun ammunition; we had our machine guns on board the tanks all the time in the turret in the motor pool. We did not keep the butt plates or the firing pins with the weapons, though we did keep them locked in our arms room.

When we had alerts, we would draw our personal weapons out of the arms room, get up to the tanks and fire them up, then do a precombat check; we had ninety minutes to be ready to move out of the motor pool. We could have done it in much less time. Our personal gear was always loaded on the tanks ready to go. We did maintenance on the vehicles every week. Prefire checks were performed constantly, so all we really had to do was get everybody in, get up on the vehicles, do some basic things, and move out.

We would then move to an area, and this was not just my unit, all units would move to an area called a local dispersion (LDP) area, where they would get their machine-gun ammunition, additional rations, and some additional POL products, and from there they would go to their general defensive positions and prepare to meet the enemy.

We did not think that there would ever be a massive surprise attack. There were just too many sensors and too many eyes on the east to be fully surprised, though we did think that something could happen as soon as maybe a week. That left a big problem for all of the family members in West Germany. The family members in our area potentially could have been cut off during the time of war, even though they did noncombatant evacuation order (NEO) exercises. My own family had a plan that they would hunker down in the cellar of our home, which was in a small village, and we just had to take it from there.

As the Cold War thawed and relations with the east improved, we began having visits from Soviet forces to our training exercises. In the summer of 1989, as I recall, we were doing a gunnery exercise at

Grafenwöhr, Germany, which is the main gunnery-training base, and the commanding general of Soviet Forces Germany and his staff came out to one of our ranges. I was not firing that day. I was going to be there the next day.

My company was in maintenance, so I went out to the range to provide support for my fellow company commander and his team, who was out there firing. The first two crews to fire in the morning were a lieutenant platoon leader, second lieutenant—as a tank commander—and on a parallel course on the same range was his platoon sergeant. They went downrange and fired a perfect score, which is difficult by any stretch of the imagination. They hit every target they shot at, the first time. At one point, one of the vehicles had some type of mechanical failure two kilometers from the base line, so they were what we call downrange; they had a problem. The crew repaired the problem, and then again, I don't remember what it was, it took maybe twenty to thirty minutes, all while they continued to engage their targets. When they came back, those two crews were debriefed. The Soviet general, their equivalent of a four-star general, awarded those two crews—eight soldiers—Soviet army tanker badges. I can't tell you how that relates to an American decoration, but it was a huge deal that these American tankers would be awarded these awards by the Soviet general. And the general, I recall his comments were to the effect of how impressed he was and that it would have required higher-level maintenance people to go downrange to fix that one vehicle in the Soviet army and that he had never seen any crews fire that well on any tank gunnery range.

So, again, it's been almost twenty years since that happened, and it's still in my mind. I think the bottom line was that he was impressed with our tankers, the same guys who a year and a half or two years later were fighting in Iraq with the 1st Armored Division, which saw some serious battles with Iraqi Republican Guard units and others. They used the same equipment and the same tactics as the Soviet Union, and I think our forces were able to distinguish themselves quite well on tank-on-tank engagements.

///COL. JOHN ANTAL (U.S. ARMY)

September 25, 1995, at the Multi-Purpose Range Complex in the Chorwon Valley, South Korea: The sky broke and deluged the mountains and narrow valleys with cold rain. The rain seemed to drop in sheets, layers and layers of water beating down on the soldiers, tanks, Bradleys, armored personnel carriers, and trucks that made up the 2nd Infantry Division's Task Force 2-72.

It was another hard day "at the office" along the demilitarized zone of Korea for the soldiers of the task force. In 1995, the threat of war in Korea was real, and today it is still possible that the world is only one decision away from a nightmare war scenario on the Korean peninsula. North Korea maintains the fifth-largest standing army in the world with an estimated 1.08 million armed personnel, compared to about 686,000 South Korean troops, plus 32,500 American troops in South Korea. And even though some of its people are starving, North Korea spends more than 20 percent of the gross national product on the military. The fact remains that all it takes for war to start is for one man, Kim Jong Il, to believe he can win.

The mission of Task Force 2-72 was to, on order, transition to crisis and/or war and deploy to initial positions near the demilitarized zone separating North and South Korea. On order, the task force was to defend or counterattack as part of the 1st Brigade, 2nd Infantry Division, to destroy North Korean People Army (NKPA) forces that crossed the DMZ, and on order conduct offensive operations to complete the destruction of those NKPA forces. The task force was also prepared to conduct force protection operations in support of the 2nd Infantry Division. Task Force 2-72 was called the Dragon Force due to the dragon on the crest of the 72nd Armor Distinguished Unit Insignia and the blending of the term *task force*. It was a name that the members of the task force—which included tankers, infantrymen, engineers, artillerymen, and support troops—were proud of.

Command Sergeant Major Roger Stradley sat in the back seat of my Humvee, watching the rain fall against his windshield. As the commander of Task Force 2-72 Armor, I sat in the front passenger seat. Corporal Stover, my Humvee driver, sat in the driver's seat and tried to stay dry from the drops of water that were plopping down on him from the edge of the door.

The sergeant major and I were almost the same age—the sergeant major was forty-three, and I had just turned forty. Both of us had soldiered all over the world in the past twenty-odd years. Duty in Korea was just one more assignment, and their job was to stare down a fanatical enemy who waited across the wire and mines that designated the DMZ. Although Stradley and I had been together as a command team for only four months, it seemed much longer, and most soldiers agreed that four months in Korea was equal to a year stateside. The pace of training in Korea was frenetic, with tank gunnery, force-on-force maneuver exercises, platoon and company training, and endless hours of talking and leading the troops we loved so much.

No one was talking, as my mood was as foul as the weather. The rain and fog were delaying the execution of the battalion's Table VIII tank gunnery exercise, and I was not happy to be wasting range time.

To break the mood, the sergeant major unzipped his rain jacket, opened the breast pocket of his Nomex uniform, and took out an envelope. The envelope contained pictures of a tactical exercise the Dragon Force had conducted two months earlier. He handed me a stack of three-by-five-inch glossy color photos. I examined the photos one at a time, smiled, and then handed them to Corporal Stover. The photos depicted a dramatic image of an M1A1 tank hanging precariously on the side of a cliff.

How did this tank get into this uncertain position? During this exercise, the task force's M1A1 Abrams tanks practiced defile battle drills down a narrow mountain road. Working hard to train each tank platoon in the tactics of fighting through the narrow mountain passes of Korea, the platoons conducted mock battles against a defending opposing force that occupied defensive positions along the narrow trail. The trail depicted in the photo was about a tank-and-a-half wide. One side of the trail was a high mountain cliff. The other side was a straight drop-off into a deep valley.

The training was going well enough. Each platoon ran the defile fight three times, with the tankers and Bradley crews learning plenty of lessons in the art of restricted terrain combat. The engagements were fought using the multiple integrated laser engagement system (MILES) on every soldier and vehicle. This equipment realistically replicates the effects of the weapon systems and registers casualties to provide an excellent opportunity for force-on-force training. As the tank platoons learned how to fight down the defiles, their tactics improved dramatically, and they often overpowered the dismounted defenders. In some of the battles, the volume of fire was so overwhelming that the opposing force infantry could not raise their heads above their prepared positions without becoming casualties.

After several successful runs, however, one of the tanks drove down the road and the road gave way under the tank's right side. Luckily, the tank came to an abrupt halt before falling completely off the cliff. The sixty-eight-ton Abrams tank clung to the side of the cliff, holding on by only a few road wheels. The rest of the tank was facing downhill. The crew, consisting of a new second lieutenant, a sergeant, and two soldiers, did the right think and quickly got out of the tank. All four crew members were unharmed but visibly shaken by the mishap.

I arrived on the scene a few moments later and radioed for our tank recovery section. The next ten hours were the longest and most difficult tank recovery operation I ever witnessed. We had to recover that tank without anyone getting hurt and, as usual, it was beginning to get dark and, to add insult to injury, it started to rain.

Not a fun situation—the tank was uploaded with about four hundred gallons of flammable JP8 jet engine fuel and forty live 120mm cannon rounds. Many of the 120mm tank rounds contained depleted uranium, so we didn't want them scattered all over the side of a hill in Korea.

I didn't want to lose this tank. Unfortunately, most of the tank was hanging over the cliff and completely blocked vehicle movement to the south. After about twenty minutes, one of our M88A1 recovery vehicles arrived on the north side of the road, and we assessed the recovery operation.

The M88 recovery vehicles at that time were only sixty-three tons, which made them lighter than the tank they are supposed to recover. The experts in the recovery section debated the problem for a while, and then tried to drag out the tank with the single M88 from the north. They first attempted to pull the tank forward. This attempt failed; the tank sunk lower over the cliff, and we almost lost it.

The battalion maintenance chief warrant officer was pretty upset, and the men of the recovery section were all doom and gloom. By then it was pitch dark, raining, and the maintenance chief suggested that we wait until the next day to recover the tank in the daylight. In the meantime, I could hear the sound of rocks trickling down the hill as the side of the mountain began to slowly give way.

It was clear that we were running out of time. If we wanted to save the tank from falling off the cliff, we couldn't wait for morning. If it fell, it would not only destroy the tank and create an ammunition and fuel nightmare, but it would also wreck all our plans for training the task force the next day.

We discussed the options. There was talk of using three M88s to hold the stuck tank in place and a few fantastic remarks about Chinook helicopters or digging the road down with bulldozers. I did not think that the tank would last on the precipice of this hill overnight, so I ended the debate and issued orders. I told the chief maintenance technician to recalculate the recovery requirements and retrieve the tank immediately.

After some further study, the chief outlined a solution requiring three recovery vehicles: one recovery vehicle in the north to hold the tank in place while two other M88s winched the tank up from the southern side of the trail. He planned to drop the M88s' front blades into the trail to brace the recovery vehicles and stop them from slipping off the hill.

Once this was done, we would attach the winch cables from the recovery vehicles to the stuck M1 tank, and then winch the sixty-eight-ton M1 tank up and onto what was left of the trail.

The only problem with this idea was that two M88s would have to drive about twelve miles around the hill to reach the rear (southern side) of the tank. It would take several hours to move and position the tank recovery vehicles, but I was convinced that two M88s using ninety-pound snatch blocks could pull it back over the hill. A snatch block is used with the cable to raise and lower loads and apply tension. It was the only way we could think of not losing the tank.

My team got with the program, and the M88s drove around the mountain and positioned on the trail. Everyone was exhausted by then, but we all knew that time was working against us, so there was no rest for the weary. We calculated that we needed 140 tons of pulling power to move this M1, but we had only 135 tons with the two M88s pulling from the southern side. Nevertheless, we decided to go for it and carefully attached cables and the snatch blocks to the tank.

It took us six long, miserable hours working in the rain with headlights illuminating the area, before we were ready. Two cables were attached at the south end to pull the tank up. One cable was attached at the north end to hold the tank steady. Finally, all was set, and we put the recovery vehicle winches in motion. Then, as the stuck tank began to creak and groan slowly upward with two-thirds of its hull hanging in the air, the clevis connecting one of the southern cables to the tank snapped! The cable swung back with tremendous force and struck the rocky cliff. We had taken precautions to back everyone off, but if anyone had been in the way, he would have been cut in half. At this point, the tank was being held by only one cable. This was the most dangerous part of the operation.

Sixty-seven tons of pulling power was now holding a sixty-eight-ton tank. The tank quivered, but somehow the single cable held. In the white light from the headlights, I could see dirt dancing on the cable from the extreme tension. Fearing the other cable might snap and kill anyone in the range of the wire, we held everyone else back, and the command sergeant major and I took on the mission to reconnect the cable ourselves. We retrieved a new ninety-pound snatch block and struggled to reconnect the cable to the tank. After a bit, we finished the job, while the taut cable to our left held the heavy tank. Once we moved back and got safely out of the way, the maintenance chief gave the order to pull again.

Slowly, the reconnected cable grew taut as the winch on the recovery vehicle pulled with all its power. The tank creaked and groaned again, but this time it began to move. The winches growled—and the tank seemed to stop. Suddenly, it pulled over the cliff and the back end moved close to the M88s. After a few anxious moments, we pulled it up onto the level road.

We were all overjoyed. The recovery crews had worked diligently in tough conditions and pulled the tank out safely without injury to anyone. This was a successful mission and a valuable learning experience. After the tank was safely back on the trail and moving to the assembly area, I smiled and lit up a cigar. After all, it was just another day at the office.

CHAPTER SIX

OPERATION DESERT STORM (1991)

///COL. H. R. MCMASTER (U.S. ARMY)

On February 23, 1991, the 2nd Armored Cavalry Regiment moved into Iraq and initiated its offensive covering force mission forward of General Frederick Franks' VII Corps. The VII Corps' mission was to envelop and defeat the Republican Guard (the elite units of the Iraqi army) from the west. The Iraqi defense was mainly oriented to the south. The Republican Guard was positioned in depth to the north to preserve their freedom to maneuver. Some Republican Guard units were in defensive positions; others were in reserve. To VII Corps' east, the marines reinforced with the 2nd Armored Division's Tiger Brigade attacked to defeat the enemy and advance on Kuwait City. To the west of VII Corps, the XVIII Airborne Corps attacked deep to cut enemy egress routes and trap the enemy. Once the Iraqis detected our effort to envelop and destroy their army in Kuwait with the VII and XVIII Airborne Corps, elements of the Republican Guard, including the Tawakalna Division, reoriented to the west.

As an offensive covering force, the 2nd Armored Cavalry Regiment led the attack to ease the forward movement of the corps, prevent its premature deployment into fighting, defeat enemy units within its capability, and develop the enemy situation. Once the regiment located the Republican Guard defensive positions, we would determine where the enemy was strong and isolate that strength, find or create weakness, and pull the divisions into the fight under advantageous conditions. Our troop was only one small part of that regimental operation, an operation that ultimately located the boundary between the Republican Guard and the mechanized divisions of the Iraqi army. Our troop's fight and other engagements gave the corps commander the information he wanted before he committed a "fist" of heavy divisions that were moving behind the cavalry.

On the first day, we traveled only about twenty kilometers into Iraq, and then waited for the divisions to close behind us. F Troop, commanded by Capt. Tom Sprowls, who led the squadron almost the entire time in Iraq, rapidly defeated several enemy infantry units. The emphasis was on getting to the Republican Guard, and we passed many of our prisoners on to units traveling behind us. Our troop had our first combat action on the evening of the 24th after moving farther to the north. It was dusk, and an enemy position fired on us as we halted. We engaged them with direct fire from Bradleys and a tank, as well as indirect fire from our mortars; we killed some of them, and then many surrendered to F Troop, which was on our right flank. Leaders emphasized to their soldiers as we continued our attack not to become complacent about our early actions because we would soon meet more capable Republican Guard units that could present us with greater challenges.

Just before sunset during the evening of February 25, G Troop, commanded by my classmate Capt. Joe Sartiano, engaged and destroyed an enemy reconnaissance unit of about twelve MTLBs, small (Soviet-designed and -built) armored personnel carriers. They were Republican Guard vehicles. G Troop took captured vehicles to the squadron command post so we could examine maps and the condition of the weapons and equipment, some of which were brand new. After entertaining ourselves by racing the vehicles around for a while, we returned to our troops to await the next day's orders. We anticipated a fight. It was clear that we had hit the Republican Guard screen line, or security zone.

It rained hard during the night of the 25th, and as a result, there was heavy fog on the morning of the 26th. We could barely see two hundred meters, sometimes less. The fog eventually lifted, but it was replaced by a sandstorm, and the blowing sand also limited visibility to short distances. It was under those conditions that the regiment ordered us to continue our attack to the east to identify the defensive positions of the Republican Guard. We had a feeling in our guts that we would soon be in a fight. The divisions of VII Corps were still far off, but were closing the gap.

After moving into the lead along 2nd Squadron's southern boundary with 3rd Squadron, our troop received orders to move out. It was about 1607 on the afternoon of the 26th. We were given a limit of advance of the 67 Easting, a north-south grid line on the map. We moved in a formation called a modified column security right. One scout platoon, Lt. Mike Petschek's 1st Platoon, led with three scout sections of two cavalry fighting vehicles, each in a V formation. The other scout platoon, 1st Lt. Tim Gauthier's 3rd Platoon, moved along our southern flank, with guns oriented south to cover the gap between us and 3rd Squadron, which was moving behind us to our south. Our mortar section followed 1st Platoon. Our tanks moved behind the mortars in a nine-tank wedge with my tank in the center. First Lt. Mike Hamilton's 2nd Platoon was to my tank's left in an echelon left formation, and 1st Lt. Jeff Destefano's 4th Platoon was to my tank's right in an echelon right.

Because we had no maps of the area, we were unaware that we were paralleling a road that ran west to east along our boundary with 3rd Squadron. The road ran through a small village and then into Kuwait.

We also did not know that we were entering an Iraqi training ground recently reoccupied by a brigade of the Tawakalna Division who had received the mission of halting our advance into Kuwait.

The enemy commander, Major Mohammed, and his soldiers knew the ground well. The unit had used the village for billets as they conducted live fire training. Major Mohammed, who had attended the infantry officer advanced course at Fort Benning, Georgia, thought it was the ideal ground from which to defend. He assumed that we would have to move along roads to avoid becoming lost in the featureless desert. He was unaware of our global positioning system capabilities. He organized his defense along the road by fortifying the village with anti-aircraft guns to be used in the ground mode, machine guns, and infantry. Mohammed's defense was fundamentally sound. He took advantage of an imperceptible rise in the terrain that ran perpendicular to the road and directly through the village to organize a reverse slope defense on the east side of that ridge. He anticipated that upon encountering his strong point at the village, we would bypass it either to the north or south. He built two engagement areas, or "kill sacks," on the eastern side of the ridge to the north and the south of the village, emplaced minefields to disrupt forward movement, and dug in approximately forty tanks and sixteen BMPs (Soviet-designed and -built infantry fighting vehicles) about one thousand meters from the ridge. His plan was to engage and destroy us piece-meal as we moved across the crest. Hundreds of infantry occupied bunkers and trenches amid his armored vehicles. He positioned his reserve of eighteen T72s and his command post along another subtle ridgeline approximately three thousand meters farther east.

The first contact came at 1607, when Staff Sgt. John McReynolds' Bradley drove right on top of an Iraqi bunker that contained an observation element positioned to provide early warning to the forces in the village. Two enemy soldiers emerged and surrendered. Staff Sergeant McReynolds took them prisoner and transported them to our trains.

McReynolds' wingman, Sgt. Maurice Harris, remained at the limit of advance and scanned into the village through the blowing sand. Evidently, the Iraqis had gotten some word back to the village and Sergeant Harris' Bradley came under 23mm and machine-gun fire. The first thing he did was to report to his platoon leader, who responded, "Well, kill them." As Sergeant Harris began to engage with 25mm, Lieutenant Gauthier moved forward and continued to report the situation.

As a platoon leader or company commander, you must be forward to have a clear picture of the situation. I asked Lieutenant Gauthier to fire a TOW (tube launched, optically tracked, wire command link guided) missile into the center of the village so that the explosion would orient our tanks. After my gunner, Staff Sgt. Craig Koch, fired a round to mark center, all nine tanks fired high explosive rounds into the village simultaneously to suppress the enemy position. Everyone in the troop was doing the right thing. There were big explosions in the village, and it would have been easy for crews to become distracted. The troop's training paid off, however, as 1st Platoon maintained its primary observation to the east.

If you know where friendly forces are, and there is not a danger of civilian casualties, do not hesitate to shoot or conduct reconnaissance by fire. Staff Sergeant David Lawrence was the commander of 1st Platoon's northernmost Bradley. When his gunner, Bradley Feltman, said, "Hey, I've got a hot spot out there; I'm not sure what it is," Lawrence responded, "Put a TOW in it; see what it is." Lawrence identified the hot spot as a T72 as the turret was ripped from its hull in the ensuing explosion.

As we fired into the village and while Lawrence was launching a missile, the troop received permission to advance to 70 Easting. I instructed 1st Platoon to resume movement east. Lieutenant Petschek did not respond immediately because Lawrence was reporting, "Contact, contact, east, tank!" At that point, I felt it was best for us to go to a tanks lead formation and instructed Green and White, the tank platoons, to "follow my move." First Platoon pulled in behind the tank wedge to cover our rear.Third Platoon retained responsibility for flank security.

As we began moving forward, 1st Platoon, responding to the contact report on their platoon radio net, started firing 25mm high explosive munitions across the front. It was a little unnerving for the tanks as we moved forward. I gave 1st Platoon a cease-fire order: "Red one, this is Black six. Cease fire."

The two tank platoons were separated slightly from our tank. When our tank came over the crest of the imperceptible rise north of the village, Sgt. Craig Koch, the gunner, and I identified the enemy simultaneously. As Sergeant Koch said, "Tanks direct front," I could see eight T72s in prepared positions to our front.

Standard unit fire and battle drills at the crew, platoon, and company levels are essential to achieving speed of action and, in armored combat, the side that shoots first usually wins. I gave the fire command, "Fire, Fire SABOT." We had a HEAT round loaded, so the order alerted the crew to index SABOT, and the next round would be a kinetic energy round. As Sergeant Koch fired the first round, I sent a contact report to the troop, "This is Black six. Contact east. Eight armored vehicles. Green and White, are you with me?"

Sergeant Koch destroyed two more tanks as the tank platoons accelerated movement. All nine tanks began engaging together as we advanced. In approximately one minute, everything in the range of our guns was in flames. Eagle Troop demonstrated great fire distribution and control, which allowed us to take out a lot of the enemy at once. Soldiers took aggressive action against a numerically superior force without hesitation.

Our tank driver, Spec. Christopher Hedenskog, knew that he had to steer a path that permitted both tank platoons to get their guns into the fight. He turned 45 degrees to the right and kept our frontal armor toward the first enemy tanks we engaged. He also drove through a minefield, avoided the antitank mines, and told me on the intercom, "Sir, I think you need to know—we just went through a minefield." He knew that it would be dangerous to stop right in the middle of their kill sack, where we would have been stationary targets. He saw that we had a window of opportunity to shock the enemy and take advantage of the first blows Sergeant Koch had delivered.

In another example of soldier initiative, Sergeant Digbie ordered Private First Class Bertubin to reload TOW missiles. Bertubin could not get the cargo hatch open, however. When he kicked the hatch release, he sheared it off. Rather than telling his Bradley commander that he could not get the TOWs reloaded, he jumped out of the back door while the vehicle was under small-arms and machine-gun fire. He climbed onto the back of the Bradley, loaded both missiles, then tapped his Bradley commander on the shoulder while yelling, "TOWs are up." Staff Sergeant Digbie nearly jumped out of skin because he thought that an Iraqi had climbed onto the Bradley. There are many other stories of soldiers taking initiative and making significant contributions to the fight.

If you are commanding tanks, use them to take the brunt of the battle and advance aggressively. Tanks drove around the antitank mines, and Bradleys and other vehicles followed in the tracks of the tanks. We ran over a lot of antipersonnel mines, but they had no effect on armored vehicles. Our squadron S3, then Maj. Douglas MacGregor, fought forward with us in his tank as was the squadron tactical command post Bradley commanded by Staff Sgt. William Burns and Lt. John Hillen. MacGregor's tank hit an antitank mine, but the blast disabled the tank only slightly, and it was able to continue, and then make a rapid repair when we stopped.

Crew drill including engagements and misfire procedures are vitally important. In one engagement, Lt. Jeff DeStefano's tank crew came around the village, destroyed an enemy tank, and acquired a second tank that was traversing on them. A round was stuck in the chamber. The loader grabbed hold of the loader's hatch, kicked the round in, the breech came up, and the gunner fired a round and destroyed a T72 at close range.

Coordination among platoons to ensure mutual support also proved critical. The burning tanks and personnel carriers of the enemy's first defensive line formed a curtain of smoke that concealed enemy farther to the east. As our tanks assaulted through the smoke, we saw other enemy armored vehicles and large numbers of infantry running to get back to subsequent trench lines and positions. We destroyed the enemy armored vehicles quickly and shot the infantry with machine guns as we closed the distance with them. Pockets of enemy soldiers threw up their arms. Our soldiers were disciplined; turrets turned away from any enemy soldier with his hands raised. Tank platoon leaders asked scout platoons to pick up observation of the enemy infantry as their Bradleys came through the smoke. The scouts saw that the enemy had used false surrender to gain a better position. Enemy soldiers were reshouldering their rifles and RPGs.

Our Bradleys surprised the enemy, however, and destroyed them before they could engage our tanks effectively. Because we pressed the assault, the enemy could not respond effectively. Just as we cleared the western defensive positions, our executive officer, Lt. John Gifford, broke in on the radio, "I know you don't want to know this right now, but you're at the limit of advance; you're at 70 Easting."

I responded, "Tell them we can't stop. Tell them we're in contact and we have to continue this attack. Tell them I'm sorry." We had surprised and shocked the enemy; stopping would have allowed them to recover. I was free to make that decision because of a command climate that not only encouraged initiative, but demanded it.

Our regimental commander, Col. L. D. Holder, told us during training in Germany that "because of the pace of the action and the size of the cavalry battlefield, important decisions have to be made quickly by junior leaders in contact. . . . Because tight centralized control of operations isn't possible or desirable . . . all regimental leaders must train their juniors to do the right things and then trust them to act independently. . . . Leaders must teach and practice mission orders." It was a message all junior leaders in the regiment internalized.

We continued to attack toward another subtle ridgeline on which the enemy positioned his reserve, a coil of eighteen T72 tanks. We destroyed the first of the reserve from long range. We could not see the others, however, until we crested the rise and entered the assembly area. The enemy reserve was attempting to move out to react to our attack, but we destroyed them at close range. There was an observation post and an elaborate bunker for the brigade commander, Major Mohammed. Major Mohammed told one of our troopers that he had not known he was under attack until a soldier ran into his command post yelling, "Tanks, tanks!" By the time he got to his observation post, all the vehicles in defensive positions were in flames. He ordered the reserve to establish a second defensive line, but it was too late. The troop stopped when we had nothing left to shoot. The main fight took twenty-three minutes. We consolidated on the ridgeline that the enemy reserve had occupied.

There was a lot of concurrent activity as we consolidated. We had sporadic contact ranging from nuisance machine-gun fire to one company-sized counterattack of T72s and BMPs. We destroyed enemy vehicles at long range from the dominating position on the ridge. Three Bradleys from 1st Platoon, led by Lt. Michael Petschek, encountered and destroyed four T72s as they moved north to re-establish physical contact with G Troop. Our medics treated and evacuated eighteen enemy wounded. Our mortar section was effective at suppressing enemy infantry farther to the east, and our fire support officer called in two devastating artillery strikes on enemy logistical bases. Scouts and a team under the control of 1st Sgt. Bill Virrill cleared bunkers using grenades and satchel charges.

A psychological operations team broadcast surrender appeals forward of the troop, and we took the first of hundreds of prisoners including the brigade commander. Soldiers organized into enemy prisoner of war teams segregated, searched, and secured prisoners through the night. Many of the prisoners cried because they had not expected such humane treatment; their officers had told them that we would execute them. We conducted logistical resupply of fuel and ammunition. Just after 2200, the 1st Infantry Division conducted a forward passage of lines in 3rd Squadron's sector to our south.

Our fight was a lopsided victory. From the initiation of our assault until battle handover with 1st Infantry Division, we destroyed approximately fifty T72s, twenty-five armored personnel carriers, forty trucks, and numerous other vehicles such as SA-9 air defense systems. Our troop took no casualties. There were many reasons for those results.

One of the principal reasons is American air supremacy and technological superiority. Although the physical destruction that the air campaign inflicted on Major Mohammed's brigade was not great, the effect of the air attacks desensitized the enemy to battlefield noise and lessened their degree of vigilance. The effect that air supremacy has on friendly troops is often neglected. Air supremacy serves to embolden ground units. Soldiers can focus their attention almost exclusively on the ground domain, and they know that the tremendous capabilities of American air power magnify their own strength. Even though the sandstorm prevented us from using air assets, they had already made an enormous contribution to the outcome.

Overmatch on the ground also stemmed, in large measure, from technological superiority. The M1A1 tank completely outclassed the T72. It is impossible for a well-trained M1A1 crew to miss with service ammunition. The round goes right in the aiming dot at the most extended ranges. Everything hit is catastrophically destroyed. The Bradley also has tremendous capabilities. Twenty-five of twenty-six TOW missiles that we fired hit their mark; many shots were near maximum range. The 25mm chain gun and the munitions it fires represent a tremendous capability against a range of enemy from dismounted infantry to T72 tanks. Our stabilized weapons systems that permit us to fire on the move with absolute accuracy allowed us to close with the enemy and achieve shock effect as we destroyed large numbers of enemy vehicles and positions. Our optics and especially our thermal sights gave us an advantage in acquiring the enemy, especially in limited visibility conditions. Finally, the global positioning system (GPS) permitted us to navigate in a featureless desert under tough conditions, including sandstorms.

Enemy technological disadvantages exacerbated our advantages. The T72 proved inaccurate due to several factors. Every tank round fired at us, of which there were at least four, fell short. Contributing factors likely included worn gun tubes and wet or damp propellant in the T72, which has an exposed ammunition compartment. It is likely that psychological and training factors caused greater difficulties. Every T72 or personnel carrier that the troop shot exploded in a fireball. There were no survivors. Seeing adjacent vehicles destroyed likely disturbed Iraqi crewmembers such that they were unable to concentrate on their engagements. The vehicles might not have been bore-sighted properly, and we knew that gunnery training in the Iraqi army was infrequent and of poor quality. Because of the slow speed of the T72 autoloader, an M1A1 crew could fire three rounds to every one of a T72 crew.

Other explanations for overwhelming victory are Iraqi tactical ineptitude and low skill level. At first glance, Major Mohammed developed a good defensive plan. He set up a reverse slope defense, developed good kill sacks with minefields, and dug in positions with good fields of fire. He established a reserve. It was, however, a defense better suited for an Iranian infantry-heavy attack during the Iran–Iraq War than a defense capable of challenging an American armored cavalry troop. Major Mohammed's conception of time and space was skewed. His vehicle positions and infantry bunkers were too close together. Once we detected the first tanks, we could orient on nearly the entire force; there were no positions designed to hit us from an unexpected angle. Antipersonnel minefields were ineffective as the mines detonated harmlessly under our tank tracks. Mohammed's reserve was too shallow, such that it lost its freedom to maneuver as soon as our troop penetrated the forward defensive positions. The defense would have been effective against a dismounted infantry assault or against lightly armored vehicles, but it was ineffective against an armored attack. Despite Iraqi tactical ineptitude, Republican Guard soldiers fought in a determined manner; the preponderance of the enemy fought until they were killed or wounded.

Surprise, shock, and the initiative gave us tremendous advantage. We did not surprise the enemy in a classical sense; it was our capabilities that achieved surprise. The enemy was unaware of the destructive power of a cavalry troop. The initial encounter action gave us the initiative. Destructive direct fires combined with a rapid advance created a shock effect that rendered the enemy incapable of mounting an organized effort against us. The enemy rapidly became preoccupied with self-preservation, and his teams at platoon level and above disintegrated due to physical destruction and psychological strain.

Perhaps the most critical factor was the offensive spirit of our soldiers and the aggressive actions of crews, platoons, and the unit as a whole. All of our soldiers attacked without hesitation a numerically superior enemy force that possessed all the advantages of the defense.

///CAPT. DAVID NORTON (U.S. ARMY)

After an extended delay caused by a maintenance problem, we were finally ready to continue our journey. The pilot pulled the 747 to the end of the runway and stopped. Over the intercom, he said there was something he wanted us to hear.

He switched the radio on over the intercom, and the main body of the 1st Battalion, 34th Armor, sat on the runway at New York's Kennedy Airport and listened as the ball dropped in Times Square. Never before, and never again, will the New Year carry such a vivid memory as it did that night. The men who would control the combat power of an M1A1 tank battalion sat in total silence. Thoughts of family, friends, home, and happier times mixed with fear, doubt, and anxiety about what lay ahead. As the cheers of the New Year's crowd swelled on the intercom, the engine's whine increased and the plane moved slowly forward. The 1st Battalion, 34th Armor, was going to war.

After the long, long flight to Saudi Arabia, we stepped off the plane, greeted by a cool breeze and a darkened airfield. I don't know what I expected, but the emptiness seemed to engulf us as we formed up. It was probably less than a quarter mile, but the walk to the point where we would meet the buses seemed much longer. When we reached the bus pickup point, we were given bottled water and told to start drinking. When we finally boarded the buses to the warehouse that would be our home for the next two weeks, most of us were sorry we had consumed so much water. We arrived at the warehouses at around 0230, and by the time we had our bags separated, it was 0330. We couldn't get an area until around 0600, so we simply dropped our bags and lay down on the cement to get some sleep.

Rumors were the order of the day for the next week. We didn't know when we would move, where we would move, or if we would use our M1 tanks or draw M1A1s. Finally, on the 10th, we learned that we would turn in our M1s and draw M1A1s sent from stocks in Europe. For the next three days, Charlie Company turned in M1 tanks, and drew and prepared M1A1 tanks for combat. The tanks we drew were not new, and our last tank was getting on a truck due to a maintenance problem, but in spite of the problems and the rush, Charlie Company had its tanks loaded and moved north on the 14th.

I had never experienced anything similar to our deployment into the desert. The company was loaded on two buses, which followed the trucks carrying our tanks. Prior to leaving the port, the company commander had called all the platoon leaders together and updated us on the situation. Intelligence was predicting that the Iraqis would attack on the night of the 14th. This was based on the January 15 deadline imposed by President Bush. So, as we rolled off to face the enemy, we were riding on buses and only the platoon leaders had any ammunition. Needless to say, this is not the picture a tanker normally imagines when he thinks of going to war.

When we climbed off the buses on the morning of the 15th, we found ourselves on the flattest piece of earth I have ever seen. Most of our tanks and the M998s with the commander, first sergeant, and support personnel had arrived ahead of us. When I went to find my tank, I was in for some bad news.

The driver offloading the tank was not used to driving in sand, and he turned too sharply, throwing a track. As we worked to get this problem corrected, the truck carrying my wing tank pulled in. Unbelievably, this truck had sideswiped another that was also carrying a tank. Only the front left side of each tank made contact, but this tore the number one and number two skirts off, crushed six track blocks and denting the bustle rack and sponson box. After replacing the bad track blocks, the tank was able to move under its own power and operate normally.

We finally got all our personnel and equipment together, and word came down for us to pull through a logistics site to get fuel and ammunition. As we were moving through the logistics site, the first sergeant came and found me. He told me that, due to the classified nature of the armor in the skirts of the M1A1 tank, we would have to retrace our route and try to find my wing tank's missing skirts. Four or five hours later, after searching up and down the main supply route, we received word that the skirts had been picked up by another unit. By the time we made it back to the company, it was dark, and we had no reference to guide on. Somehow, we found the company, and I returned to my platoon. As a new platoon leader with only three months in the company, my first day in the desert had not exactly been a rousing success.

January 16 was a better day. We organized our tanks, secured our gear, and prepared our weapons for combat. We also drew a mine plow per platoon, and one of the tanks in 1st Platoon was fitted with a mine roller kit.

Nothing exciting happened until I was awakened at 0330 on the morning of the 17th. We were told to go to REDCON 1 and stand by. At 0400, we began to see flashes to the north as Operation Desert Shield turned into Operation Desert Storm. I remember having my gunner and driver pop their heads out of the tank and look north. As we sat and watched the explosions flash across the sky, I told my crew they were watching the start of a war.

The next six weeks were filled with fear, anxiety, and extreme boredom as we waited to see if a ground war would be necessary. The days turned to weeks, and then we learned that if a ground war came, our parent unit, the 1st Infantry Division (Big Red One) would be the breach force for VII Corps. In preparation for a ground war, we moved to a firing range and tested all our weapon systems. After ensuring that all our systems were functioning properly, we started a series of rehearsals. Beginning at the platoon level, the rehearsals grew in size and scope. The final rehearsal was the movement of VII Corps to its attack position.

We also contacted leaders' recons into the neutral zone that separated Iraq and Saudi Arabia. These recons gave us a good feel for what we would see when we moved into the attack. I can't imagine a force ever being better equipped or better prepared than we were.

When I talked to people who weren't there, I hear how Desert Storm was such an easy war. Sometimes I even feel that way when I look back at how things turned out, but sitting in the desert waiting, I sure didn't feel that way. As we prepared for our mission, we were told that as the breach force, the Big Red One could expect 10 percent killed in action (KIA) and 30 percent wounded in action (WIA). As a tank platoon leader, that equals four or five soldiers and at least one tank lost. When you look at numbers and turn them into names and faces of men you are responsible for, *easy* is not the word that comes to mind.

On the morning of February 24, I climbed out of my sleeping bag and secured my gear, knowing that in a few hours we would begin our attack north. I went from tank to tank in the platoon to ensure each crew and vehicle was ready to go. As I checked my tanks, I found a stenciled picture of Cecil, the cigar-smoking rabbit, on the front slope of each turret. I soon learned that Cecil was the combined work of all the junior enlisted members of the platoon. Prior to our arrival in Saudi Arabia, 2nd Platoon had been looked upon as a bunch of troublemakers. Cecil was a sign that this group ranging from nineteen to forty-nine had finally pulled together. I was proud to carry Cecil's image on my tank as we moved off to face the Iraqis.

With every weapon checked, every bustle rack secure, and every crewmember in his place, we waited for the order to move. Finally, the company radio net came to life: "Short count follows five, four, three, two, one. . . ." As the number one rang out, forty radios were switched off and the sound of fourteen M1A1 tank engines filled the desert air. A minute later, the company commander was back on the radio, and we began our move. We were on the right side of the company wedge formation and waited for 3rd Platoon to move so we could form up on their flank.

When the time came for us to move, I keyed the intercom and told the driver to move out. Instead of hearing the engine gain power and feeling the tank move, I heard the driver yell, "Sir, it won't move!" There we sat as the rest of the company moved around us. I was frantic; I called for the maintenance team, and the entire crew began to troubleshoot the problem. Five minutes later, we were screaming across the desert as fast as we could go to gain our place in formation. My driver, who was tall and slender, had accidentally bumped the throttle cable when we climbed into his seat, jarring it loose. This simple and unforeseen problem was in some ways a sign of things to come.

I can't begin to describe the feeling that ran through me as we moved north. We passed units of all types, and everyone must have been out to watch us pass. Each unit we passed greeted us with waves, cheers, and shouts of encouragement. Knowing that we had the support of our families, the American public, and the rest of our comrades in arms was a great feeling.

When we moved past the field artillery, I knew we were getting close. Shortly after passing the artillery, we stopped. We were waiting on orders to continue or to wait until the following morning. While we waited, contact reports began to come across the radio. The first report was that enemy attack helicopters were spotted moving in our direction. This report was followed by a report that the unit to our right was under chemical attack. These reports all proved to be false, but they did help to keep us alert while we waited. Finally, orders came down to continue the attack.

The battalion shifted forward and left, to get lined up on the lanes that would be cut by Task Force 5-60 Infantry and Task Force 2-34 Armor.

As a tank-pure battalion, 1-34 Armor would move through these lanes, destroy enemy second-echelon forces, block any enemy counterattack, and open the way for follow-on divisions to pass through. Once in position, we watched as truckloads of Iraqi prisoners of war moved past us to the rear. More concerned with what was going on to my front, I didn't really notice the battery of eight-inch guns that set up a couple hundred meters behind me. This quickly changed when the first volley of the prep fire exploded over our heads. I nearly had to change my pants. Watching and listening to the size and violence of the prep fire, I closed my eyes and thanked God that we were not the ones on the receiving end.

Even before the last rounds impacted, the lead elements moved forward. I have to admit that after watching the prep fire, having sixty tons of steel wrapped around me gave me a real safe feeling. On the other hand, I began to think of the men who would have to dismount and clear the battle-hardened Iraqis from their trenches. To everyone's surprise, word that the trenches were clear and the lanes were open came quickly from the breach task forces. We moved forward, and as we neared the breach lanes, I was glad that we were not facing serious resistance. Dust and smoke made visibility a real problem that was compounded by the large number of vehicles in such a small area. Several vehicles nearly collided as we moved through the lanes with everyone trying to maintain position in line.

The training and rehearsals paid off as the battalion quickly moved into a diamond formation after exiting the lanes. Buoyed by the limited resistance during the breach, we moved forward with careful confidence. Leading the task force, the scout platoon and Charlie Company were first to make contact with the enemy. Hot spots began to appear in our sights at ranges in excess of three thousand meters. Unable to identify what was out there, we continued to move. We stayed under tight fire control, and no one was given permission to engage until we identified the hot spots as towed guns and wheeled support vehicles. The guns and some of the support vehicles were destroyed with main gun rounds as we continued to move forward. These guns were antiaircraft guns and were part of an enemy trench and bunker system. We rolled right over the top of the bunker system using machine guns to suppress suspected enemy positions as we moved.

We didn't see any Iraqi soldiers around the equipment or in the first set of bunkers as we passed. It wasn't until we crested a small ridge at the rear of the bunker complex that we began to pick up movement in the distance. Approximately two thousand meters to our front was a second bunker complex. Through our thermal sights, we could now see soldiers moving in these distant trenches. The turret distribution valve went out on my tank at the same time that we first identified what appeared to be the main bunker in the complex ahead. No longer able to traverse my turret quickly, I told my driver to pick up a tight weave. This made it possible for us to scan our sector and enabled me to control the platoon. My three tanks had also identified the large bunker to our front, and after clearing fires, I told my gunner to hit it with a HEAT round.

The impact of the HEAT round and the Iraqi reaction were simultaneous. Before the dust had even cleared, a sea of white flags went up throughout the enemy position. The battle area that just seconds before was filled with machine-gun fire and the crash of tank main guns grew deathly quiet. We pulled into an overwatch position as the scouts, assisted by the engineers, rounded up the enemy prisoners of war. We soon learned that we had captured an Iraqi infantry brigade, including the commander and staff. Information that the Iraqis had no idea who was to their front filtered back to us on our tanks; they expected to see an Arab force comprised primarily of infantry. The sight of fifty-eight M1A1 tanks was devastating, and they lost all their will to fight as soon as that tank main-gun round impacted their bunker.

Day quickly turned to night as the last enemy prisoners were gathered up and the command bunker cleared. With the day's objectives secured and the battalion arrayed to defeat an enemy counterattack if it came, we stopped for the night. As soon as we got word to stop for the night, soldiers began to clear the area around their tanks. Knowing that tankers are not really trained or equipped to clear bunkers, and with all the unexploded artillery bomblets in the area, the battalion commander ordered everyone back on their tanks. We had come too far to get someone hurt or killed needlessly.

The adrenaline that pumped through our veins during the day began slowly to leave our systems. Soldiers began to wind down, and as soon as we established security, we rotated guards so soldiers could get some rest. I was still too wound up to rest, so I teamed with my loader to take the first watch, allowing my gunner and driver to get some sleep. Near the end of our watch, Alpha Company, to our right, reported three Iraqi dismounts moving across their front. They were told to continue to observe but not to engage unless necessary. A short time later, my three tanks reported that the dismounts had moved into his sector. Tired of manually traversing my turret, I decided to use my tank to watch the Iraqis. This left my three good tanks free to scan our sector.

Time passed slowly as I continued to track the Iraqis moving from right to left across our sector. Watching them, I noticed that one of them was carrying something over his shoulder, but I could not make out what it was. I became concerned as they moved between our scouts and us. Each time they came near a Bradley, they would stop, drop to their knees, and face the Bradley. I could see well enough to know that they never pointed any type of weapon at the scouts, but I wasn't sure of what they were up to. After a minute or so, they would get back up and continue on their way. Once they crossed in front of my tank, the battalion commander, who was about one hundred meters to my left rear, decided they had gone far enough. He ordered the scouts to button up, and then had his gunner fire a burst of coax a safe distance in front of the Iraqis. The Iraqis dropped to the ground and didn't move. Several minutes later, they got back to their feet and continued to move. This time, the battalion commander told his gunner to fire a little bit closer. Once again, the Iraqis dropped and didn't move for what seemed like a long time.

I was surprised when I again heard the rattle of machine-gun fire. I called on the radio to ask the executive officer what was going on. Apparently, the battalion commander's gunner had seen the four Iraqis start to crawl toward the scout vehicles and awakened the commander. The commander, concerned for the safety of scouts, told his gunner to fire a burst at the Iraqis. I stayed awake all night keeping an eye on the three forms on the ground eight hundred meters to my front. Two of the men lay perfectly still, but the third one reached his hands out like he was in pain. Soon he quit moving, and as I watched through my thermal sight, his image turned from green to gray as the heat of life drained from his body.

At the first light of morning, two of the Iraqis got up, and with hands raised began to walk toward our position. They came up between my tank and my wingman. While we covered them from my tank, my wingman checked them for weapons. They said that their friend had been wounded and needed a medic. Not wanting to send a medic out alone, my commander told me to move out and secure the area. When we neared the Iraqi, I knew he was dead before we had even stopped moving. We were told to search him for documents, identification, and any personal property that his family might want returned. We were then told to bury the remains and mark the site for future recovery. This presented a situation that I don't know if anyone is ever really prepared for. This was the first time I had ever handled a dead body. The smell and the gore caused by a single 7.62mm round surprised me. No movie or picture can come close to real life. When we finished, we turned the soldier's belongings in to the battalion commander, and I was glad when we moved out of the area.

I honestly don't know how far we moved, or where we ended up. We were off the maps that we had, and the entire company was relying on the company executive officer, who had a GPS and one large-scale map. When we stopped, we pulled into a blocking position and received word that follow-on divisions were passing forward. The Big Red One had successfully completed its mission and would become the corps reserve.

We completed resupply and maintenance checks, and once again moved out, only this time we were following VII Corps. Even as the reserve, we maintained our battalion diamond formation and never let our guard down as we moved across the desert.

On the afternoon of the 26th, we began to receive reports that the 2nd Armored Cavalry Regiment was in contact with an armored division of the Republican Guard. Unknown to any of us, someone at an extremely high level decided to move the Big Red One forward to destroy the Tawakalna Division of the Republican Guard in a night attack. Unaware of what was going on, we were relieved and happy when we stopped to refuel just before dark. After hours of riding through wind-blown sand and dust, any rest was welcome. Not until later, when we were once again on the move, did the company commander come up on the radio and tell the platoon leaders to go green. Riding through the night with the wind in my face and the sand in my eyes, I learned of what was to come.

I don't remember being afraid when we went through the breach on the first day of the war. I was excited, nervous, and anxious, but I don't remember any real fear. That changed as I listened to what the company commander had to say. Not only were we going to conduct a forward passage of lines with a unit in contact, but we would be doing it from the march and at night. When we exited the passage lanes, we would face a Republican Guard division equipped with T72M1 tanks, dug in, and waiting.

Fanning the flames of doubt and fear was a briefing the company had received prior to deployment. The briefers told us all about the T72M1, and that it was a great tank, almost as good as the M1. We were going to conduct one of the most dangerous maneuvers possible against a well-equipped and -prepared enemy, and I couldn't even brief my platoon properly. The shortage of secure communications equipment made it impossible for everyone to have a secure system in their tank. So over a nonsecure radio net, I became creative in letting my platoon know what was happening.

Unbelievably, the passage of lines went smoothly. We simply used battle drills to move through the lanes and redeploy on the far side. The fact that it went smoothly didn't make it any less exciting. We flowed through the lanes as artillery fired overhead, and the horizon was dotted with burning Iraqi combat vehicles. Soldiers who just moments before were dead tired and dragging came to life as the adrenaline of combat once again began to flow. We used the burning vehicles to guide on, and as I passed a burning Iraqi tank, we were told that we no longer had friendly forces to the front.

The 2nd Armored Cavalry Regiment (ACR) had destroyed everything in range of their weapons, allowing us to deploy before we made contact. We began to pick up vehicle movement to our front as we moved in front of the 2nd ACR. The scout platoon, approximately one thousand meters to my front, was using 25mm and machine guns to recon by fire. They were firing at bunkers and unidentified hot spots. Suddenly, a SABOT round went right through the Bradley to my left front. We weren't sure who fired at the scouts, but we did know that it came from the direction of friendly forces. The scout platoon leader, not knowing where the round came from, moved his vehicle to support his damaged track. His vehicle was also engaged as it moved into position. The battalion commander quickly moved Bravo Company forward to secure the area so the medics could treat the injured. The gunner on the platoon leader's Bradley was killed, and the platoon leader was injured. Miraculously, no one on the first vehicle hit was seriously injured.

Only the soldiers involved in evacuating the wounded knew the extent of the damage, but everyone in the battalion knew we had suffered our first casualties. The battalion commander moved the remaining four scout tracks back, and Charlie Company moved out to lead the attack. With no one to our front, we began to engage targets at ranges of 3,000 to 3,500 meters. We were not going to take the chance of getting too close and giving the enemy a chance to fight back. Riding up in an open hatch, I used AN/PVS-7B night vision goggles to keep track of our place in formation. I dropped into the turret only to look through the sight to identify long-range targets. After destroying several vehicles to include at least one tank and some armored personnel carriers, we began to see numerous trucks and trailers. I told my guys not to fire unless they identified a combat vehicle or an enemy fighting position.

We identified a large logistics site and were soon moving through a corps-level supply area. Along with all the trucks and trailers were a large number of enemy dismounts. We also skirted a large fenced-in area that turned out to be a major ammunition holding area. Most of the dismounts we came across didn't want any part of a fight, so they simply dropped their weapons and we sent them to the rear. My platoon sergeant's wingman reported eleven dismounts three thousand meters to his front. I told him to keep an eye on them but continue to move. A few minutes later, he reported that the dismounts had taken up a position in a bomb crater. I told him to watch them, and if they did anything stupid, we would deal with them when we were within machine-gun range.

The company's direction of travel put the Iraqi position right in front of my tank. We kept them under continuous observation, and they didn't move or take any hostile action as we approached. When we were close enough and they got a good look at our tanks, they began to stand and drop their weapons. I pulled my tank up beside their position and yelled for them to leave their weapons and move west. Most of them started to move, but just at that moment my loader and I noticed two guys with machine guys trying to sneak around a berm.

Knowing that we couldn't traverse fast enough, I screamed at my driver to back up, right track! The engine roared, the dust flew, and a squad of drop-jawed Iraqis found themselves looking down the barrel of a 120mm smoothbore cannon. Mouths were open, hands flew up, and a couple of them began to pray. I nearly came out of my turret yelling at them to drop their weapons. I can't begin to list or even remember the stream of profanity that came out of my mouth. All I remember is that I really didn't want to kill these guys just because of a couple of idiots.

After a few seconds of yelling, I suddenly stopped and calmly asked if any of them understood English. One guy, who was white with fear, slowly raised his hand. I said okay and began screaming again. I told them that if they didn't all want to die, the guys with the machine guns better drop their weapons.

Paralyzed by fear and the sight of a crazy American yelling at them from the top of a tank, it took the Iraqis a few seconds to react. Finally, one of the Iraqis near the last guy with a weapon reached over and knocked it out of his hands. Knowing that I was falling farther and farther behind the company, I was out of the turret and on my way down the front slope before the machine gun hit the ground. Without stopping to think, I found myself on the ground in the middle of a Republican Guard infantry squad. I realized as I collected weapons and sent the Iraqis marching west to be picked up by follow-on forces that I was armed with only a 9mm pistol. In reality, I wasn't armed at all because my pistol was still holstered, and I didn't even have a round in the chamber. Fortunately, I didn't need a weapon, and my loader dismounted to assist in destroying the captured Iraqi weapons.

We smashed the Iraqi weapons between the track and the sprocket of the tank, ensuring that they could not be used in the future. I scanned the area after remounting the tank and saw M1A1 tanks about five hundred meters away. I told my driver to kick it so we could catch up quickly. When we were close enough to identify the tanks, I realized that they belonged to Delta Company. Delta was at the rear of the task force diamond, meaning we would have to pass through the center of the task force formation to catch our company. I quickly called the company executive officer to have him notify the rest of the task force that our tank would be moving through the center of the diamond. I was worried that someone would see a lone tank out of formation and mistake us for the enemy. When I received word that it was clear, we moved as fast as possible to join the company.

We attacked through the night, stopping just before sun-up. I can't say exactly when the passage of lines started or exactly when we stopped, but I do know that the night of 26–27 February was the longest of my life. Morning held little change from days past. Fuel and ammunition came forward, allowing us to resupply, and we did some basic maintenance on our tanks. Later, with no sleep and only an MRE, we once again moved out in pursuit of the retreating Iraqi army. We moved all day and into the night. We passed through the worst tank country I have ever seen. The S3 called it the "valley of the boogers," some type of strip mine in the desert. As we started through it, we went to platoons in column, then companies in column, and then the entire task force was in a single column. We moved along a single trail, all aware that a relatively small force with light antitank weapons could have stalled our move indefinitely. We didn't meet any resistance, but we did see a number of dismounted Iraqis as we continued to move. The night grew extremely dark. Due to the hazardous terrain and soldier fatigue, we were forced to stop. The commander ordered the task force to halt, establish local security, and get a few hours' rest so we could move again at first light. I stopped my tank and had my platoon jockey around to provide all-around security. The road was so narrow that by the time we were in place I could jump from tank to tank.

I knew how tired everyone was, so I told my tank commanders to get their soldiers as much sleep as possible. We went to 50 percent security, with two soldiers up in each turret. We heard reports of Iraqi dismounts in the holes and ravines around our position, but no one in the platoon saw any. Approximately one hundred meters to our front, where the rest of the company had stopped, we heard machine-gun fire as tank crews tried to frighten Iraqis out of the area. After making my rounds, checking on soldiers, and ensuring security was in place, I rolled out my bag for some much-needed sleep.

I had my bag rolled out on the blowout panels and was just getting ready to pull my boots off when the tank commander of my three tanks jumped across to mine. He informed me that his gunner had spilled boiling coffee on himself. I grabbed my helmet, mask, and weapon and went to check on the injured soldier. After being briefed by the combat lifesaver, I called to get a medic to evaluate the burn. The medic vehicle was up with the rest of the company and, due to the narrow road, couldn't get to us. Because of dismounts in the area, we didn't want the medic to cross the one hundred meters to our position on foot. I told the commander to have the forward platoons hold their fire, so I could come get the medic. I started up the road to get the medic, and the injured soldier's tank commander joined me, because he didn't want me to go alone. As it turned out, the burn wasn't serious, and the soldier was able to continue to perform his duties. After returning the medic to his vehicle, I climbed back on my tank.

Before going to sleep, I thanked God that we had come so far without serious injury in the platoon. I also thanked Him for the way 2nd Platoon had come together, then I drifted off to sleep. A short time later, I was awaked by the explosion of two mortar rounds near our tanks, but exhausted by the past three days, I asked if anyone was injured, rolled over, and went back to sleep.

We moved out at 0600, amid rumors of a pending cease-fire. Charlie Company moved out ahead of the task force, taking the shortest possible route to block the route of Iraqi forces retreating north. The company executive officer (XO) who was leading the company used a GPS to navigate our way out of the "valley of the boogers." Topping a small rise in the road, the XO reported an enemy tank to his front. A SABOT round at five hundred meters set the enemy tank ablaze, and we continued to move. A few minutes later, my platoon passed the burning tank, and the XO reported more enemy vehicles to his front. These vehicles were facing in the opposite direction and appeared to be unmanned. The commander told the XO to continue to move and not engage the enemy vehicles. We could use thermite grenades to destroy the vehicles and save our main-gun rounds. I asked the commander to allow my platoon, the trail platoon, to destroy the vehicles. The road was so narrow that I was worried about my tanks passing so close to burning vehicles as their ammunition exploded.

We destroyed three tanks, one ZSU 23-4, and some APCs prior to battalion telling us to leave the rest of the vehicles for follow-on forces. We picked up the pace of our move as word came down that a cease-fire would go into effect at 0800. We moved through the fog and haze, bypassing several enemy vehicles and dismounting soldiers to establish a blocking position facing south just prior to 0800. Sitting in the desert under a sky darkened by the smoke of oil well fires, we all slumped a little and felt the fatigue wash over us as 0800 passed, and the war ended.

Exact dates, times, and places on a map hold little importance in my memories of Operation Desert Storm. The things that stand out are the people and the emotion that can never be fully explained by those who fought, or fully understood by those who didn't. I remember the immense pride that swelled within me when my loader pressed the play button on his Walkman and I heard Lee Greenwood's "God Bless the USA" as we moved forward into the breach. I remember the loneliness and pain I felt writing letters home to my wife, kids, and family, knowing that we would soon be fighting. The fear of the unknown: Was I ready? Was there anything more I could do to prepare my platoon or myself? This was the self-doubt that soldiers at all levels must feel prior to combat. Aside from my love for my wife and family, I have never experienced such strong emotions. I learned more about myself as a soldier, an officer, and a man in the hundred hours of Operation Desert Storm than I had in the rest of my thirty-five years.

CHAPTER SEVEN

OPERATION IRAQI FREEDOM (2003–PRESENT)

///MAJ. CLAY LYLE (U.S. ARMY)

In 1996, I was commissioned as a second lieutenant of armor. Eventually as I rose in rank, I assumed command of Apache Troop, 3d Squadron, 7th Cavalry, in January 2003. The following January, I deployed my troop to Kuwait in support of Operation Enduring Freedom in order to prepare for combat operations in Iraq. My story begins a couple of weeks after the beginning of Operation Iraqi Freedom.

We had charged nonstop across the desert for forty-eight hours to reach As Samawah and the Euphrates River. We had encountered the Fedayeen for the first time in As Samawah. We had battled dug-in infantry and Fedayeen all night south of Najaf, crossed the Euphrates, and fought through a sandstorm for two days east of Najaf. We had been the first U.S. troop to approach and coduct the initial screen of the Karbala Gap.

We had done it all with our every move being reported live to the world via the troop's embedded CNN reporter, Walt Rodgers. All that said, we were about to attack into Baghdad, the heart of Saddam's regime, and I knew it would be nothing like anything we had already encountered. I got off my tank and moved to the rear of it. I wanted a few minutes to just stand there and think. We had planned and read for months about the defense of Baghdad. I believed we would face fighting far worse than anything we had seen previously in the war. I tried to clear my mind and relax for a few final seconds. Walt came up and asked, "Will we be going soon?" I said, "Yes, very soon." He knew the importance of what we were about to do, and we told one another to be careful.

My loader, Specialist Posey, leaned over the side of the tank and said, "The SCO (squadron commanding officer) said for us to go REDCON One." I said a little prayer for my soldiers, and then I climbed onto my tank. I gave a short count, and all of Apache Troop's engines started simultaneously as always. Apache Troop was ready to lead the squadron across the Euphrates River and into Baghdad.

I called Lieutenant Garrett on the radio, "Red one this is Apache six. Execute your move to objective Peach. Over." He excitedly acknowledged. My troop began moving toward the Euphrates River for the second time of the war. This time, however, Baghdad awaited us on the other side. I considered the population of more than five million people and the composition and disposition of the Republican Guards and Special Republican Guards forces defending the city. I envisioned horrible street fighting with black and white visions of World War II footage running through my head. I thought of the historical implications of laying siege to a nation's capital. Many issues ran through my mind as we moved up the road in column toward the bridge over the Euphrates River. All of those things reinforced my belief that we would shortly be in the fight of our lives.

It took more than an hour to cross a series of bridges and get out from behind 2nd Brigade Combat Team, which was attacking into Objective Saints. We moved onto an alternate route that took us through some farmland and allowed us to move onto Highway 1 just southeast of Saddam International Airport.

I could see the light poles and an overpass on the highway; we were approaching it quickly. At approximately 1500, Apache Troop turned west onto Highway 1 south of Baghdad. Both 1st and 2nd platoons ran over the guardrails to cross the median and occupy both the eastbound and westbound lanes of traffic in staggered column. The SCO and Major Gavle pulled in behind my troop.

Suddenly, coax and 25mm fire erupted to my right. Specialist Wheatley reported, "Engaging dismounts and a 23-2 ADA (air defense artillery) gun." All the vehicles on the right side of the road were firing at twenty Iraqi soldiers and an ADA gun. The ADA gun was quickly destroyed, and the ammunition stacked next to it began cooking off. The enemy infantry desperately fired their AK-47s at us.

Lieutenant Garrett reported that the twenty dismounts had all been killed. Small-arms and ADA fire erupted on both sides of the road. The troop was encountering enemy positions on both sides of the highway. Each position was composed of an ADA gun being used in direct fire mode with anywhere from ten to twenty soldiers supporting it. All twenty-four of my combat vehicles were firing to both sides of the road.

I did not want to stop and maneuver on the enemy. I possessed enough combat power to pass the enemy soldiers from one vehicle to the next, and then from platoon to platoon and continue to move. I refused to lose my momentum.

The constant fire from both sides of the road continued for more than five kilometers. In every situation, the large quantities of ammunition stacked next to the guns began to explode and cook off. In total, we had encountered and destroyed fifteen of the 23-2 ADA guns and more than one hundred dismounts. Several bursts from the ADA guns and hundreds of rounds of small arms had flown over and in between our vehicles, but none of my soldiers were wounded. I could observe the first interchange of Objective Montgomery I was to seize less than three kilometers ahead.

Both 1st and 2nd platoons moved onto the interchange, and most cars began turning around and leaving. Lieutenant Garrett reported more Iraqi infantry firing at them, but did not report that they were impeding his seizure of the intersection. He quickly reported that his hunter/killer team had killed the fifty dismounts that were firing on them. The interchange was secure, and I ordered Lieutenant Linthwaite to begin his attack up the expressway. I followed closely behind.

The 3rd Platoon moved little more than five hundred meters up the expressway before they began receiving fire from two heavy machine guns dug in to bunkers and fewer than twenty scattered dismounts. Specialist Chase reported the gun's destruction, and Lieutenant Linthwaite soon reported the dismounts' demise. One of the machine guns was sandbagged in the median, and all of its ammunition was violently cooking off.

Both 3rd and 4th Platoons rapidly moved onto the interchange of Highway 10 and the Abu Ghraib Expressway. I told Lieutenants Linthwaite and Fritz to assume some risk on the south side of the expressway, as it was the direction we had come from and 1st and 2nd Platoon were blocking access onto the expressway from that direction. I ordered him to focus his combat power east and west down Highway 10 and northeast up the expressway. A small town was immediately adjacent to the Highway 10 overpass. The only terrain available was the actual overpass itself and the on and off ramps, so the Bradleys and tanks pulled up onto the overpass and oriented the appropriate direction. They were sitting completely exposed and silhouetted blocking Highway 10 and observing into the small towns. Two Bradleys and one tank remained down on the Abu Ghraib Expressway and oriented northeast down it, blocking all traffic leaving Baghdad.

Lieutenant Garret and Specialist Wheatley continued to report sporadic contact with Iraqis attacking both on foot and attempting to shoot their way through the checkpoint from a car. Specialist Fuentes reported that the mortars were set and ready to fire. First Sergeant Woodhall reported that the trains were set.

Lieutenant Linthwaite reported that his vehicles were set. He, Staff Sergeant Pizzino, and Specialist Chase controlled the west side of Highway 10. Lieutenant Fritz, Specialist Gilmore, and Staff Sergeant Williams controlled the east side of Highway 10. Staff Sergeants McDaniel, Knight, and Julian controlled the Abu Ghraib Expressway. Staff Sergeant Campbell was protecting the rear of the 360 degree perimeter.

Almost instantaneously, from three different directions, all hell broke loose. Heavy volumes of small-arms fire, machine-gun fire, and RPG fire began to consume 3rd Platoon, 4th Platoon, and myself. Iraqis were firing on the vehicles on the overpass from in and around the town. All vehicles began returning aimed coax and 25mm fire where they could identify enemy positions. This intensified over the next thirty minutes.

Word of our presence must have spread rapidly, because within an hour of our arrival, vehicles carrying Fedayeen and uniformed Iraqi soldiers began to pour into the area on all three of the contested routes. The volumes of fire of both the Iraqis and my vehicles were relentless. Within the first thirty minutes, tanks and Bradleys were having to empty their coax-spent brass boxes. It was tight terrain, and everything was occurring in close proximity of the town. I began using my FBCB2 (a wireless tactical Internet system) to request artillery and mortars right at the edge of the town on likely dismounted infiltration routes. From that moment forward, Lieutenant Wade and I would process almost constant indirect fire missions to my mortars and the artillery battery throughout the remainder of the night.

I realized I needed to get the CNN crew and their truck that had followed me out of this situation and back to the slightly more secure area my first sergeant had occupied. As I began my move, I observed five Iraqis running through some sparse palm trees toward the town to go join the fight against my troop. My M16 was at the ready, and we were moving slow. I aimed and fired at one of the Iraqis. For the second time in this war, I watched a young Iraqi soldier fall down dead from my rifle. The others began scrambling around, but Sergeant Davis was now on them and he peppered the other four Iraqis with coax until they were all dead.

As I arrived at Lieutenant Shea's location, he told me two jeeps with soldiers firing from them had just attacked the location. The engineers and the TAC (tactical air controller) personnel began engaging them with small arms. One engineer destroyed both of the jeeps with his Mk-19 40mm grenade launcher.

The sun began to fall, and it turned into a night battle. The Iraqis began using dump trucks to bring groups of fifteen to twenty-five reinforcements at a time to the battle. I instructed the troop to engage the dump trucks as soon as they identified a uniformed soldier or a weapon. Eight dump trucks attempted to bring soldiers to the battlefield, and all eight were destroyed; 120mm HEAT from the tanks was completely destroying the truck and all its occupants in one large blast. The Iraqis were blown from the dump trucks like popcorn out of a hot kettle.

One uniformed soldier attacked the vehicles on the expressway firing his rifle as he approached on a motorcycle. He was quickly cut down by machine-gun fire from the Bradleys. Every form of vehicle imaginable tested our defense. An uparmored truck attempted to tow an ADA gun into position and was destroyed with 25mm fire. Several of the Iraqis' most popular weapons, pickup trucks with machine guns mounted in the back, pulled into range and began to fire, but were rapidly shot by the tanks and Bradleys.

Two hours into the battle, a bus charged Staff Sergeant Knight and Staff Sergeant McDaniel; it was going almost seventy miles per hour and was heading directly for them. Fortunately, I had briefed the troop on the Iraqis' use of suicide bombers. My vehicles fired three bursts of warning shots, and then I ordered them to destroy it. As the tank and Bradley shot the bus, it stopped, and two wounded uniformed Iraqi soldiers attempted to get clear of the bus. Then, there was a huge explosion, much larger than that of a normal bus. The bus had been carrying explosives. The explosion killed the already-dying Iraqi soldiers.

I was having difficulty keeping up with the sheer numbers we were killing as I reported to squadron. For more than three hours, from the time we first reached Highway 1 until this time, I was reporting another fifteen to twenty Iraqis killed every ten minutes. Each dump truck contained fifteen to twenty-five Iraqis alone. The vehicles on Highway 10 were still receiving constant small-arms and RPG fire and returning devastating fires themselves. Specialist Chase and Lieutenant Fritz could observe the mortars and artillery falling directly on and destroying Iraqi soldiers and equipment.

To keep my line of communications between 1st and 2nd platoons and 3rd and 4th Platoons, I instructed Specialist Birdsong to lead two Bradleys from his position up the expressway to the Highway 10 overpass and destroy any threat he identified. I ordered him to conduct, at random, one of these "gun runs" every forty-five minutes.

My every thought went into to trying to anticipate the enemy's next move and identifying any and every action I could take to improve my troop's survivability and lethality. I wanted to bring every system to bear at my disposal against our attackers.

The constant hail of gunfire continued at the Highway 10 overpass. It truly was beginning to look like the highway of death. Destroyed, mangled, or burning vehicles littered both the Abu Ghraib Expressway and Highway 10. The number of dead Iraqis continued to rise rapidly. Bullets and RPGs had been impacting my tanks and Bradleys for hours, but none of my soldiers were wounded. As the night continued, it seemed the carnage around that location began to take its toll on the enemy. The level of gunfire tapered off, and the vehicles finally stopped approaching.

Shortly after 0400, Specialist Chase and Lieutenant Fritz almost simultaneously reported dismounts near the west and east towns. I used my FBCB2 to plan an artillery target on the west side of the expressway and a mortar target on the east side. I planned the targets as close to the town and the location of the activity as I could. The mortars and artillery quickly began firing with their usual ground-shaking affects. The grid coordinates from my FBCB2 and the mortars' and artillery battery's fires again proved deadly accurate, falling directly on the Iraqi infantry.

The rounds ceased impacting, and all vehicles reported negative contact with any enemy activity. Both towns had fallen silent. It was 0430 on the morning of April 4, and we had been slugging it out on that overpass for twelve hours.

Just when everything seemed to have completely subsided, it happened, the radio call I had trained my entire career to hear: "Contact, T72s (Soviet-designed tank). Out." The sky began to light up with Bradley 25mm and tank main-gun fire. I could not engage the enemy from my position and frantically got the tank ready to move forward. Lieutenant Linthwaite reported: "Blue Two, Blue Five, and Green Three are in contact with nine T72s, three MTLBs (Soviet tracked armored personnel carriers), and fifty dismounts (infantry). They are attacking down the expressway." I reported the situation to the SCO as my tank began to move toward Staff Sergeant McDaniel's position. I wanted to get artillery firing. I used my FBCB2 and plotted a grid 1,200 meters down the expressway from Staff Sergeant McDaniel's position. I called the grid to Lieutenant Wade and Specialist Fuentes: "I want immediate suppression with mortars and artillery. Apache Thirty, you work the fires net and get the guns firing ASAP. Out."

Stanight and his gunner, Sergeant Coward, hit three of the T72s with HEAT rounds, resulting in huge fireballs and explosions illuminating the predawn sky. I pulled behind Staff Sergeant McDaniel. The battle was near its end as the tank and two Bradleys finished the destruction of the dismounts with their coax machine guns. It had lasted little more than five minutes. The artillery was impacting down the expressway. I wanted to destroy or suppress any additional tanks coming down the expressway. I ordered Lieutenant Wade to end the mission of indirect fires, as we could not observe any other vehicles approaching.

I talked to Staff Sergeants McDaniel, Knight, Julian, Pizzino, and everyone else who had witnessed the short battle on the radio to capture what had occurred. The nine T72s and three MTLBs had attacked down the expressway in staggered column in both lanes of traffic just as we had moved up the highway the day prior. They passed the carnage of Apache Troop's highway of death presumably assuming the destruction was caused by artillery or the air force. The tanks appeared to be confused and lacking night vision capability, because they fired few main-gun rounds. Most of the vehicles, the MTLBs, and most of the T72s had been carrying infantry on top of them. The tanks carrying infantry and the MTLBs stopped to let the infantry on the ground. Some of my soldiers reported one of the tanks firing its commander's machine gun in desperation. The infantry began firing AK-47s and RPGs immediately, but they were not the primary threat. Many of them were killed as the MTLBs were destroyed.

Five of the T72s had been destroyed by the Bradley's 25mm chain gun. The gunners, Sergeants Poss and Patterson, used 25mm depleted uranium armor-piercing rounds to engage the tanks. They were at ranges varying from four hundred to one thousand meters. They aimed at the turret and the turret ring. The T72s destroyed by the Bradley guns did not experience the huge explosions inflicted by the tank HEAT rounds. The 25mm rounds hit and penetrated the turrets causing spall (fragments of the turret) to shoot into the turret, killing the crews. It appeared that components inside the turrets and hulls were damaged. When the crews were killed, the vehicles were rendered ineffective.

The tanks Staff Sergeant Knight destroyed with HEAT rounds continued to spew deep black smoke and cook off ammunition for almost an hour. The MTLBs continued to burn until only charred metal hulks remained. Some of the infantry and one of the MTLBs had progressed relatively close as the priority to engage targets remained with the T72s.

The sun began to rise, and the death and destruction that occurred during the night was only magnified in the daylight. It was hard to grasp what I saw before my eyes. Everything appeared as hot spots through the thermal sight in varying shades of green at night. Destroyed, burned, or still-burning vehicles filled the expressway. The expressway appeared to be impassable with the amount of destroyed vehicles strewn across all six lanes. The expressway, the towns, and the surrounding farmland were littered with bodies.

The dead Iraqi infantry lay all around. A severed boot with part of the leg still attached lay within sight. The driver of one of the T72s shot by the Bradleys crawled out of his driver's hatch and made it halfway onto the top of the turret before he died. All that could be seen of the tank commander of the same T72 were two motionless hands frozen in the air as they began to emerge from the turret. A soldier was still burning on top of one of the MTLBs; he burned until there was nothing left but an ash outline of a human being.

There was no time to stand in awe of the carnage; the sun brought a new day's worth of attackers. The majority of the enemy was now in the towns, using building windows, roofs, and walls to fire from. Bullets and RPGs flew overhead and exploded around every vehicle. Fuel arrived, and the tanks desperately needed to refuel. I began rotating one Bradley and one tank back at a time. I decided to stay and man the position while Staff Sergeant Knight and Lieutenant Devlin rotated back. Lieutenant Wade arrived with Walt. Walt immediately began raising the dish to begin reporting live. The small-arms and RPG fire was relentless throughout the day as we repelled attack after attack.

About 1500, the SCO called, "Apache Six, the is Saber Six. How would you like to go attack twenty-two T72s?"

I replied, "Sure, you coming?"

Lieutenant Colonel Ferrell replied, "I wouldn't miss it. Here's the deal, stud. The air force has identified twenty-two stationary T72s. You will have to move about three kilometers down the Abu Ghraib Expressway. The air force is going to attack the target. I'll also have Assassin fire the target. I want you to move forward and observe, then complete the destruction of any remaining T72s. Let me know when you can be ready."

I answered, "Roger. I will take a force that is tank-heavy. I have to reposition a couple of Bradleys to maintain my blocking positions. I can be ready in ten minutes. Over." He replied and said the TAC (tactical air command) would move on the expressway and trail behind us when we moved.

I issued a radio order to my troop, assembled my force, and began to move. We passed through Staff Sergeant McDaniel and began to drive past the death and destruction on the road. I drove within five to fifty feet of all the destroyed vehicles and dead bodies. It stunk. I realized when I had passed the Highway 10 overpass that the hundreds of bodies in the immediate area were beginning to fill the air with the stench of death. Some of the T72s and MTLBs from the morning were still smoldering.

Apache Troop finally passed all the destroyed vehicles and continued up the expressway. My force was composed of seven M1A1 tanks, two M3A2 Bradleys, and the M7 BFIST (an artillery command and control vehicle based on the Bradley). Lieutenant Garrett reported that he had reached the grid I had given him to stop at. I had to allow two kilometers of safety standoff for the air force. The grid the pilots reported was nine hundred meters north of the expressway, and my unit could not observe the target because of palm groves and buildings. I reported to the SCO that I was set but could not observe the target.

The SCO reported, "An A-10 (U.S. Air Force ground attack aircraft) is finishing a gun run right now. As soon as it is clear, I am going to have Assassin fire ICM (improved conventional munitions) on the target until the F-15s (U.S. Air Force fighter-bomber) come on station." I responded, "Roger, continuing to observe." The A-10 cleared the area; I could hear A/1-9 FA begin firing. Assassin fired twelve rounds of ICM and appeared to be on target. The F-15s began making their approach, so A/1-9 FA ceased firing. The F-15s dropped four 1,000-pound bombs. The sound and shock from the explosions was impressive even from two kilometers away. The pilots reported they were now clear and the SCO ordered A/1-9 FA to fire again. This time, Captain Schwartz fired twenty-four SADARM (sense and destroy armor) munitions. Those munitions are made to seek out armor as they descend. I observed that the impacts and both the artillery and air force were on target.

A great deal of dust and white smoke began filling the sky. I noticed something odd based on my experience with the T72s in the morning. I called Lieutenant Colonel Ferrell: "Saber six, this is Apache six. Everything seems to be on target, but I am not observing deep black smoke from burning vehicles. There is a ton of white smoke and dust, but no black smoke from metal burning." He responded, "That is a good point, we'll see. Two Tornadoes (British air force fighter-bombers) are inbound and will fire Maverick (antitank) missiles, then I'll move you forward." In five minutes I heard the planes overhead and the missiles firing. I saw big explosions, but still no black smoke.

Lieutenant Colonel Ferrell called, "Apache six, begin your attack. Try to get eyes on the target area and destroy anything left. Over." I acknowledged and began moving my element forward. I told Specialist Wheatley to assume the lead and for the two Bradleys to get behind the tanks.

My force had been sitting on the expressway with a town on the right/south side of the expressway. Two kilometers to our front, another overpass crossed the expressway. To the left/north side of the expressway were a palm grove and some farm houses. I still could not see the target area the air force had engaged far off of the left/north side of the expressway.

The column began moving. The massive artillery and air force barrage had created a large amount of dust and smoke, which the wind was blowing back our direction. The artillery and air force attack had also lasted more than forty-five minutes, and dusk was approaching. We had moved eight hundred meters forward and were beginning to move past the town that had been adjacent to the Abu Ghraib Expressway on the right/south side.

Suddenly, Specialist Wheatley fired a main-gun round. Simultaneously, small-arms tracers and large rounds began flying toward us from the front and flanks. Specialist Wheatley reported, "I've got T72s and dismounts at the overpass." Specialist Chase immediately keyed the net: "There are T72s on the right."

I didn't need the radio report. I was right behind them and saw an entire defensive position. I quickly ascertained the situation. Four T72s and approximately one hundred dismounts were in a strongpoint on each side of the expressway in the vicinity of the overpass to our front. A canal ran in front of the entire enemy position. On the enemy side of the canal was a (earthen) berm running along the bank the entire length of the canal. Hull-down fighting positions for the T72s were dug in to the berm. The positions were well dug and only the T72s' turrets were exposed. I could see a great deal of activity behind the berm; there were soldiers and vehicles moving behind it. I could observe several ADA guns being used in direct fire mode as well as some artillery pieces. The town on the right side of the expressway had concealed us from the Iraqis and vice versa. The engagement ranges were from 800 to 1,500 meters. Nothing in the enemy defense had been reported or engaged by the air force.

I commanded, "Contact tanks, front and right. Slow your move, but do not stop. Bradleys concentrate on the dismounts to the front."

Sergeant Davis yelled, "I'm laid on one, sir."

I said, "Fire, fire at will." Sergeant Davis fired, and a fireball from the T72 exploded almost forty feet into the air.

I dropped inside the turret and looked at my FBCB2 screen. I touched my pin to the screen where the center of the enemy position was. I keyed the net: "Saber Six, this is Apache Six. I have contact with T72s and dismounts; center of mass grid to the enemy defense is MB 215865. I am engaging with direct fire. Break. Assassin Six, this is Apache Six. Over." Captain Schwartz quickly responded. I continued, "Assassin Six, this is Apache Six, immediate suppression, grid MB 2152 8653, T72s in the defense. Over." He confirmed the grid and said he had high-explosive rounds on the way.

Every vehicle commander was cross-talking with the others on the troop net to control fires and report targets destroyed. Specialist Wheatley called me, "Apache Six, this White Four. The expressway is about to dip down below ground level, and we won't be able to see or shoot anything."

I responded, "Stop and continue to fire. There isn't anything on the left; all guns right."

Captain Schwartz called on the squadron command net, "Shot. Over." His guns were firing. I was so impressed. It had been less than ninety seconds since I called the eight-digit grid coordinate to him and requested artillery.

Lieutenant Ferrell called, "Apache six, SITREP. Over." All my adrenaline was flowing and Sergeant Davis was preparing to fire again. I replied, "Saber Six this is Apache Six . . ." Sergeant Davis firing the 120mm gun again and destroying another T72 interrupted my transmission. I called again to complete my transmission: "There's a lot of shit out there. We are taking fire, but most of it is just dying. Over."

Captain Schwartz' rounds began affecting exactly where I had wanted them. They were landing right on all the soldiers and vehicles I could see moving just behind the berm.

I could see the fast-traveling, glowing 125mm main-gun rounds from the T72s flying over my vehicles or falling short. The gunners and crewmembers of the best tanks in the vaunted Iraqi Republican Guards were obviously poorly trained.

A round exploded less than twenty-five meters short of my vehicle. It rattled Posey and shook the entire seventy-ton tank. It had been the closest round yet to any of my vehicles. The last T72s were burning. The huge fireball explosions had been occurring every twenty to thirty seconds since the engagement began. Specialist Wheatley, Staff Sergeant Suzch, and the Bradleys were still firing at the dismounts to the front, but had destroyed all four of the T72s around the overpass ahead. The remainder of my force had destroyed the twelve T72s to the right and was continuing to engage the ADA guns and infantry.

I made a count of the enemy. The sixteen manned and fighting dug-in T72s were all burning. Ammunition was cooking off and fuel was exploding. Specialist Wheatley reported that almost all of the one hundred dismounts were dead. My vehicles continued to engage the

ADA guns and artillery pieces we could see. There was still a great deal of activity behind the berm. We surprised the Iraqis as much as they had surprised us. There was no surprise left; Americans were soundly defeating the best the Iraqis had. I wanted to disengage and retrograde back down the expressway before they reinforced their position with more tanks or counterattacked.

Iraqi artillery began impacting on the expressway between my vehicles and the TAC, which was stopped one kilometer behind us. The Iraqi defense even had planned artillery targets in support of it. It was somewhat surprising that the Iraqi defense was so well established and coordinated, just poorly executed. The Iraqi artillery proved to be slow and inaccurate, but it was falling. I wanted to move before the rounds were adjusted onto my stationary force.

I reported the situation to the SCO: "Saber six, this is Apache six. I have engaged and destroyed sixteen manned and fighting T72s, approximately one hundred dismounts, and several ADA guns and artillery pieces. I am observing enemy artillery behind my position. Request permission to disengage and move back to my position. Over."

He said, "Roger. Let's get moving." The entire battle had lasted little more than ten minutes.

I was willing to trade speed for the survivability of keeping my tanks' frontal armor oriented toward the enemy. I told everyone to begin backing up. All my vehicles began backing up. A/1-9 FA fired ICM at the same grid to cover my displacement. The SCO called, "Let me know when your trail vehicle is clear of the 20 degree Easting. Division is going to fire MLRS (multiple-launch rocket system) at that grid you reported."

Slowly, as dusk was falling, we moved clear of the enemy engagement area. My vehicles passed back through Staff Sergeant McDaniel's wire and were now relatively safe. The impact of what we had just done began to hit us like a tidal wave. We realized how much exhilaration and adrenaline we were all feeling. We had just encountered the best the Iraqis possessed. They were dug in and prepared. We had slugged it out in true armored warfare. We had just lived through a tank fight, a tank fight we decisively won.

///COL. RICK SCHWARTZ (U.S. ARMY)

On April 5, 2003, at 0600, U.S. forces from the 3rd Infantry Division attacked into the heart of Baghdad, Iraq, focused on penetrating the reinforced city defenses, determining the level of resistance, and demonstrating coalition resolve. Simply put, this was an armored raid into a city of more than six million people. In fact, the Battle for Baghdad was the first armored raid into a major city since World War II. Moreover, it was certainly the first of its kind involving the M1 Abrams main battle tank. I was the task force commander (TF 1-64 Armor, Rogue) who led the charge on that early spring morning.

The events of that day are captured in print, still photos, and video clips. Each form of media captures the Battle for Baghdad in its own unique way, however, so many unspoken words will stay with the soldiers who fought that day because it is truly indescribable. And, no matter how hard I try, my words will provide only a glimpse into one battle on one day. If the words that follow seem to lack emotion, I apologize. I have tried on numerous occasions to capture the feelings of battle on paper. In the end, I cannot find the words to describe courage, fear, intensity, sadness, and brotherhood. I also do not have the audacity to use the word *I* in writing about the Battle for Baghdad; I actually did little. If anything, I was on the battleground serving as a point of reference for the boys. If Rogue 6 was ready to go, then so was I.

The planning for the Battle for Baghdad was quite simple—move and attack. After receiving the attack order the previous night, it would be an understatement to say that emotions were high. The Rogue plans team exited the brigade operations center with limited information: the direction of attack, projected timeline, and a hearty "Good luck." We were going in as the information collectors and were planning and anticipating for the worst. The information about the defending Iraqis was spotty at best. For many months after the battle, I was angry at the lack of information available before the fight. Eventually, I came to accept this information void.

Following the mission brief, we brought together the operations officer, intelligence officer, and artillery officer and I prepared to issue my commanders planning guidance. Up to this point in the war, planning for each battle was simple. Most battles occurred by chance contact, and battle orders where issued over the radio. However, the Battle for Baghdad was going to be different—not simply the tactics of the battle, but the leadership required to motivate a group of men to attack into the true unknown. As the plans team assembled, I had an inclination that this was going to be a defining moment in our lives. In particular, I knew that my greatest life challenge at this point was going to be looking into the eyes of the company commanders, first sergeants, specialty platoon leaders, and staff and convincing them that we would fight hard and we would win, without question.

The morning of the attack was without incident. Tankers, infantrymen, and engineers moved to the ready line as if preparing for a race. At 0600, Task Force Rogue crossed the line of departure and unleashed heavy volumes of main-gun and machine-gun fire. The pace was slow, and our actions were methodical. The lead company/team received the greatest volume of enemy fire but remained selective by handing off targets to follow-on companies. Conserving ammunition and handing off targets was going to be our most effective strategy for destroying the estimated four thousand enemy fighters.

Most crewmen were fighting well exposed in the turret. Tank commanders were chest high, placing them in great danger. We fought exposed for the five previous battles leading up to Baghdad. Fighting exposed was a matter of personal preference. Staff Sergeant Stephon Booker chose to fight exposed. He was a tank commander and a motivator. He was considered by most to be a high-energy tanker and not one to sugar coat words. Booker also chose to use an M4 machine gun from the turret of his tank in order to get at those hard-to-reach targets. At 0730, Booker was shot and killed while firing his M4 at close-range targets. The next moments in the turret are understood only by his crew, however, their actions that day are a testament to the high training standards enforced by Booker. They adjusted to the chaotic situation and continued to fight.

The Iraqi defenses appeared to be emplaced in two rings of fire. A protective cordon, or outer ring, created the initial defensive while an inner ring was the primary defensive body. The lead attacking forces quickly breeched the Iraqi outer ring with most of the Iraqi fighters seeming genuinely surprised by the attacking lead tanks. High volume of machine-gun and RPG fire was the initial threat. Some Iraqi fighters fought from complex underground fighting positions while others fought from buildings, apartments, schools, shops, and mosques. Some chose to attack our column on foot, in cars, and even on motorcycles. Highway 3, the attack route, was virtually abandoned. The air strikes against strategic targets were enough to keep most nonfighters home. That said, not all vehicles on the highway were considered hostile, and this made it necessary to discern the intent of any vehicle on the road.

Collateral damage during the attack was considered an *unacceptable outcome;* Rogue leaders didn't use that term, nor the term *unintended consequences*. We called it exactly what it was: *killing innocent civilians*. Therefore, leaders in our outfit remained sensitive to life as opposed to fixated on death.

The gap between the inner ring and the outer ring was noticeable. We entered that zone low on ammo and with a flaming M1 (C12) that had been struck and penetrated. The air filters were on fire, and the tank quickly became engulfed in flames. Crewmembers poured cans of water on the engine, all the while exposing themselves to massive enemy fire. Soldiers were hit and the tank continued to burn. After attempts to extinguish the flames and tow the tank to friendly lines, it reignited and became unmanageable. Orders were given to abandon the tank and evacuate the crew.

The last vehicle in the attack column shot the burning M1 multiple times at close range. The sabot shots were precision strikes intended to destroy it; yet the tank refused to explode. Seeing this, we were sure the tank would end up in Iraqi hands and make headlines. The thought of that made me sick.

Reaching the inner ring was met with the command, "Button up." Every vehicle in the attack column was struck. Numerous tanks and Bradleys were hit multiple times by RPGs. One Bradley was hit five times, eventually knocking out the fire control system. The engineers in the personnel carriers seemed to be taking the most enemy fire. They were also the most exposed and least armored. They fought with small-arms machine guns and demonstrated unbelievable courage. On that day, of the many lessons I learned, one stands out: engineers are incredible war-fighters, and their ability to fight should never be underestimated.

In the last moments of the battle, the lead company reported that they identified tanks to their front that appeared hostile. The battalion operations officer checked the digital tracking device and responded that they were friendly tanks from the unit in which we were intended to link up. The Rogue tankers held their fire under incredible stress. The patience and discipline demonstrated by those lead tankers was remarkable. Link-up complete, the armored strike into Baghdad ended.

In forty-eight hours, we would do it all again.

///GUNNERY SERGEANT NICK POPIVITCH (U.S. MARINE CORPS)

I was the tank commander of Charlie 1/4, and the platoon sergeant of Charlie Company's 1st Platoon. We had just relieved the army in Fallujah. My platoon had been operating with relatively little rest in support of the 1st Marine Regiment, although the contact had been pretty light. We had been operating on the east side of town, and the enemy insurgents there had little desire to tangle with marine tanks.

My platoon had just come in from three days' duty at a coalition strongpoint out in town. Regiment had nothing planned for tanks that day, so it appeared my marines would get some overdue rest and a chance to turn a few wrenches on the tanks. We had been back only about an hour when bad news arrived. We were eating breakfast in the base chow hall when word arrived about some Americans killed out in town. Worst still, their bodies were being desecrated in the streets. Shortly after that, I received the word to ready the platoon to move out again.

I informed the marines of 1st Platoon about the morning's events. I told them, "Nobody does that to Americans," and to mount up and prepare to move out! The looks in their eyes and on their faces told me that the insurgents had made a grievous error in picking a fight with the U.S. Marine Corps.

By the time we departed the base, more details had arrived. The enemy *insurgents* (I use this term only to describe them for lack of a better one as there really is no good term for such a dishonorable excuse for a human being) had hung the corpses from a train trestle and were vowing to turn Fallujah into a graveyard for Americans.

The first couple of days of the Fallujah offensive were mostly uneventful. We did a lot of reconnaissance of the enemy, and they occasionally probed us. After a couple of days of this, the marines were itching for a fight. We would get one soon.

I received orders to take my tank section (with two tanks, mine and my wingman's) to support the Fox Company that had been in contact with enemy probes the night before. I arrived at Fox's AO (area of operations) northwest of Fallujah and located their CO. After a brief meeting, we agreed the best place for my tank was at the center of their company's defensive line, with my wingman protecting my flank. My position was good. I was about two hundred meters from the first row of buildings; I had a good berm in front of my tank to protect from RPGs, a train trestle overhead for mortars, and a lot of grunts in elevated positions. Life was good except that we weren't there to defend, we were anxious to attack!

About mid-day, Fox conducted a security patrol to prevent the enemy from working in close for a mortar or RPG shot. We were unaware of how close the enemy had already come. About ten minutes into their patrol, the infantry squad was ambushed. I couldn't see it, but I heard the insurgents open up with RPGs, AK-47s, and RPK machine guns. This was a little more committed than the enemy usually engaged.

The infantry squad took a casualty, set up a base of fire, and called for support. I asked the CO if he needed the tanks. He agreed, "Roll tanks!" At last, we were on the offensive.

I took the lead with my wingman behind me. As I passed through the infantry squad, I saw a corpsman rendering first aid to a marine who had been shot in the face. I later learned that this marine not only survived but also returned to his unit to finish the deployment. *Semper fi!*

My tank crew and I were like sharks with blood in the water, and the enemy insurgents were eager enough to fight with tanks. There was no coordination or reason to their attacks. They would pop out of buildings or doorways and take a shot at my tank. Usually their RPG shot wouldn't hit, but usually my tank's machine guns or main gun would. In a short while, I had taken a couple of RPG hits (resulting in no damage) and had inflicted more than a dozen kills on the enemy. By now, Fox Company, 2nd Platoon, had worked their way into the city alongside of my tank. Fallujah was going to be a graveyard all right, but not for Americans.

We began to work our way into the city. The plan was that I would lead with my tank. My wingman would trail about a block back, covering my flanks and rear. The infantry would work building to building, covering my move from the rooftops. This technique was successful, as enemy insurgents would attempt to shoot, and then flee into buildings not knowing our infantry were over the top directing the tank's main gun on to target whatever room in whatever building the enemy thought he was safe.

We used this tactic to take block after block. Soon we had a pretty good tally of enemy kills, and the remaining enemy was getting less eager to tangle with a marine tank. The next tactic we employed was this: after a period of more than ten minutes without a contact, I would start to back up the tank as if I were leaving. The enemy would come out for one last shot. I would then order the tank forward again and continue to kill the enemy. I was amazed how often this worked.

My tank crew and I fed off one another's motivation and intensity. My gunner, Corporal Chambers, surgically removed enemy from the face of the earth with the tank's main gun and coax machine gun. My driver, Lance Corporal Frias, flawlessly maneuvered the tank down tight city streets. We took block after block. The infantry rallied behind the carnage the tank was dispensing. The only problem was that we were expending a lot of ammunition.

Late that afternoon, I began to run low on ammunition. Because I was in the lead, I had expended much more ammunition than my wingman, Staff Sergeant Escamilla. His tank still had a relatively full combat load. I backed up closer to his tank, and the infantry put down some good suppressive fire. Our two crews quickly transferred ammunition from his tank to mine. The problem was solved, at least temporarily.

Back into the lead and back into the attack I went. I was monitoring only my platoon's radio frequency and that of Fox Company, so my situational awareness of what was going on with the rest of the task force was limited. The CO informed me that we were the deepest penetration into the city, which was motivating. This also was good news because with no friendly units to the left, right, or ahead, there was no need to de-conflict fires before I shot. The enemy fights were asymmetrical in Fallujah, and the ability to engage more quickly resulted in less insurgents getting away. A tank in a city is like a bull in a china cabinet. All the friendlies well behind us was good for us and bad for the enemy! The attack was going well, but the enemy had prepared to make a stand against us up ahead.

About two blocks to our front was a courtyard. Blocking the entrance were two telephone poles with power lines strung between them like a fishing net. Generally, all obstacles are covered by fire, and it was obvious that the courtyard was the kill sack for this ambush. As I closed on this obstacle, I observed many sandbagged fighting positions in the courtyard. I didn't know if the power lines were electrified, and I really didn't want to find out the hard way. The one thing that the enemy didn't count on was that about a half block short of the obstacle, I could see almost the entire courtyard. I stopped there and showed the insurgents that a few sandbag bunkers against a sixty-eight-ton main battle tank was hardly an even fight, and it was a quick end to your life. We killed about ten enemy; only a few were quick enough to escape. The power line obstacle had brought our advance to a halt, however.

I called up higher on the radio and asked if we had any engineering assets available. I don't think anybody thought that a bangalore torpedo or line charge would be an overly useful item in an urban fight. We had none. I looked for a bypass. There was an alley unblocked to the right. About ten meters down that alley a fuel tanker truck trailer was parked. I was sure it was full and wired to blow. I began to plan other options. I couldn't stand the fact that our attack had been halted, and I began to grow impatient.

Luckily, there was a building in the courtyard that must have been a stockpile point for weapons for them. About every ten minutes, an insurgent would attempt to make it across the courtyard to enter it. Sometimes they would actually make it only to get killed taking an RPG shot at us on the way out. This kept my gunner busy while I plotted.

I figured the power lines would tangle my track and possibly halt my tank in the courtyard. In addition to this, I still didn't know if they the power lines were electrified. I eliminated the bypass as an option, due to the fuel trailer. I didn't have any main-gun ammunition to spare to attempt knocking down the telephone poles that supported the power lines. That would be a difficult shot, and I figured it would take too many rounds before I hit it. Also there still was a small portion of the courtyard that I hadn't been able to see up to now.

The success we had caused me to grow more impatient with this halt in our attack. I had a plan. I wasn't overly thrilled with it, but I couldn't stand the thought that the enemy insurgents had stopped me even more. I informed my wingman and the infantry platoon that I intended to ram the obstacle at an angle where I would hopefully hit mostly telephone pole and entangle as little power line as possible in my track. If I sealed my hatches shut, I figured that the distance from the fuel trailer was enough that it would do no damage other than spray burning fuel on the outside of the tank. I was mostly concerned about the fire I would inevitably take when I entered the courtyard. I knew that between the power lines and the certain RPG shots, there was a good possibility that I would be immobilized in the courtyard, so I needed Staff Sergeant Escamilla's tank and the infantry platoon to be prepared to enter the courtyard closely behind me and take the lead if my tank was immobilized. As I said, I wasn't thrilled with this plan, but it was the best I had. Luckily, just prior to executing, the CO called on the radio and presented another option.

I was informed that a C-130 gunship would be on station, but not until after the sun went down. The next problem was how to mark the obstacle for the aircraft. First, I tried to give them a grid, because we were deep in the city and the CO no longer had visual contact with us. I had only a 1:100,000 map, so I couldn't give an accurate grid for an air strike. The aircraft could identify my tank, but not the obstacle. The only solution was for me to drive up to it to designate it. Under the cover of darkness, I took my tank up to the obstacle. Just to be sure, I threw an infrared chem-stick into it. The aircraft reported that it had a tally on the target.

I must admit that I was a little nervous being this close to the obstacle without taking any fire. I was anxious for this obstacle to be gone. The aircraft informed me to let them know when I was 125 meters away from the target. I thought they were being overly cautious, so when I was about one hudnred meters away, I gave the green light. As it turns out, they were not being "overly cautious." The first impacts from the aircraft were most impressive. The burst of the first salvo went all the way to my tank. Impressive. The gunship continued to pound the target. The resulting explosion confirmed my suspicion that the tanker was full of fuel. Soon the air strike ended, and it was time to access the damage.

I drove my tank up and reported the following: "The obstacle has been reduced. The IED, the tanker truck trailer, has been destroyed." Half of a city block had been destroyed (to include the previously mentioned stockpile point). I could sense the increase in motivation among the marines at the overwhelming success of the air strike.

What next? Night had fallen and the CO of Fox had asked for a situation report. I told him that the road was open and that I wanted to continue to press the attack! The enemy had surely been decimated and demoralized by the gunship's strike. We definitely had the initiative, and as a bonus, the gunship was going to remain on station for a while more. The CO gave the go ahead to continue the push deeper into the city.

I used the gunship's overwatch to search for enemy out ahead. With this and the tank's thermal sights, I really had the advantage at night. I chose to take the fight to the enemy. The insurgents had poor night vision and were easily caught in the open at night. Due to the rotor wash of the gunship, they often didn't hear the tank coming until the first burst of my machine guns. The speed that my tank section and the gunship could take the fight to the enemy meant that the infantry were going to be left out of the night's festivities. They went firm in two three-story structures as my tank section sped off into the night.

We moved fast and shot accurately. We pushed deeper and deeper into the city and left a trail of dead insurgents. Hunting was good that night. I really think we caught them offguard being so deep into Fallujah. Their communications weren't good, so few escaped our fire. That, combined with the speed we moved, consistently gave us the advantage and what seemed like complete surprise on the enemy. I became so caught up in the attack that I lost track of my ammunition situation.

At approximately 0400, my gunner, Corporal Chambers, informed me, "Gunny, I'm down to my last two hundred rounds." I informed the CO that I was black (almost empty) on ammo and could no longer continue the attack. He ordered my tank section to return to where we had left the infantry, go firm, and await resupply.

My tank crew and I alternated standing watch so that we could all get at least a little rest. I shut the tank's engine down, and we became a big metal bunker in the middle of that Fallujah city street for the next two hours. After the previous sixteen hours of firing and destruction, everything seemed amazingly peaceful. It was strangely quiet. The enemy was going to take one last attempt at my tank before dawn, though.

I was standing watch while the rest of my crew slept in their crew positions. They had earned the rest even though they weren't going to get much. Out of the predawn quiet came the crack, crack, crack of an assault rifle. It was not an AK-47, but it was close. About a second later, just as I was figuring out that the shots were from an M16, came a short burst from a SAW (squad automatic weapon). It was the infantry in the building next to me who were firing, and they were shooting close! The firing then stopped as suddenly as it had started, and it was eerily silent. Shortly after that, I heard the marine infantry who had shot start to laugh a little. Marines are amazing in our ability to find humor in just about anything.

"What's going on up there?" I called to them.

"Three of them were trying to infiltrate you, Gunny. You'll see them when the sun comes up," they replied from the rooftop.

Soon the dawn broke on Fallujah. I must admit that I was surprised to see the dead enemy insurgents were only about ten meters from the rear fender of my tank. Quickly, thoughts of what could have happened were it not for the infantry came into my head. I forced those thoughts out and focused on the task ahead. I then had a great sense of satisfaction. I thought of how the enemy had vowed to make Fallujah a graveyard for Americans. Today, they would awaken and see two marine tanks and a platoon of infantry defiantly set up in the middle of their city. Many of the dead enemy combatants still littered the streets around us. I figured this would serve as a warning to any other insurgents as to the consequences of tangling with us.

Soon civilians slowly began appearing in the streets. I knew some of them were certainly insurgents with weapons hidden nearby. I was sure they were looking for an opportunity to attack, and I didn't plan on giving the one. We stood poised for a fight, but due to our ammunition situation, we could not continue to push forward into the city again.

I called on the radio and inquired about the resupply. I also informed them that my tanks were running low on fuel and that by tonight that would be an issue also. I was informed that we were pretty far into the city and moving ammunition to where we were at would be difficult and to get fuel to me would be impossible. I could not stand the thought of giving back to the enemy any of the ground we had taken, so I figured we would deal with the fuel issue later. While I waited for more ammo, I watched Iraqi civilians picking up off the streets all the expended brass from my machine guns. I wondered if I should stop them from doing that, but I could not think of a reason why.

The resupply arrived about an hour after daybreak. It came on foot! Resupplying a main battle tank is not a small task and is usually done with large trucks. The high volume of RPG fire in this area of Fallujah meant that no trucks were coming in here, certainly not a fuel truck! I looked behind me and saw a column of marines running. They were in pairs, with ammo crates slung between them. The U.S. Marine Corps' commitment to mission accomplishment is amazing, and the Fox Company marines were going to get ammunition to me if they had to carry it by hand, which they did!

The infantry platoon surged out of their building and pushed forward ahead of my tank, to provide an overwatch while my section uploaded. The civilians saw the infantry moving; due to the insurgents' experience, they know how to anticipate when a firefight is going to break out in their streets. They disappeared. In the Iraqi theater of operations, whenever civilians are not present at all, it indicates an impending insurgent attack. They know who the enemy is and protect themselves from their violence.

The infantry's surge forward must have caught them off-guard. No attack came, and we were resupplied with machine-gun ammunition. Main-gun ammo was again transferred from Staff Sergeant Escamilla's tank to mine, but again, this was only a temporary fix as both of our tanks were extremely low on ammo. My crew and I linked up 2,600 rounds of 7.62mm and loaded it into the ready bin of the tank.

I called the Fox CO and informed him that the resupply was complete and that we were prepared to continue the attack. I reminded him of my low fuel situation and told him I was also low on main-gun ammunition. He was going to resupply the other two tanks in my platoon (the platoon commander's tank and his wingman) because they were not yet into the city. They would then relive my tank section, and we would go upload fuel and main-gun ammo outside the city because those trucks couldn't come in.

The infantry moved back into the two buildings that they had been occupying, and I moved back into the lead. We were ready to take the fight to the enemy again. The CO told us to hold. We were much farther into the city than anyone else at this point; that combined with our fuel and ammo situation wasn't the best scenario for an attack. Much to our disappointment, we stayed defensive and held the attack.

In Fallujah, the enemy has the ability to move around unarmed as civilians and conduct reconnaissance on us for their attacks. All we could do was present as tough a target to them as possible; be hard to kill. We must have done this well, because it took about an hour and a half before the first attack came. The urban environment allows the enemy the ability to get close before he has to commit. The first enemy RPG shot was a good one, taken from close. It passed right between Lance Corporal Hernandez' head and my head. It was so close that I felt the heat of its rocket propulsion on my face. The shooter was gone as quick as he shot. Not many got away from my tank, but this one did. He must have inspired the lesser-trained insurgents to fight.

Just like the previous day, they came out to attack my tank. Again, there was no coordination to their attacks. The results were the same. A few hits on my tank, producing no damage but many dead insurgents. The only thing different about today was that we were stuck sitting on the defensive, and the enemy had the advantage. The attacks were coming from a lot closer. I was getting anxious to get back on the offensive. I wanted to take the fight to the enemy, not the other way around.

One of the infantrymen on the rooftops spotted a dozen insurgents gathering three blocks ahead. I called the CO and requested to go back into the attack before they could get away. "Go get 'em!" was his reply. That was the best news I had heard all day.

I commanded, "Red Three, this is Red Four. Follow my move. Driver, move out." We were back on the attack, and I was happy.

The speed that we were going to move with again meant that the infantry would stay behind. My tank charged ahead a couple blocks. We had caught them in the open on a city street. They were assembled outside of a mosque. All were males of what we referred to as "military aged," and most had weapons, AK-47s. Half tried to flee into the mosque; none of them made it. The other half of them ran around the corner down a narrow street. It appeared to me that the mosque was a staging area and almost certainly a stockpiling point for insurgent weapons. I could stay and secure the mosque or pursue the fleeing insurgents. I decided to stay on the attack and take the fight to the enemy. I commanded my tank and wingman to move out around the corner down that narrow street.

Once I entered the street, I observed that the fleeing insurgents had taken cover. My gunner, Corporal Chambers, searched with the tanks' high-powered optics while Lance Corporal Hernandez and I scanned from our hatches for enemy. The insurgents quickly darted from doorway to doorway. Some we got; some got away. They were definitely attempting to get down this street away from my tank. I didn't want to give them a chance to dig in and defend, so I kept up the pursuit.

The street got narrower as we went farther down it. Soon, I could no longer traverse my tank's turret. I still had the two machine guns on top to fight with, so I continued. I couldn't stand the thought of giving back any of the ground we had taken. I passed a small crossroad about eight feet wide. As I entered this intersection, I scanned to my right for enemy. I spotted one about fifty feet away just as he fired an RPG at my tank.

I dropped into my hatch to swing my machine gun over and kill him. His rocket hit the side of my turret, doing no damage. As I was swinging my .50-caliber over, I didn't see the second insurgent firing from the rooftop of a three-story building next to me. I heard a hiss about a split second before it hit me. The RPG hit struck inside my hatch striking me on the head. I saw a bright flash of light, and then nothing but blackness. I had been blinded in both eyes. It felt as though I had been hit in the head with a sledgehammer, and it knocked me down onto the turret floor. I was still conscious, so I stood back up. I couldn't hear anything except a dull static-like humming in my ears.

I knew at the time that it was an RPG that had hit me. I couldn't see anything, so I reached up and felt my face. It felt wet and gooey. My first concern was to get the tank moving out of what was obviously a bad place to be. Because I could not see to direct the tank, I grabbed Corporal Chambers by his flak jacket and said to him. "Chambers, you've got to get the tank moving. You've got to start working on a medevac for me."

I could feel Chambers moving, but he was not answering me. I repeated my commands to Corporal Chambers again and received no response. I was to figure out later that he had been answering me, but I couldn't hear it. Corporal Chambers had been wounded himself yet he unhesitatingly moved out of his gunner's position and into the tank commander's hatch, the same hatch I had just been blown out of. I felt the tank begin to move forward, and I felt good about that.

The RPG had hit me on the head inside the commander's hatch. The majority of shrapnel ended up in my flak jacket, helmet, and head. Shrapnel struck Lance Corporal Hernandez in the left and Corporal

Chambers in the left tricep. I wonder what the insurgent who fired the rocket must have thought after seeing it score a direct hit inside the hatch, and then seeing all the crewman of the tank still on their feet, to include the one he had hit with the rocket. He must have thought, *What do I have to do to kill these Americans?*

The gunner of a main battle tank has the most restricted field of view and perception of the world outside of the tank, even though he is the second in command. Corporal Chambers got the tank moving, but he didn't know exactly where we were. We were deep in the city at this time. Lance Corporal Hernandez, because of his position on top manning a machine gun, knew the way back. He directed Chambers which way to go. Hernandez' hand was bleeding profusely, and he had to drop down to apply a pressure dressing. At this point the driver, Lance Corporal Frias, took over direction of the tank. There would be no medevac to where we were, so my tank had to return to the Fox Company's defensive line, and Frias knew the way.

I must wonder again what the enemy must have thought after hitting this American tank with everything he had only to see it drive right through their ambush and continue on its way. I was truly lucky to be in command of what I believe to be the best tank crew in the U.S. Marine Corps. Pressure brings out the best in some people, and I am alive today because of their actions under fire.

During the trip back to the Fox defense line, I began to try to figure out how bad I had been hit. I couldn't see, I couldn't hear, and I knew that wasn't good. I could feel that I was bleeding badly from my head and neck, which also wasn't good. I was still conscious, and I was still standing up. That was good. I was in little pain, my whole head felt somewhat numb. I felt both nauseous and sleepy; sleepy as if I could just lie down on the turret floor and go to sleep I would feel better. I knew that was bad, so I focused on staying awake. I grabbed onto the tank's turret to help me stay on my feet.

The next thing I remember was feeling the tank pitch back and then slam forward forcefully. I knew this could only be one place. We had just crossed the same berm I was set up behind two days ago in the Fox

Company defensive line. I knew the medevac would be soon. I felt good about things at this point and knew that everything was going to be all right. The tank stopped, and I climbed to the top of the turret and waited for someone to come and get me.

Soon marines and corpsmen came, pulled me down from the tank, and began to render first aid. During this, mortar rounds began to impact near us. The corpsmen who were treating me took off their own body armor and piled it on top of me to protect my wounded body. The dedication and skill displayed by these men was truly extraordinary.

Next, I was placed on a Humvee and transported to a surgical unit. While I was there, I could hear (I was starting to get a little hearing back in my left ear) a commotion going on near my stretcher. I asked who was there. The response was, "General Hagee." Although the commandant of the U.S. Marine Corps was not a doctor, there was something about his presence in the hospital that made me feel that everything was going to be all right. Marines take care of their own!

I was then sedated for the removal of what remained of my right eye. I awoke and felt as though I was moving. I asked into the darkness, "Where am I?"

"You're on a plane to Germany, dude" was the response.

///LT. COL. PAT WHITE (U.S. ARMY)

I commanded the 2nd Battalion, 37th Armor Regiment, of the 1st Brigade, 1st Armored Division in Iraq from June 2003 through July 2004. My impressions of armor in urban operations in Operation Iraqi Freedom are much based on the situations I was presented with. What I remember most about how we operated as armor crewmen, as we tankers call ourselves, in the urban environment that we were in, the most powerful machine that the world had seen on the ground in ground combat in years.

We knew that we possessed both technological advantage and firepower advantage over any enemy that we would confront. But what we found out early on was that the enemy was not a stupid enemy. He was actually a thinking enemy, and he understood where our weak points were. In our understanding of the enemy he knew where are vulnerabilities were, we weren't trying alleviate that if we went on a mission.

I think the first time I ever realized that we had issues was working in an urban environment in Sadr City, Baghdad. It's a suburb of Baghdad, heavily populated by Shiites. When an uprising occurred that trapped a patrol from the 1st Calvary Division and they had no heavy armor to relieve that patrol, we were called upon to send in a tank company.

The tank company went in. You've got to understand that at the time I sent the tank company in, we were two days away from traveling to Kuwait to transition back to Germany. We were low on ammunition—and all the soldiers (the tankers) were thinking about was home. We had been in Iraq for almost twelve months, and our focus was not on combat operations.

I have to say that was the first time we really were bloodied as a unit. As we rolled our 1st Company, John Moore's Charlie Company of the 2nd Battalion, 3rd Armor, into Sadr City, we encountered multiple engagements from every angle you could think of. We had young Iraqi men rushing at us shooting RPGs, snipers from second- and third-story windows, RPG-gunners on rooftops, all trying to disrupt our ability to relieve the patrol that was trapped with dead American soldiers caught in an alleyway.

As John Moore's company fought that afternoon, we rolled our tanks back out of the motor pool from Alpha Company and a headquarters company, my tank personally, to begin movement toward Sadr City, which was about five kilometers away from our headquarters. John's company was running low on ammunition, and because we were planning on going to Kuwait, there was limited tank ammunition available.

We consolidated all the ammunition available on my tank from my battalion's 8-3 tank, and we moved to Sadr City in an attempt to resupply John's company. In communications with John's company, I couldn't directly talk to him, I could only talk to his executive officer. I got a location on where the center mass of his company was within the urban environment of

Sadr City. I moved in that direction with all the ammunition on my tank and on the 8-3's tank. My 8-3's tank was pinned by obstacles and sniper fire. We moved the ammunition off his tank because he unable to move forward onto my tank. He moved back to the rear, while I continued moving forward.

I got up to where John's company was deployed. I found his 1st Platoon, and the first thing I heard was reports of "black," meaning they had no ammunition left. My first duty was to get them ammunition—and I'm talking boxes of machine-gun ammunition that weighed anywhere from fifteen to thirty pounds, depending upon what type of ammunition it was.

I immediately told my gunner, "Come up into the turret; you man my commander's weapon, continue to scan the area." The loader had his M16, and I began throwing cans of ammunition onto the ground thinking that I would run them from tank to tank and throw them up on the turret after getting their attention.

The funny thing was, after about the second tank, with bullets flying everywhere, I realized that I was exposed outside the tank trying to heave thirty-pound cans up on the tanks of gunners and tank commanders who were inside their tanks trying to kill people that were shooting at them. Call it epiphany, but I realized at that moment, that was the stupidest thing I'd ever done in my life.

I had a completely functional seventy-ton tank that I could have just driven up next to their tank, jumped out, thrown it over, and gotten back into it. In the end, we were successful—and alive. We relieved the column, and we saved the six remaining soldiers—and the road march out of that city was quite eventful as John's company continued a mission for 1st Calvary Division from Fort Hood and I was left alone to find my way back to our base. That was really the first time I experienced urban combat, and it was a good experience.

I think the next eye-opening event was when we were moved all over central and southern Iraq over about a two-week period between April and June 2004. This was again in response to Muqtada al-Sadr's Mahdi army uprising. His Mahdi army came and attacked a number of places, blew up bridges, attacked houses, basically took them over from a coalition division, which was a U.S.–led CPA (coalition provisional authority) that helped Iraqis rebuild cities after the war.

We were assigned to go to Al Kut, which is near the Iranian border. That mission lasted about six or seven days. At that point in time, the central part of Iraq was under heavy attack by the Mahdi army; the Spanish and the Polish were really in charge of that sector and they had no heavy armor and required assistance. After seven days of settling in and patrolling around Al Kut, we moved to the east by heavy equipment transport about 250 kilometers in one day's travel to link up with U.S. units that were there to support the Polish and the Spanish.

Over a number of days of operating there, we became the sole proprietors of that particular area of operations. The 2nd Armored Calvary Regiment to which I was attached extended all the way back to the Iranian border, but our battalion was really responsible for cities of An Najaf and Al Kufa.

Al Kufa and An Najaf are strongholds—both of which are religious icons for Islamic people. In An Najaf, there is the second holiest mosque in all of Islam, and next to that is a cemetery that is probably the size of a small city in America, accommodating somewhere between ten and fifteen thousand people and numerous buildings that house any type of monument to the dead. It was a multi-storied city from ground to subterranean. It was really not built for tanks to operate in.

We found that one of our toughest fights in the next six weeks up until June 2004 occurred there. Basically, the enemy would hunker down inside of the cemetery and fire mortars and RPGs at our soldiers who were securing police stations.

We encountered a seven-hour battle that initially started as a platoon fight—a platoon of tanks—and ended up being a two-company-plus fight with Humvees, tanks, mortars, and artillery, all battling the fanatic fighters in the area. Upon conclusion of the fight what we found was numerous piles of drugs—amphetamines, barbiturates, hashish—all piled up. The fighters would use, and then run to attack coalition forces; this time it happened to be my battalion.

That was actually the second most shocking event in my stay in my fifteen-month stay in Iraq, because we could never really figure out up until that day why these young eighteen, nineteen, and twenty year olds would rush a seventy-ton tank firing a rifle or firing an RPG and get within fifty or sixty feet of the tanks when they were surely going to die. They'd seen their friends do it, and their friends had died, but yet they continued to do it. I can't attribute every attack to that, but I can say that at least in our stay in An Najaf we thought that the amount of illicit drugs in the area probably contributed to a number of deaths there.

I think the last real event that I recount from fighting tanks in urban terrain—because there are numerous examples now that it's been a few years—was when we were moving from Al Kut to An Najaf. I had loaded all my tanks up on the heavy equipment transports (HETs) I mentioned before. Chains tied them down; they were not mobile; the gun turrets on top of the tanks did not move; we couldn't swivel them; the crew were positioned in those tanks on top of huge trucks as we drove. And they were vulnerable. As those tanks moved from the east to the west during evening hours, the HET drivers became disoriented and passed through a town called Diwaynia, which was also a stronghold of the Mahdi army.

During their disorientation, they came under attack from four different directions simultaneously, destroying a number of vehicles. In order to escape the fire and to counterattack, my tanks actually broke the chains that were holding them onto the HETs and drove off the HETs without ramps to assist A5 back into the city to free the people who were being encircled; we killed a number of enemy fighters in that area.

At the end of our stay in An Najaf and the time that we returned back to Germany in July, the Iron Dukes, 2nd Battalion, 37th Armor, were the most decorated unit of Operation Iraqi Freedom: six Silver Stars, numerous Bronze Stars with Vs, and an even greater amount of Purple Hearts. It was just an amazing unit of American young men and women who were thinking they were going to go home. Then just two days later they were embroiled in a fight that would last eight weeks across central and southern Iraq. That would make any mother, father, sister, brother, cousin, aunt, or uncle proud of what we produced.

///CAPT. JOHN MOORE (U.S. ARMY)

After the insurgency in Iraq began on April 4, 2004, the company I commanded was engaged in some of the fiercest fighting we would see in one hundred days of constant subsequent urban combat. The Crusaders (Charlie Company, 2nd Battalion, 37th Armor Regiment) had fought a brutal hasty attack on April 4 into Sadr City to relieve and extricate an encircled infantry platoon (1st Platoon, Charlie Company, 2d Battalion, 5th Cavalry Regiment) that had taken casualties. The actions on April 4 in Sadr City have received a great deal of attention in the media, and many accounts and even a book have been written about this day. The days that followed were every bit as brutal, but we adapted to the battlefield quicker and more effectively than the Mahdi army. These battles remain largely unknown because we suffered almost no casualties, and hence, there is less attendant drama. Nonetheless, the fighting was ferocious, at close quarters, and we inflicted grievous losses on the enemy.

The 2nd Battalion, 5th Cavalry Regiment (Lancer Battalion) assumed responsibility for Sadr City on April 4, and the Crusaders were attached to them until April 10. During this period, the Mahdi army made every effort to assert dominance in Sadr City. The Crusaders were committed to the defense of three police stations in various portions of the center of Sadr City during this time. We provided tanks to serve with infantry from Lancer Battalion in defending police stations. This mission was twenty-four hours per day from April 4 to April 10. Given that a tank company is assigned fourteen tanks and that some are not mission capable for maintenance reasons and battle damage, this meant that all of the tankers were forward in Sadr City more than fourteen hours a day, leaving the rest of the time for maintenance, refueling, and crew rest.

Tanks would return to base, get a new crew, and go back. I slept twice in those six days, the first time on April 7, when my first sergeant, Vince Bacon, literally put me to bed. I had become so tired that he diplomatically prohibited me from going back in after refueling one time. I slept ten hours. I had fought three distinct fights since I had last slept three days before.

While forward, our engines ran constantly for a week so that we had full power to our turrets and were ready to fight immediately. It was a surreal experience. During the days, life progressed as normal in the dismal slum of Sadr City. I commanded the combined infantry and tank element required for the central Iraqi Police Station on Route Delta just north of the Meredi Market, a portion of the wide street with innumerable shop stands where people bought and sold all manner of things. We fought for hours every night, sometimes all night. The next day, the area around the police stations looked exactly like one would expect: a battlefield. Dead Mahdi army soldiers littered the streets. Destroyed Iraqi vehicles burned or smoldered. After sunrise, the population of Sadr City went on with their lives, set up their shop stands, and subsisted. Eventually, someone would cover the bodies with rugs or plastic bags. At some point, well after sunrise, ambulances would arrive and take away the remains. It was usually about eighty degrees during those April days in Baghdad, but it was much warmer in the tank. We were forward in exposed positions, and the sniper threat was too great to stand around outside the tank. There were no breaks. I would run as fast as I could several times a day into the police station to coordinate with the infantry lieutenants leading their platoons in and around the station. I would talk to either Lt. Dan Hines or Lt. Shane Aguero, both from Charlie Company 2/5 (2nd Squadron, 5th Cavalry Regiment) Cavalry usually about the coming night's fight and plans for relief of my tanks or their Bradleys. Shane was still bandaged and limping from the wounds he sustained on April 4 when my company fought its way in to get them—the fourth attempt to rescue them.

On the night of April 5, I was forward with four tanks at the central station. Staff Sergeant Henry Eldridge was holding the left flank position as we oriented south down Delta, a broad crossroads. My executive officer, Lt. John Caulwell, was on the right with me in the center. Staff Sergeant William Deaton commanded the sole tank oriented north. The infantry all defended within the buildings of the police station and were not directly threatened by the fight in the crossroads a mere fifty meters away. A few hours after sundown, the enemy began their nightly ritual of setting fire to large roadblocks that blocked all access into or out of the area. They would continue to roll burning tires and other debris into these roadblocks to sustain them. This constituted hostile intent and naturally had an effect on the thermal sites we depend on to fight at night. It always preceded an attack. I ordered my men to kill anyone constructing and improving obstacles, and they did. That night, Staff Sergeant Deaton identified individuals in his thermal sites throwing more objects onto an ignited roadblock. He requested clearance to fire, which I granted. He and his gunner killed and wounded a number of them before they dispersed. This tactic worked, and over time, the obstacles moved farther and farther away until they were tactically irrelevant. Actually, these obstacles started to work to our advantage: they signaled impending enemy attack.

Around midnight, the Mahdi army attacked. That night is memorable for a variety of reasons. Chief among them was that I made a tactical mistake that night that could have cost the lives of my men.

We knew that most of them concentrated around the Sadr Bureau to our south, and the wide avenue of approach from the south was where I positioned the bulk of our defense. We were aided by the fact that there was another police station defended by Americans just to our north. The enemy would not be able to concentrate well there. I pushed all three tanks defending to the south into the intersection. This was the mistake. They could cover the wide intersecting road, perhaps seventy or eighty meters wide, and I would orient down Route Delta, straight to my front, which was just as wide. Thus, we could cover three of the four roads to the intersection. I thought the tanks needed to be forward to cover the entire breadth of this critical crossroad that bisected our position.

The flanks of the tanks, where the armor is thinner, were exposed. No gunner, no matter how attentive or lucky, would be able to kill all threats in such a wide sector before they would get a shot off in the event of an attack. Although I have felt penitent about this mistake over the years since, there is some satisfaction in knowing that the enemy selected me first to teach the lesson of my folly.

A parachute flare went up to our south and drifted noiselessly downward. We clearly had not fired it. I had my head just out of the hatch enough to see over the vision blocks when an RPG slammed into the right side of my tank. The blast pushed me down in the hatch, and the driver, Spec. Peter Zuhan, immediately screamed out that we had been hit. I am sure the concussion was severe in the sealed driver's compartment. Other gunfire commenced, and the tanks responded with every weapon available. RPGs zipped in from the west and east. My tank was hit again. The sight of my loader, Spec. Omid Zehtab, calmly reloading the main gun and checking me and the gunner in the turret reinforced my confidence. Based on reports of the driver, I was concerned that we were a mobility kill, unable to move because of damage to the suspension or track. Moving and throwing a track would be an indescribable nightmare that would take hours to repair leaving exposed men on the ground. We continued to fight where we were.

One RPG gunner in an alleyway to the front right was incredibly persistent and got several rounds off at us from a range of about seventy meters. I laid the main gun on the alleyway using the tank commander's override, and told my gunner, Sgt. Patrick Jordan, to fire the main gun when he adjusted to the optimum site picture of the near corner of the alleyway. He fired, but we never knew the result. However, the next morning, after the fight, a tremendous amount of people gathered at this location to observe what was obviously carnage. Our XO, Lieutenant Caulwell, and his gunner, Sergeant Anthony, were fighting off a series of attacks assailing our right flank. Most spectacularly, a Toyota truck came barreling down the road at fairly high speed from the west, the bed packed with armed men. Sergeant Anthony destroyed this vehicle and all of the enemy troops aboard with a HEAT round—a thirty-five-plus-pound high-explosive projectile designed to destroy tanks—at a range of 150 meters. There was almost nothing left of the truck. For days afterward, there were pictures of this truck, and local Iraqis' reaction to it, on several Internet news websites. Fighting became sporadic. The enemy would consolidate, reorganize, and come back at us.

Toward the end of the night, one lone soldier with an AK-47 came up Route Delta from the south walking carefully, oblivious to the fact that we could see in the dark and he could not. He was 150 meters away. All three of my forward tanks saw him. I gave the order to fire, and all three tanks opened fire with coax machine guns. He was down but kept moving. We fired again. He kept moving. The third attempt finally succeeded in killing this militiaman. I heard Staff Sergeant Eldridge finally report it was over. In the immediate aftermath, we joked about him being the toughest man in Baghdad. Humor is morbid in combat. By the end of the night, we had killed a few dozen Mahdi army soldiers and suffered no casualties. About a dozen enemy KIA were visible immediately at the crossroads, and it is impossible to know how many they had evacuated. All four tanks were damaged but all of them were still mission capable. The M1A1 is an absolutely amazing piece of equipment.

There were two big lessons that night. First, company commander analysis of the terrain has to be in the context of the mission. We were there to defend a police station, not cover wide roads with our weapons systems. I became too fixated on the enemy and did not use all of the advantages of my tanks. The mobility of a tank is as much an asset as the armor or the weapons. Subsequently, I ordered tanks and Bradleys to stay close to buildings on the north side of the crossroad on Route Delta, backed out of the intersection, where they were unexposed on their flanks. I ordered them to use a cross-pattern of firing so they could cover the most terrain and not limit themselves by the close proximity of buildings. This means that the right tank fired to the left across the area to the front of the other two tanks and vice versa. When I felt that there was probably infiltration to the flanks, we would pull forward, look, shoot if necessary, and then move back. Take advantage of terrain.

Second, the flare issue prior to the fight had been interesting. I asked Lieutenant Hines if he had any flares, and he said he did. That was good. The next night at about the same time, I called him on the radio and told him to send up a flare and to pop it to the south so the parachute would open over the enemy like the one had the night before. I had let my tanks know, and that night, a section of Bradleys from Lancer as well, that they were probably coming. The Mahdi army attacked right after the flare just as they had the night before. This was like firing a machine-gun table at a gunnery range. Everybody was completely ready and looking through their sites. All weapons had been double and triple checked. Fingers were on every trigger. We slaughtered them. There were fewer than the previous night, but we were learning fast, handing off targets on the radio, getting great spot reports from the infantry on what they saw and heard, and crew and section drills got sharp. Perhaps there were fewer enemy because we had inflicted such heavy casualties on them in the opening seconds of that fight. A key in gaining and retaining advantage is inflicting casualties on the enemy faster than he can react.

The enemy was learning, too, and on subsequent nights, the flare routine did not bait them into an attack. It is a thinking man's game. The difference between the first night's defense and the second night's defense is that on the second night, the Mahdi army never had the advantage and we were never forced to react to them. The attacker generally has the advantage of initiative. As a defender, stripping the enemy of this advantage is a critical step. Get him to react to you and you are starting to win. You can palpably feel whether you have the advantage or the enemy does. It is almost more of a physical sensation than a perception.

The Crusaders went on to fight dozens of engagements in Sadr City and subsequently in An Najaf and Al Kufa until early June. Starting in late April, we fought as part of our own battalion: 2nd Battalion, 37th

Armor, the Iron Dukes. We conducted many defense missions including Iraqi police station defense again there. However, in both of these cities, we conducted a tremendous number of offensive missions to attrite the Mahdi army. The Mahdi army had shifted its center of gravity to these two cities late in April. I will never forget how well the troops fought and performed their duty through our fifteenth month of a planned twelve-month deployment to Iraq. Our first day of fighting in Sadr City was supposed to have been our last day of duty in Iraq. We were going home. All of the combat occurred during an extension of the tour of duty of the 1st Armored Division. We lost one killed, Sgt. Mike Mitchell from California, as well as two wounded in Sadr City. We suffered two more killed in Al Kufa, Lt. Ken Ballard, also a Californian, and Pfc. Nick Zimmer from Ohio. We also suffered several more wounded. I was witness to incredible acts of courage, performed by great American soldiers in the tank, infantry, and cavalry platoons task organized to the Crusaders.

Fifty-six tank crewmen and two tank mechanics earned four Silver Stars, twenty Bronze Stars for Valor, and forty Army Commendation Medals for Valor. Some soldiers in my company were awarded twice, and in one case, three times for bravery. I will always be in awe of their service. Among these characteristics, I would name the will to sacrifice, incredible technical proficiency, superior personal initiative, applying humanistic principles to limit unnecessary casualties often at personal risk, and a mission focus shared by all ranks that transcended concerns for personal welfare.

We learned innumerable lessons during all of that combat. Some of what we learned was specific to tank troops. Fighting in tanks is unique. Every soldier, from the lowest private to the lieutenant colonels commanding battalions and squadrons, wears a combat vehicle crewmen's helmet, the CVC. Unlike in any other branch, it is completely normal in the tank corps for the most junior eighteen-year-old soldier to key his CVC and report to captains, majors, or lieutenant colonels. Every soldier has his own radio call sign, and you know who he is and where he is as soon as he says it. There is an incredible level of information exchange. In conventional land combat, only in the tank corps can a commanding officer receive a spot report over the radio from every single soldier under his command all the time. It is important for us to cultivate a command climate where all soldiers feel comfortable reporting on comparatively high command nets. There are platoon nets, just like in the infantry and the cavalry. However, if you need to skip the middle man, that young soldier can transmit on whatever command net he needs to in order to make sure everybody has an idea what he saw. The spot reports of a private may well change a battalion scheme of maneuver.

The M1A1 can absorb incredible levels of punishment. My M1A1 was RPGed nine times. There were never significant problems. RPG impacts caused problems that limited but did not end our ability to fight. We were never penetrated. The damage was usually superficial but did serve to point out to nearby tanks where the enemy had fired from, which often proved fatal for their antitank teams. Any enemy concentrates on the primary weapons systems of the tank and disregards other potential threats. This means other tanks can kill them if they are concentrating too much on a near tank. It also means that they forget there are living, thinking crewmen in the turret close to them who can see them or hear about them on the radio. We can come up fast in our hatches with carbines, pistols, or even grenades, and dispatch these enemy troops. As a tank commander, I fired at the enemy only one time with the tank commander's override, which would allow me to fire coax machine gun or main gun at the enemy from my position. I let the gunner do that, occasionally laying him on so he could get his bearings. I fought with my M4 carbine from the commander's hatch all the time. You could sense this shocked them. They missed this threat. It was ironic at close ranges when they would successfully avoid the incredibly destructive primary weapons systems of the tank only to be dispatched by an attentive tank commander or loader with a carbine.

The coax machine gun is the most deadly thing on the urban battlefield. Tanks and Bradleys have an incredible advantage with the coax machine gun.

It is slaved to the site laterally and inputting laser range finding data immediately induces the necessary elevation for the machine gun to hit any target. Hitting a man-sized target at five hundred meters is easy. It is normal and is expected. At ranges under two hundred meters, hitting an enemy in the head, as he looks at you, is commonplace. At night, they usually don't even know they are exposed until it is too late for them. In urban fighting, the main gun is critical in killing enemy in hardened positions. At extremely close ranges, the concussive effect alone can be sufficient to kill the enemy. Still, the coax machine gun is the most effective weapon in urban combat.

Fighting in tanks, day in and day out, is an unbelievable experience. You are sitting inside a vehicle with a turbine engine that generates a lot of noise. Imagine sitting next to a jet engine for days on end. With your CVC on, you can talk to the men in the tank and the people on the radio with you. Take the CVC off for a second and you realize that no matter how loud you yell, nobody can hear you.

During one of our last battalion attacks in An Najaf with the Iron Dukes in June 2004, I had an incredible experience. It was hot, we had been fighting for hours, and I was drenched in sweat. The earpieces of my CVC had filled with sweat. Somehow, there was a minor electrical short. Every time I keyed my radio, it shocked me in both ears. It hurt. After the second or third time, I could taste the metal fillings in my mouth. I remember laughing at the absurdity of it, all while we were still in contact with the enemy. There was nothing I could do. I had to keep talking to Lieutenant Colonel White about my observations. I knew in advance that every time this would be painful and my fillings would howl. We laughed about it in the turret. It changed my feelings about dental work for the rest of my life. Dental work is just not as bad as combat. No matter how bad the dentist is, he is not trying to kill you.

This is dedicated to the Crusaders, both those who survived and those who fell, in the battles of 2004.

///LT. NICK MORAN (U.S. ARMY NATIONAL GUARD)

In January 2005, we found ourselves sent to Mosul, to help the Stryker brigade of 1/25th ID (1st Brigade, 25th Infantry Division). Strykers are great vehicles, but they lack the "we mean business" attitude that heavy tracked vehicles like tanks and Bradleys exude. Mosul is one of the larger cities in Iraq, and it is a combination of Sunni, Kurd, and Shia. The town had been quiet for most of the occupation, but in late 2004, after the Fallujah campaign, there was a dramatic upsurge in violence, and so the call went out for reinforcements. Our tank company was the most visible part of these reinforcements.

After a couple of weeks working with Deuce-Four Infantry, we were assigned our own sector to patrol, on the east side of the river from FOB Marez, our base camp. Every day, thus, we would commute to work, in our tanks. Quite literally, we were just another vehicle on the road, albeit one that weighed more than sixty-five tons and had tracks, machine guns, and a cannon. We tended not to worry about traffic lights, but would otherwise merge in traffic, get caught up in traffic jams, and so on. Kind of surreal, really, driving down the market street, waving at people on the footpath, watching out for people reversing out of parking spots, and so on, while also keeping an eye on the roofs with one's rifle at the ready.

Of course, being tanks, we weren't all that worried about observing the rules of the road. (Do as I say, not do as I do!), and it really isn't safe for a tank to be stationary in urban terrain for any length of time. Sometimes if our lane of traffic was stopped, we would cross over the median, or if traffic was bad going both ways, we'd just straddle the median (really just two curbs with a two-foot-wide cement footpath between them) and make our own lane. This resulted in a couple of near misses as people would make left turns without thinking about checking their driver's side mirror for the possibility of an armored fighting vehicle bearing down on them on the wrong side of the road.

One day, as we were trundling slowly down the median between lanes of stopped traffic, we saw this Iraqi chap, about twenty-five years of age, standing on the median, looking to one side of the street. As we got closer, he didn't move out of the way, or even acknowledge our presence. We figured he was just being obstinate, so we continued to creep forward. An M1 tank has a turbine engine, and it is surprisingly quiet. The loudest thing is the noise of the track pads hitting the road, and when creeping at five mph or less, that's not loud at all. Of course, we had no horn. Eventually, we were about twenty feet away, with the gun tube about to bop him on the head when either he caught a glimpse of movement out of the corner of his eye, or a little voice in his head said, "Look left."

The expression on his face made it quite clear that he was not being obstinate; he was just being oblivious. I didn't notice the woman he was presumably ogling so intently that he didn't see the tank until it had snuck up on him, but he jumped four inches into the air, and then took off like a rocket across the far lane of traffic to the other side. We fell apart laughing inside the tank, and looking around; I could see that the Iraqis who had witnessed this were also struggling to remain upright from laughter. That probably did more for east Mosul/U.S. Army relations than anything that month until the elections.

Being as we were just roaming around in traffic, we had the same risks that the average policeman would suffer in his squad car, people flagging you down for questions and those high-speed pursuits. (We didn't have flashing lights, but if you see a tank doing more than forty mph in your rearview mirror, chasing that blue car that just whizzed past you, you're likely to get out of the way.) And traffic accidents.

As we were commuting back to base, we were about to make a left-hand turn from a smaller road to a main road. It was a wide main road, with three lanes in each direction and a wide flat center median. There wasn't a curve for more than a half kilometer, but it had been raining earlier. Once we a bit of a gap in traffic, I had the driver pull out. A white car was approaching but was four hundred or more meters away, plenty of time for him to stop as our little convoy of tanks, Humvees, and an APC (armored personnel carrier) crossed the street. Sure enough, he slowed to a halt. The driver of the car behind him, a red Opel Vectra, obviously didn't stop to think why the car in front had come to a halt in the middle of a straight, wide road, and just saw an opportunity to pass him. He pulled out from behind and kept going. I saw the maneuver, and told my driver to stop.

Presumably, at this point, the Vectra driver was looking to his right, examining the obviously idiotic and uncivilized driver he was overtaking who was daft enough to stop on the main road. The fact that he then looked forward again was evidenced by the sudden and hard application of his brakes, but that model of Vectra evidently didn't have ABS. With wheels locked, he continued to slide toward us.

Although the thought that it was a suicide car bomb had crossed our minds, the overall tone of the maneuvers made it seem quite likely that it really was just a normal, everyday, run of the mill, car-meets-tank accident that was about to occur. Just in case, though, I had my loader and myself both drop down into the tank. I continued to observe the really quite long slide of the Vectra as it came toward my tank through my periscopes. When impact finally occurred, there was a small rocking of the tank. So slight, indeed, that only the driver and I who were able to watch the impact coming and make the timing association felt it. The gunner even asked, "Did he hit us?"

Hit us, he did. He ran the hood of his car squarely under my left track, and I seriously doubted the car was ever going to run again. To add insult to injury, he broke his nose. I sent our medic over to check him out, with an interpreter. When he returned to the APC after having applied a dressing, the medic was laughing. I asked him, what was it that made the driver ram a ten-meter-long, 2.5 meter high, sixty-eight-ton stationary tank on the open road. The answer, "I didn't see the tank." Well, it was painted camouflage . . . !

///MAJ. NICK AYERS (U.S. ARMY)

"Never take a tank into a city." This is what our instructor told us in officer's basic about urban operations. He also showed us diagrams about how tanks were vulnerable in close quarters and about how our weapons couldn't elevate high enough to reach enemy in high buildings. The bottom line, which he repeated many times was, "Don't go into a city."

A couple of years later, I found myself in Kosovo as a tank platoon leader with the mission as the quick reaction force for U.S. operations in Mitrovica in the spring of 2000. Things went relatively peacefully, and I was relieved that I didn't have to test the tank's ability in urban combat.

In the summer of 2003, however, my instructor's cautionary tale came back quickly as my unit was alerted to deploy to Iraq. I was a company commander in the 1st Brigade Combat Team (1st Infantry Division) and we were deploying to the city of Ramadi, Iraq, with the 82nd Airborne Division. We had all just watched the nonstop news coverage of the initial ground war, and although we had seen tank units heavily engaged in fighting we were confident in the M1's ability to take care of whatever could come our way. As we quickly found out, though, like many tank units that were deploying to the theater, we wouldn't be bringing most of our tanks. Although we were going to be taking "tanks into cities," we re-equipped many of the tank crews with Humvees, and thus prepared for both motorized and mechanized operations.

The transition away from tanks is not a subtle change for armor units. For many tankers, the motto "Death before Dismount" is deeply ingrained. Operating on Humvees meant that crews had to leave the relative safety and comfort of their seventy-ton, steel war machines. Operations in the Balkans had shown most armor units that operating on Humvees meant that tankers had to be prepared to conduct dismounted operations. This can be a difficult adjustment as *walk* is often an evil, four-letter word for tankers (only surpassed by the word *run*).

Despite these misgivings, however, the unit soldiered on as others have before. In a matter of weeks, we changed from a sixty-five-man tank company with fourteen M1s to a motorized and mechanized company team with six tanks, five Bradleys, fourteen Humvees, four M113s, and 125 soldiers. The transition required extensive training on not only how to fight dismounted, but also how to integrate tanks and dismounts in the fight. As we arrived into the urban terrain of Ramadi, a city of a half million people and the capital of the Al Anbar province, this close integration became invaluable.

In the months that followed, we found out that my instructor's warnings were somewhat misleading. Although there are certainly vulnerabilities for tanks in the city, they are a critical asset in urban operations for several reasons. First, as we quickly found out, nothing creates a bigger impression than a tank; their size and sound alone have a psychological effect than cannot be matched by any other type of vehicle. Whenever an area was heating up, the presence of a tank or two would quickly quiet things down. When the policemen at our local station became afraid of showing up to work because their sister stations had been attacked, we could park a tank outside the station and suddenly the policemen would all return with big smiles.

Second, tanks have an ability to destroy things quickly and dramatically. Whether it is from their awesome firepower or their ability to run things over (cars, walls, etc.), a tank can deliver. As we found out, missiles (whether they are TOW, Javelin, or an AT4) are often good weapons to use against enemy vehicles, but are not useful in destroying buildings. For that job, tanks are needed.

A third value of tanks in the urban terrain that I will highlight is the reassurance that having a couple of tanks in the company provides to the dismounted and motorized soldiers in the company. With tanks accompanying a dismounted operation in the city, all of the soldiers were confident that a tank was nearby to lend support if needed. The fears of a "Black Hawk Down" scenario were seriously reduced because we knew that if need be, the tanks could clear a path to get to any soldiers in need or clear an exit for the company out of a hostile area.

My instructor was right, though, there are some vulnerabilities with the tanks, but we found that these were quickly remedied by the close integration of motorized and dismounted forces. This was not something well taught in the schoolhouse several years ago but is something that units on the ground are quickly learning in Iraq.

The other thing that units are learning is that American units adapt tactics and techniques to adjust a difficult and asymmetric enemy; that same enemy is trying things with us, as well. One of the most innovative (and thankfully unsuccessful) attempts made occurred in the summer of 2004. To deter the placement of IEDs (improvised explosive devices), we often positioned tanks and other vehicles on highway overpasses. From these elevated positions, we could see for great distances. However, we were worried that because these positions were static (not moving), they would be targets for a suicide bomber. We took several protective measures against this possibility, but even with these, the enemy tested our defense. They did so, however, not with a car, or even a person; instead, they used a donkey.

Yes, the donkey IED or DBIED (donkey borne improvised explosive device) was attempted against our position. For those who haven't had the pleasure of traveling to the wonderful country of Iraq, donkeys are quite common. One day, we noticed a lone donkey walking slowly up the overpass. It was approximately two hundred meters away from our position, and it had stopped. Although this was odd, even more odd was that there seemed to be some individuals at a local soda stand urging it forward (that stand was about three hundred meters away). My soldiers on the overpass used their long-range sights to get a better look at this donkey and noticed that the donkey had a few satchel bags on its back that seemed to be full. Although we didn't really want to believe that the donkey could be carrying an explosive, we had to entertain the idea.

While we kept a watchful eye on the donkey (who was now grazing on some weeds), another vehicle went to the soda stand to investigate the situation further. As they approached, those who were urging the donkey on quickly left. The remaining individuals claimed that they didn't know anything about the donkey and that we shouldn't be concerned. However, having been in Iraq for nine months already, we weren't going to let it go just yet. So, after some additional questions and us telling them that we were prepared to shoot the donkey, one of them said that he would "show us the donkey was safe," so he walked over to it and reached in the satchel bags.

Through our binoculars we could see the man stop at the donkey, looking somewhat puzzled and scratching his head. He looked back at us several times, and finally he reached in the bags and took out two 82mm mortar rounds. In doing so, he had pulled out the wires and set it on the side of the road. As he ran back to us, he quickly apologized and said, "The donkey is now safe." Although we were concerned with the man's safety (and told him that he was one dumb SOB), we had to shake our heads and laugh a little at the incident. EOD came and disposed of the rounds, and we took the donkey back down to the soda shop where we turned him over to man who had "saved" the donkey.

The incident left us puzzled about a couple of things. First, we wondered how the enemy expected it to work. We wondered how did the man who took the rounds out not know and how could he be that stupid and still be able to take the rounds out and pull the wires? We were most curious about how they found a donkey willing to do be a suicide bomber. Later in the summer, as the temperature passed 135 degrees (one day it was 143!), we realized that while most Iraqis go inside, the donkeys are left outside in the sun. I guess that donkey had had enough. So, now when people ask me, "How hot did it get in Iraq?" I respond, "Hot enough that a donkey tried to kill himself."

But as a quick epilogue, don't fret over the donkey. As we ended our tour in Iraq, we saw the man again at the soda shop and inquired about the donkey. He assured us that the donkey was doing well and was not involved in any anticoalition activity.

///1ST LT. JOHN W. CAULWELL (U.S. ARMY)

I served as a tank platoon leader for Bravo Company (Battle-cats) and as executive officer for Charlie Company (Crusaders) of the 2nd Battalion (Iron Dukes), 37th Armored Regiment of the 1st Brigade, 1st Armored Division during this unit's first tour in Iraq for Operation Iraqi Freedom from May 2003 to July 2004. As long as I live, I'll never forget those fifteen months and the great men and leaders I served with in the Iron Dukes.

For the first twelve months of this tour, I did not fire my rifle once. We drove around Baghdad in light-skinned (unarmored) vehicles, stopping to share ice cream with the local kids. We concentrated our efforts into rebuilding schools, unifying neighborhoods, and establishing the new Iraqi army among many other things. There were some violent incidents, but these were few and far between. For a long time, it seemed as though the country was heading in the right direction to unification in a post-dictatorship era. All this changed after April 4, 2004, which marked the official beginning of the insurgency. I'll always remember my commander, Capt. John C. Moore, saying after the battle in Sadr City that "things have changed in this country, and there's no telling what can happen now." Our unit was set to redeploy in a matter of weeks, but instead, and rightfully so, our unit's tour was extended to help defeat the Mahdi army stronghold in Najaf and neighboring Kufa.

As stated before, our mission in Iraq up to this point was relatively without incident. This did not mean that it was easy. The operational pace needed to secure Baghdad was indeed excruciating. We conducted countless raids, traffic control points, IED sweeps, static guard, base security, and constant, rotational patrolling.

In the spring of 2004, there were growing indications that a significant change was taking place among the people. It's very hard to describe, but as soldiers who patrolled the streets for a year straight, we could just feel the disdain from the populace. I imagine it can be comparable to an experienced police officer's premonition of a bad night to come. We could feel a very thick current of unrest in the air. Anyone who was there could tell you about it, but they cannot describe it adequately.

Friendly smiles and hand waves from people on the streets turned into icy glares. I distinctly remember one occasion when one young man in a group of several others on a street corner looked at me as I passed in my tank and made the gesture of cutting a throat by dragging his index finger across his throat.

Our soldierly instincts and keen perception of the people were confirmed as they gave way to undeniable actions of hatred from certain groups of Iraqis, particularly among the young men who formed to create the Mahdi army. There were more direct fire engagements, ambushes, and IEDs. Sadr City had become filled with traveling truckloads of military-aged men wearing green and black uniforms, sometimes blatantly carrying rifles and shouting at American troops.

Green and black flags flew from almost every rooftop to signal their support for the Shiite militia. Rallies and gatherings formed in Sadr City, as Muqtada Sadr became a very attractive figure and force for young Shiite Iraqi men to follow. In the midst of this growing unrest, an ambush ocurred in Fallujah in which civilian employees were killed and then dragged in the street and their bodies mutilated. This only empowered the mob mentality of the growing Mahdi army. The truckloads and crowds of young men chanted "Fallujah! Fallujah!" mere meters away from our traffic control points and patrols, taunting us. It was always very tempting to slam a 120mm HEAT (high explosive anti tank) round center mass into one of their trucks full of men. But that opportunity would have to wait.

By the time the Iron Dukes settled into and around Najaf, we had lost two of our men. We would go on to lose more. These were men who would be alive today if the insurgents, and particularly the Mahdi army, had not forced us into an extension. The extension, and the loss of our men, had the effect of creating a phenomenon among our men that still gives me goose bumps to this day. We all felt robbed. Not only were the lives of our men taken, but all the backbreaking effort we put forth for the good of the Iraqi people for an entire year—the sacrifice, the blood, sweat, and tears we spilled for this country and its people—was completely undermined by the actions of a rogue mob in just a few weeks. We spent millions of dollars in Sadr City to try and help them clean up the raw sewage in the streets, our engineers built soccer fields and repaired water mains, we refurnished schools, we guarded their government buildings and trained their army. The greatest irony was the enemy we now faced was made up entirely of Shiites, the downtrodden religious sect under the Saddam Hussein era. In essence, we rid them of their worst fear and enemy, helped to rebuild their city, and now they were shooting at us.

The phenomenon among our men I speak of really might just have been a natural reaction to all of this. I doubt I will ever see morale in a unit as high as it was in the Iron Dukes during this period and following the deployment. Although it was the most challenging time of my life, I look back to this period with the fondest sense of nostalgia. We became a well-oiled machine. There was no hint of a complaint from anyone. Everyone was eager for payback, and it was evident in the way we furiously completed each task leading up to the fight in Najaf. Obviously, our mission had changed. For the time being, we had no interest in anyone's heart or mind. In Charlie Company, we unofficially titled our mission Operation No Love. What the Mahdi army now faced was a very well-trained, battle hardened, pissed off, cohesive tank battalion.

We fought in Kufa and Najaf for nearly forty-five straight days. When we first got there, we could not patrol through the streets in anything but M1 tanks. There were enemy mortars, IEDS, small arms, machine-gun fire, and RPGs. It was all over the city. We could always tell an attack was coming when the street cleared of all pedestrians and it got really quiet. Then we knew shit was about to hit the fan. There were numerous battles on a daily basis. We used a vast amount of 120mm main-gun ammunition to diminish the enemy's will to fight. The majority of our missions were oriented toward enemy attrition. We would take several tanks to spots we knew the enemy would frequent, establish direct fire contact, kill as many as we possibly could, and remain in the sector long enough to deplete their resources. Sometimes we would have three or four operations going on at the same time throughout the city in order to gnaw away at the enemy.

My two most memorable battles in Najaf and Kufa both centered around one common location. My favorite place to go during this time was a mosque near our base located on the western side of Kufa. It came to be known as the "Rock-em Sock-em Mosque." Every single time we went anywhere near this place, there was a knife fight. The terrain was restricted, and there were plenty of alleys that enemy could laterally move among to get keyhole shots with RPGs or small arms. After taking a shot, they would duck into another alley or behind a civilian house. Often they would fire mortars from the courtyard of the mosque as well, knowing we could not return fire with our mortars for fear of hitting the mosque.

As I said, this mosque was located close to our base. We could see its tower during the day, and at night we could see the glowing green light on top of the tower. Our base security was manned by the El Salvadorian army, and they were an angry bunch just like us, because prior to our arrival, the Mahdi army raided the entire compound, killing several El Salvadorians and nearly overthrowing the base completely. On top of the roof, right outside the window I slept near, an El Salvadorian sniper team maintained a .50-caliber sniper rifle and an M240 machine gun. They fired these weapons in such a constant state that the report of their weapons just became background noise.

When we took indirect mortar fire from the courtyard of the Rock-em Sock-em, the El Sals would fire right back at them and not stop until the mortars stopped. One night I watched from the balcony of our building as the El Sals worked through one of these exchanges. The first mortar dropped and the El Sals returned fire until the glowing green light was extinguished at the mosque and the mortars stopped. The next night it happened again—the green light was lit, mortars dropped, the El Sals returned fire for fifteen straight minutes, the green light was extinguished once more, and the mortars stopped. This was the relationship that the El Sals had with the Rock-em Sock-em, and it remained so for the majority of our time on this mission.

Our relationship with the mosque was a bit different. One night Charlie Company was put on alert as a QRF (quick reaction force) because our Bravo Company was to conduct a movement to contact in and around the vicinity of the Kufa mosque, the enemy stronghold, and continue movement until reaching the Rock-em Sock-em to destroy any enemy in this vicinity.

Our entire company laid out on our tanks listening to the radio for the word to react if need be. In an unlucky turn of events, the Bravo Company tanks went to having only three mission-capable tanks due to mechanical and fire control malfunctions. The decision was made to proceed as planned with Bravo's three tanks. Naturally, after they started their move, Charlie Company went to REDCON 1.5, meaning all our personnel were in our respective positions in the tank, ready to go with nothing left to do but start the engine.

Bravo Company immediately came under extremely heavy fire near the Kufa mosque. Two of the tank's turrets were penetrated from the top, and some soldiers were wounded. The third tank had an RPG actually hit and penetrate the main-gun tube. Bravo had to turn their three tanks around. We knew what was next. We got the call to go to the Rock-em Sock-em and complete the mission.

By this time, it was early morning and a beautiful dawn was beginning to spread across the sky in Kufa. It was still dark enough to see the faint glow of the Rock-em Sock-em's green light as they played their morning prayer over the loudspeaker. The monotonous sound of the prayer was drowned out by the wining scream of the 1,500-horsepower turbine engines as the Charlie Company tanks went to REDCON 1 and we began our move. As we left the gate, we were able to see a lot of dismounted activity in and around the courtyard of the mosque.

They were scrambling around because they knew right where we were headed. Although the Rock-em Sock-em was only 1.5 kilometers away in a straight-line distance from our base, we had to maneuver through the neighborhood south of the mosque to get there. By this time there was enough light to see the huge dust cloud that marked our positions as we zig-zagged through the small streets, getting closer to the mosque.

At one point, due to the outlay of the town, we had to emerge from the southern neighborhood and take a paved road, which ran laterally beside the mosque at a distance of about three hundred meters. As we emerged from the southern neighborhood, all the tanks were in a column running along the paved road exposing our left flank to the enemy at the mosque courtyard. Although our flank was exposed, and although they took the opportunity to get early shots at us, it didn't matter. We calmly continued our move, neither slowing nor speeding our space. I don't even recall anyone even making the effort to turn the turret to face the enemy. We marched face forward like robotic, colonial-era British redcoats in a column. We were heading right up into the Rock-em Sock-em Mosque courtyard, and there wasn't a damn thing any of them could do to stop it.

We filed into the courtyard and immediately came under heavy machine-gun and RPG fire. I was second in order of march and directly behind my commander, and we went straight to the twelve o'clock position at the west side of the courtyard, 2nd Platoon covered north, while 1st Platoon covered east and south. I'm pretty sure most of the drivers put the tanks in park and set the parking brake, knowing we were going to remain in place until we were finished. We fired the main-gun anywhere an RPG or bullet came from. We must have fired fifteen to twenty main-gun rounds—mostly HEAT and OR (obstacle reducing). At one point, I was looking out the front vision block in my TC (tank commander) hatch when it shattered in my face. I had eye protection on and was not injured, but it certainly made me sit back in the TC chair and collect my thoughts for a second. After the battle I dug out a 7.62 AK-47 round that nearly penetrated the periscope. The round sits on my bedroom dresser to this day. We continued firing until the enemy simply didn't fire anymore and stopped moving. It was hard to see because there was so much dust from the main-gun rounds. In thermal view there were hot spots all over the place.

By the end of the battle, dawn had painted the sky an astounding fiery pink. Breakfast at the air-conditioned DFAC started at 0600 and we wanted to get there before the biscuits got stale and while the coffee was still fresh. So we left the Rock-em Sock-em in the same manner we arrived, calmly, at our own pace in column file. Not a word was spoken over the radios on our movement back to base. Moreover, the biscuits were still soft upon our return.

The next encounter I had at my favorite mosque wasn't so calm, at least from my and my tank crew's perspective. Our battalion coordinated several missions throughout our area of operations to channel enemy movement. My commander and I established a blocking position at a key intersection approximately 1.5 kilometers east of the Rock-em Sock-em in an attempt to block enemy routes of movement. At some point, a scout chase team in Humvees bypassed our blocking position headed toward the direction of the mosque. When they got to the vicinity of the Rock-em Sock-em, they could not get through and continue their chasing task because the enemy dismounts in the mosque courtyard were putting too much fire on them with machine guns and RPGs. At that time in OIF (Operation Iraqi Freedom), our scouts had only M1025 light-skinned vehicles. My commander and I were ordered to move to the Rock-em Sock-em, suppress the enemy in the courtyard with our tanks, and establish a screen in order to enable the scouts to pass through and continue their mission.

On that day I brought along our FIST (fire support team) NCOIC (noncommissioned officer in charge), Staff Sergeant Demo, who wanted to serve as my loader for a mission. Sure enough, when we arrived at the Rock-em Sock-em, it was like a circus, only there were no elephants or clowns and everyone was firing a weapon. My commander quickly analyzed the terrain and correctly determined that in order for our screen to work with only our two tanks, we would have to separate. He would stay at the intersection that had direct line of sight into the mosque courtyard to suppress enemy located there, and I would have to move ahead down the road that runs laterally to the front of the mosque, this being the same road we used to enter the courtyard a week earlier during the dawn mission just described.

As I moved ahead, I did not initially take fire from the enemy after falling out of the courtyard's line of site. I moved down the lateral road far enough to scan down the scout's intended route but not far enough to lose sight of my commander, as I was his wingman. As we were just about set, I saw the unmistakable back-blast of an RPG tube from an alley to our left, but the shooter ducked away too quick for us to even turn the turret. The RPG impacted the number three side skirt on the loader's side of the tank, and although it was loud as hell and shook the vehicle, no damage was done. The problem now was, my loader, Staff Sergeant Demo completely lost his hearing from the percussion blast. I noticed this when I told him to load a HEAT round and he didn't acknowledge me. The second time I said it, he saw my lips move but he couldn't hear. I could tell he became quite worried and he yelled that he couldn't hear anymore. At this time my gunner, Sergeant Schroeder, finished clearing a jam in the coaxial M240 machine and lowered the sights in time to see more men with RPGs moving laterally between alleys. The last sequence of events I described all happened in mere seconds. It made me understand how quickly things can turn to shit in combat.

I was still out of the TC hatch at name tag defilade after learning Staff Sergeant Demo lost his hearing. I was scanning to the left talking to the gunner when a bright orange fireball and blast from the right knocked me to the left side of the TC hatch. My legs went limp, and I slouched down inside for a second. I quickly realized I was okay. My gunner and driver both asked, "What the hell was that?" while Staff Sergeant Demo was still not hearing a thing. As much as I didn't want to, I had to pop my head out of the hatch because I had to determine if the last blast was from a grenade or an RPG. I preferred the latter because that meant we at least still had some standoff distance between us and the enemy. If it was a grenade, it meant dismounts were close and that's the last thing we needed right now. When I rose out of the hatch I noticed the sponson box lid was gone; of the contents that weren't missing, the rest were on fire. I grabbed a bottle of water from inside the tank and put out the worst of the fire while my gunner continued to scan. We were in pretty bad shape, and it was just a matter of time before the enemy realized they had a lone tank that they could keep hitting left and right. My gunner laid suppressive fire in sweeping zig-zag patterns and kept the tank under control while I finished off the last of the fire with water. Again, from the time we set into position until now, no more than twenty-five to thirty seconds had passed.

At this time my commander was moving to my position with the scouts behind him. He saw the impact of the RPG on my side of the tank and the sponson box lid fly into the air with of its remaining contents. He later told me when he saw me fall into the turret that he thought I was gone. He was also in a position to see who fired at me. He sent a HEAT round down the alley at the men who shot at me. I'm sure that took care of them. My commander linked up with me, and the scouts were able to pass through safely and continue their mission. The rest of the day was uneventful.

Thankfully, Staff Sergeant Demo regained his hearing twenty-four hours later. A few weeks later, our battalion was given permission from higher command echelons to conduct a joint raid on the mosque with Iraqi army forces. The decision was based on reliable intelligence that the Mahdi army was stockpiling weapons and mortars inside the mosque. Some lucky Alpha Company tanker got to slam a HEAT round into the heavy front gate of the mosque courtyard to initiate the breach for the raid. I would have spent a month's combat pay to squeeze that round off from my TC override handle.

Sure enough, inside the mosque were piles of mortars and weapons. It took a few truckloads to empty it all. One other peculiar thing was found in the mosque during the raid, my gunner's DCU (desert combat uniform) top, which was half burned up. He often wore only his brown T-shirt in the gunner's station necause the temperature would reach 135 degrees inside the tank during the summer. Sergeant Schroeder placed his DCU top in the sponson box the day the RPG hit it. The militiamen retrieved it after the battle and probably used it as some sort of trophy.

After I returned to base that day, I sat alone in my room and thought long and hard about what had just happened. That was the closest to death I had ever been or ever would be for the rest of the deployment. Honestly, it troubled me, but not for too long. My good friend, our 1st Platoon leader, 1st Lt. Dave Fittro, said something to me one day as we often talked and shared such concerns. He said, "You know, I'm not really afraid of dying, I'm afraid of not living." This statement makes complete sense to soldiers, otherwise they wouldn't do what they do. I can honestly say that I did not come across one soldier in our unit who was scared to die. I personally witnessed eighteen- and nineteen-year-old young men tirelessly complete the most amazing and courageous tasks day after day.

It's clear to me now, looking back at the phenomenal camaraderie we developed in the wake of the harshest of times during our fifteen months together that the possibility of dying was not as severe as failing one another or our fallen brothers. We were only afraid of not living to fight alongside one another and avenge our fallen.

///CAPT. DEREK PING (U.S. ARMY)

April 4, 2004, marked our battalion's transition of authority with the 504th Parachute Infantry. It's been all hell since then. Though our relief in place seemed to paint the picture of an area of operations with limited violence, this was before the CPA (Coalition Provisional Authority) decided to go into Sadr City. My tank platoon of four M1A2 SEP (system enhancement package) tanks sat in our FOB (forward operating base) with a quick reaction force mission that evening. Protests had been occurring all over our battalion's sector and the mood was tense. One of the other platoons in my company, equipped with Humvees, was monitoring a mosque in an area known as Abu Discheer, which was a Shia slum in southern Baghdad. At approximately 1900, the platoon was ambushed with small-arms and RPG fire, resulting in two friendly casualties. My platoon could see the tracers rising up in the distance. I immediately brought the platoon to REDCON 1, and we were moving toward the gates of the FOB before we had even been activated.

The battalion ordered us to go to the Yemama traffic circle, which was only a short distance from the FOB. Once we arrived I sent my platoon sergeant to retrieve the plan from the battalion S3/A. We were given an ambiguous plan that was something to the effect of "move down Powerline Road and gain contact with the enemy in order to allow the battalion to develop the situation."

Powerline Road was essentially a diagonal two-lane road with a large median that created a gap of about fifty meters between the two roads. Two- to three-story buildings were close to the roads. It was hardly tanking country.

Our first engagement occurred before we even got to Powerline Road. My wingman spotted an insurgent with a rifle on Market Street. I used an explicative and told him to kill him. I didn't want any hesitancy in the platoon before we went down a road that would have a plethora of insurgents. Staff Sergeant Gutierrez's gunner did in fact freeze, but the staff sergeant dispatched the enemy with his .50-caliber machine gun.

I ordered the platoon to move down the road in a staggered column, with two tanks on each side of the road. We did a crossing firepower because the main gun could not traverse to fire outward. Though we had permission to travel in protected mode, we would have been too vulnerable to top down attack. The tank commanders and loaders remained outside the hatches to watch the rooftops.

My two tanks saw something in the middle of the road. Because we had not been in Iraq long, we thought it might be an IED, so I brought the platoon to a halt. (It would later turn out that it was a concrete block.) Again, because of unfamiliarity with the sector, we did not realize we were right outside of the mosque. At that point, the insurgents started engaging us. The shots seemed to be coming from everywhere. The tightness of the alley made all of the shots reverberate, and initially there was a lack of muzzle flashes or tracers to observe the location of those firing.

We used our thermals, however, and quickly acquired our targets. The insurgents were haphazardly raising their AKs (assault rifles) and firing them at us without even looking. They must not have realized we had thermal sights, but they would pay for their mistake. Our coax and .50-caliber machine guns lit up the insurgents' positions. What I am most proud of, however, is that the platoon acted professionally, identified its targets, made sure it showed hostile intent, and engaged. During the entire firefight, I could see a family watching the battle from their window. Though I would occasionally check them with the flashlight attached to my M4, they were safe from us.

Eventually, the pace of firing slackened and we stopped identifying insurgents in our sights. I still had the uneasy feeling that the insurgents were maneuvering around us and trying to use the tank's dead space against us. We continuously used flashlights to scan the areas immediately around our vehicles. Thinking back to basic doctrine, I realized that we should have some sort of dismounted support to protect the tanks. I immediately told my platoon sergeant to request dismount support. I will admit, though, that we had probably already been in the fight for more than an hour at that point.

Unfortunately, our battalion did not have any infantry, but they did send a motorized platoon to assist us from Alpha Company, led by Lt. Andy Forney. I personally felt much safer when they arrived. Lieutenant Forney's platoon moved through the narrower allies on my platoon's flank. At one point, an insurgent fired an RPG that went right between one of Forney's trucks and my two tanks. Private Simpkin, the loader on the tank, engaged and destroyed the insurgent with his M240 and Lieutenant Forney killed an insurgent with his pistol. My loader, Specialist Howell, identified an enemy moving up the alley on the left of our tank, and then killed him with his M240. After about thirty minutes of negative contact, the battalion gave us the order to withdraw back to the FOB. We estimated that we killed twenty to thirty insurgents in the engagement. The battalion cordoned the mosque the next morning, and they told us the rooftops of some of the buildings were saturated with blood.